Mothering and Welfare

Depriving, Surviving, Thriving

edited by Karine Levasseur, Stephanie Paterson, and Lorna A. Turnbull

DEMETER

Mothering and Welfare
Depriving, Surviving, Thriving
Edited by Karine Levasseur, Stephanie Paterson, and Lorna A. Turnbull
Copyright © 2020 Demeter Press

Demeter Press
2546 10th Line
Bradford, Ontario
Canada, L3Z 3L3
Tel: 289-383-0134
Email: info@demeterpress.org
Website: www.demeterpress.org

Demeter Press logo based on the sculpture "Demeter" by Maria-Luise Bodirsky www.keramik-atelier.bodirsky.de

Printed and Bound in Canada

Cover artwork: *Drowned Nest,* Corey Hardeman (Oil on Canvas, 30"x30")
Cover design and typesetting: Michelle Pirovich

Library and Archives Canada Cataloguing in Publication
Title: Mothering and welfare : depriving, surviving, thriving /
Karine Levasseur, Stephanie Paterson and Lorna A. Turnbull, editors.
Names: Levasseur, Karine, editor. | Paterson, Stephanie, 1972- editor.
| Turnbull, Lorna A., 1963- editor.
Description: Includes bibliographical references.
Identifiers: Canadiana 20200257080 | ISBN 9781772582420 (softcover)
Subjects: LCSH: Mothers, Social conditions. | LCSH: Mothers, Economic conditions. | LCSH: Mothers, Services for. | LCSH: Mothers, Government policy. | LCSH: Motherhood, Social aspects. | LCSH: Motherhood, Economic aspects. | LCSH: Public welfare.
Classification: LCC HQ759.M68 2020 | DDC 306.874/3,dc23

We dedicate this collection to our mothers and to the children in our lives, who add to our wellbeing every day and who inspire us to keep working towards thriving for all who mother. Always.

Acknowledgments

The editors would like to thank all the authors for their thoughtful and diverse contributions to an important global conversation about how we provide care for the vulnerable among us. In this time of a global pandemic and demonstrations against racism and inequality, diverse voices that centre the work of mothering are absolutely vital. None of us knew, when we began this project in 2017, that we would find ourselves in this place in 2020, but your contributions are a glowing reminder of how interdependent we all are, and how urgent the need is to address the structures and systems that shape the space for the work of mothering.

We also thank Concordia University (Faculty of Arts and Science) and the University of Manitoba (Department of Political Studies, Faculty of Arts, and Faculty of Law) for their financial support on this project.

Contents

Part III
Reimagining Mothering
185

Chapter 11
"Money Isn't Everything, But It's Involved in Everything":
Young Mothers' Experiences with Poverty, Their Survival Strategies, and
Demands for Systemic Changes
Heather Bergen
187

Chapter 12
The Missed Bus: Intersecting Law, Motherhood, Advocacy, and Privilege
Shauna Labman
203

Chapter 13
Single and Desperate? Lone Mothers and Welfare
Rachel Lamdin Hunter
215

Chapter 14
Mothering, Welfare and Political Economy of Basic Income in Australia:
Potentials for Mothers with Disabilities
Jenni Mays
227

Chapter 15
Lesbian-Parented Families: Negotiating the Cultural Narrative of
Heteronormativity through Leisure and Sport Experiences
Dawn E. Trussell
243

Chapter 16
Storytelling Motherhood with Katniss, Hermione, Tanya, and the
Warrior Cats, or Owls and Ravens Raising Wrens
Gillian Calder
259

Notes on Contributors
275

Mothering and Welfare: Depriving, Surviving, Thriving

Karine Levasseur, Stephanie Paterson,
and Lorna A. Turnbull

In the closing years of the second decade of the twenty-first century right-leaning forms of populism appear to be displacing more pluralist and social democratic forms of government. The June 2016 referendum in favour of Brexit and the resulting political turmoil in Great Britain, the November 2016 election of Donald Trump as president of the United States, the election of, or formation of coalitions with, populist and anti-immigrant governments in several countries in the succeeding years, and continuing instances of rhetoric and violence against minorities worldwide are but the most reported examples of this phenomenon. Although neoliberal ideologies and austerity measures reign in many places, some states, such as the Nordic ones, continue to advance supports for mothers and families and others take tentative steps in that direction. Canada, for example, has expanded the child benefit program; it has increased in value and is now indexed to inflation. Meanwhile, in Kenya, the government has experimented with various basic income programs.

In what ways do these policy environments affect mothering and welfare? Who do we think of when we think of mothering and what do we mean by welfare? These are some of the questions tackled by the authors in this collection. Over two years ago, when we put out the call for papers, things were already looking grim, especially in the United States and the United Kingdom, and they do not seem to have improved and may, in fact, have become worse in the intervening months while our authors wrote their chapters. Indeed, the arrival of a global pandemic during the publication process has created new strains on the welfare of many, especially those who are mothering, and has revealed more starkly the gaping chasms that carers and their vulnerable charges fall into. Similarly, the increasingly global Black Lives Matter movement illuminates the additional challenges facing Black mothers and their families at the hands of white supremacist state agents. In the call for papers, we were clear that we understood welfare to include both the income support programs and social services that are so essential for the wellbeing of the many people doing the unpaid motherwork of caring for the next generation. It has also been clear for us from the beginning of this project that mothering is done mainly by mothers, but not exclusively by mothers. Fathers, othermothers, and queer parents also mother, and their welfare is equally a concern within the pages of this volume. Still, policies that support or disadvantage those doing mother-work disproportionately affect women. Social policy, and welfare policy in particular, in many rich and developed Western nations has not meaningfully met the needs of mothers, as evidenced by women's continued lower income and earnings, their precarious employment, the lack of affordable and regulated childcare, and the ongoing state surveillance of marginalized mothers through social service agencies, child welfare systems, and the criminal justice system.

All of these ideas are reflected in the cover art we selected for this collection. We wanted an image that would convey the labour and love that goes into mothering without attaching a particular kind of mother to the image. We were thrilled to find the work of Canadian artist Corey Hardeman, titled "Drowning Nest". A mother of four, she says "my paintings of nests are entirely about motherlove, about trying to make a structure that contains love and nurturance, and, of course, I put them in these perilous situations because, well, here we are." Indeed, here we are. Many of us who are mothering are doing so in perilous situations, yet we continue to strive to create safe spaces where our offspring are raised and where mothering takes place, even though many of us may feel as if we are drowning and unable to protect and care for our children. The nest may have fallen from the tree, but the tide may change, and the nest may wash up on the shore again, safe on dry land. And those who are doing motherwork are resourceful and resilient; they have to be.

Although this volume is a rich and diverse collection that gives voice to many perspectives on mothering and welfare, it is not a textbook of political or economic theory. Nonetheless, many, if not most, of the chapters in the collection rely upon certain theoretical descriptions of the social environment in which mothering takes place, today and over the previous several decades. Neoliberalism is the label attached to the twentieth-century manifestation of Western Enlightenment ideals that intend to limit the power of the state, the crown, and the church, thus protecting the rights of individuals. According Milton Friedman, government's only role is to provide the regulatory framework and infrastructure for the free functioning of the market, supporting the logic of a minimalist state. Of course, such a regulatory framework contains laws that protect the superiority of individual rights over collective ones and support a system of private ownership, accumulation of capital, and rent seeking (Stiglitz). To protect the interests of the one per cent, states have moved steadily away from progressive taxation and broad social safety nets, and from protecting labour unions. Instead, markets are freed to determine the conditions of employment (wages, job protection, etc.) while carrying reduced tax burdens. Multinational corporations, Western foreign policy, the International Monetary Fund, and the World Bank have been the mechanisms by which neoliberal regimes have been established in the Global South. Creditors (financial institutions and nation-states) have gained influence over governments, and laws are made to benefit their interests, often over the interests of the nation's people.

Neoliberalism is established and maintained through a redirection of resources away from the public towards private market actors. Austerity is the means by which these neoliberal objectives are achieved, allowing private actors to provide 'public' services, for profit. Healthcare, education, social security, prisons, and other services previously provided by the state are outsourced to private providers. Workers soon find themselves in a state of precarity, in which many jobs are temporary, casual, or intermittent—usually at the discretion of the employer. The vulnerabilities of women and other marginalized people are exacerbated in this widespread and precarious working norm, and the authors in this book bring their own perspectives in order to interrogate how these norms are leaving those who are mothering our next generation drowning like the nest on the cover of this volume.

The chapters in this collection are organized into three sections. The chapters in the first section, "Depriving: Mothering in the Face of Austerity," illustrate the many ways policies and actions of the state, especially the neoliberal state, deprive mothers and their children of the supports and frameworks that allow them to live rich and meaningful lives with dignity. In the second section, "Surviving: Images of Mothering," the chapters explore how mothers are portrayed as well as the ideals that they are expected to embody in order to achieve the social expectations of a good or worthy mother. In the final section, "Thriving: Reimagining Mothering," the chapters offer different ways of reimagining the place of motherwork in our societies and the kinds of support that can help ensure that all who are mothering, and their children, can thrive.

Depriving: Mothering in the Face of Austerity

Statistics Canada does not track all who are mothering, but it does publish a report every five years tracking the situation of women in Canada, and they have found that women's wellbeing is adversely affected by their caregiving responsibilities. This is not good for these women or their children. It is not a good foundation for welfare. In contrast, mothers who are empowered, thriving, and have adequate food, safe shelter, and access to safe and affordable childcare raise children who do better and are themselves able to contribute to building stronger communities (Crittenden 112; O'Reilly 70; Smith 240). Andrea O'Reilly, in *Matricentric Feminism*, articulates a theory of empowered mothering. She sees a direct connection between neoliberalism and intensive mothering. As neoliberal policies shrink the public realm (welfare becomes workfare, and budgets of schools and community programs are cut) and the wage gap persists, mothers replace the shrinking public services with their own private and unpaid labour.

The first section of the book opens with a poem by Tara Kainer that captures the violence done to mothers and their children who are condemned to live in poverty. Kainer draws the reader in to feel the desperation of the mother who is numb from the constant battle of trying to survive; the poem sets the tone for the chapters that follow, illustrating the many ways the current economic system deprives those who have taken on the vital function of caring for the next generation. First, Marie

Lovrod, Stephanie Bustamante, and Darlene Domshy show how systemic barriers discourage and fail to support young mothers who have grown up in the child welfare system and how stereotyped assumptions frame these young women as unsuitable for mothering. Then, Lynsey Race and Lorna Stefanick describe how mother-child programs in prison are another tool in the state's repertoire to control mothering practices and enforce women's vulnerability and gendered norms. They show how this disciplining of care work falls more heavily upon women who are already marginalized, as it is precisely their marginalization that has left them reliant on disappearing state support, including housing, childcare, income assistance, and transport, which makes their resort to criminalized activity (for example, drugs and sex work) more likely.

Cuts to basic services and supports, such as healthcare, have devastating consequences for low income, especially racialized, women. In their chapter, Lynda Ross and Shauna Wilton outline how Trump's attack on healthcare in the United States further marginalizes vulnerable groups in the United States, especially women and children. And to conclude the section, Nathalie Reis Itaboraí underlines how precarity for mothers is not limited to the dominant stories from the Global North. Brazil is considered a global economic success story, as it now ranks as the eighth largest economy in the world. Yet income inequality is significant and social supports are far from universal in the country; urban and formally employed mothers are privileged, whereas rural, racialized women largely work outside the formal sector and have access to only meagre and conditional maternity support.

Surviving: Images of Mothering

Contemporary discourses of mothers and motherhood conjure images of warm, nurturing, and selfless caregivers. Such images pervade popular and political discourses, shaping how we think, speak, and feel about mothers and motherhood. In Canada, for example, the turn of the nineteenth century saw motherhood emerge as a policy problem, in part due to efforts to populate the nation (Valverde). As such, these dominant images of the nurturing caregiver were embedded in policy discourse and texts, which served to fix meanings of motherhood to white, middle-class ideals. In problematizing motherhood and mothering, public policy interventions resulted in the emergence of a wide range of experts with the authority to diagnose and treat issues related to fertility, birth, and parenting (Ehrenreich and English). In effect, all mothers, though in unequal ways, were subject to state intervention and surveillance, and disciplined accordingly.

The persistence of these disciplinary forces—which are gendered, racialized, ableist, and hetero and gender normative—is compounded by more recent policy problems that challenge the reproductive labour undertaken by mothers. In particular, a key challenge for contemporary policymakers is how to enable mothers to balance both unpaid and paid work. The best policy responses trouble the gendered division of care work, such as paternity leaves that encourage fathers or other parents to contribute to care work. More typically, however, policies include various leaves aimed at the birth parent, which assume and encourage short-term exits from the labour market to engage in unpaid care work while promoting privatized care arrangements, often relying upon racialized and migrant labour.

All of the chapters in this section illuminate these disciplinary forces at work and reveal that the lived experience of motherhood and mothering is much more complex than contemporary images suggest. Roberta Garrett investigates the emergence of the "mumpreneur" against the backdrop of austerity politics in the United Kingdom. She argues that the mumpreneur figure reconciles the competing discourses of the caring mother with the cutthroat capitalist and reinforces the maternal role of women in an advanced capitalist society. Similarly, Rebecca Wallace examines the role of the media in edifying particular images of mothers in her study of English print media in Canada. Her analysis reveals a complex and contradictory discursive terrain that gives rise to multiple maternal framings in which discussions of race and class are more subtly conveyed than in the United States.

The expected maternal role of women and the work mothers do are directly addressed by the remaining chapters in this section. Lindsay Larios illuminates how contemporary discourses on mothering often render invisible work that does not directly involve a child. She reveals how immigrant mothers work to contribute to and shape their communities and how this is directly linked to their identities as mothers. Sara Cantillon and Martina Hutton link the concepts of "self-sacrifice" and "role captivity" among women to the ideology of "intensive motherhood" (Hays). They examine how such forces work to constitute this particular form of mothering as aspirational and how they serve to perpetuate inequality and undermine maternal wellbeing. In her chapter on the Canadian government's Muskoka Initiative, Jacqueline Potvin examines how maternalism is embedded in international assistance policy and argues that the Muskoka Initiative deployed discourses that aimed at making mothers responsible for not only the health and development of their own children but also the entire developing world.

Thriving: Reimagining Mothering

The first two sections of this collection outline the challenges associated with how mothering is seen (or not) as well as the destructive effects neoliberal austerity has on mothers. This section begins to trace a path towards more positive understandings of mothering—the type of mothering that O'Reilly suggests can be a site of power. Black feminist and Indigenous scholars have long argued that motherwork and families are important sites of resilience and resistance (e.g., Collins, hooks). Indeed, Kim Anderson argues that Indigenous women draw on cultural and collectivist norms to build families as sites of resistance (762). The authors in this section provide a sense of hope that mothering can be reimagined through literature, culture, administrative reform, and public policy. This sense of hope is in keeping with of theme of the nest. To be sure, the image on the front cover is of a nest that has fallen out of a tree and into the water, but it is still intact; it was skillfully built, and it may yet become a home again for raising the young.

In her chapter, Heather Bergen shares the lived experiences of low-income young mothers she works with in Toronto; she makes it clear that these young parents see themselves as agents of change who speak out about structural barriers and what young parents need to succeed. Shauna Labman also picks up themes of agency and voice in her chapter, as she challenges school transportation rules that presume that mothers are always available, always at home with their children, and not occupied at work while their children attend daycare. Recognizing her own privilege, she also acknowledges that these same assumptions make reconciling mothering and market work even more difficult for marginalized mothers whose voices she strives to amplify. Rachel Lamdin Hunter in her chapter directly invites the reader to reimagine mothering and to explore the role that antenarratives can play in reshaping how "street-level bureaucrats" (Lipsky) can more meaning-fully support single mothers engaging with the welfare system. She maintains that antenarratives can challenge the dominant narrative of how society views lone mothers on welfare and can open a space for progressive policy development. Jenni Mays takes us even further in her chapter, as she argues that a basic income, in the form of an unconditional cash transfer, can better support mothers living with disabilities in Australia—increasing their freedom and reducing their vulnerability to domestic violence. Next, Dawn Trussell explores the stories of two lesbian parents and their nine-year-old-child to highlight the impor-tance of leisure and sport for the wellbeing of individuals and families. She identifies opportunities for both public policy and administrative bureaucracies to make public spaces more welcoming and safer for all families.

The last contribution, from Gillian Calder, reimagines mothering and offers hope through shared storytelling. Structured as a book to be read aloud, her contribution explores children's literature, which she, as a parent, reads to her child. The style is unconventional and unexpected, intended to both capture the orality she writes about (reading aloud) and to model, through provocation, an embodiment of othering. Calder illuminates how children's literature challenges the dominant under-standing of families, and the format and rhythm of her chapter are designed to do the same. Through literature, non-traditional families, Indigeneity, and new kinds of care models emerge to produce different understandings of mothering and of welfare.

Together, the chapters in these three sections invite readers to critically engage and reflect on the diverse experiences of mothering and to consider ways to better support and, indeed, transform its practice. In these uncertain times, we hope these chapters not only offer insight into what's currently wrong but also inspire alternative ideas about the sort of society we can achieve when we centre mothers and motherwork as well as the policy interventions necessary to achieve it.

Works Cited

Anderson, Kim. "Giving Life to the People: An Indigenous Ideology of Motherhood". *Maternal Theory: Essential Readings*, edited by Andrea O'Reilly, Demeter Press, 2007, pp. 761-781.

Collins, Patricia Hill. *Black Feminist Thought*. Routledge, 2000.

Crittenden, Ann. *The Price of Motherhood: Why the Most Important Job in the World Is Still the Least Valued*. Henry Holt and Company, 2001.

Friedman, Milton. *Capitalism and Freedom*. University of Chicago Press, 1962.

Hays, Sharon. *The Cultural Contradictions of Motherhood*. Yale University Press, 1996.

hooks, bell. *Feminist Theory: From Margin to Center*. South End Press, 1984.

Lipsky, Michael. *Street Level Bureaucrats: Dilemmas of the Individual in Public Service*. Russell Sage Foundation, 2010.

O'Reilly, Andrea. *Matricentric Feminism: Theory, Activism and Practice*. Demeter Press, 2014.

Smith, Janna Malamud. *A Potent Spell: Motherlove and the Power of Fear*. Houghton Mifflin Company, 2003.

Statistics Canada. *Women in Canada: A Gender Based Statistical Report*, 2017, www150.statcan.gc.ca/n1/pub/89-503-x/89-503-x2015001-eng.htm. Accessed 14 July 2020.

Stiglitz, Joseph E. *The Price of Inequality*. W.W. Norton and Company, 2012.

Valverde, Mariana. "When the Mother of the Race Is Free: Race, Reproduction, and Sexuality in First-Wave Feminism." *Gender Conflicts: New Essays in Women's History*, edited by Franca Iocovetta and Mariana Valverde, University of Toronto Press, 1992, pp. 3-26.

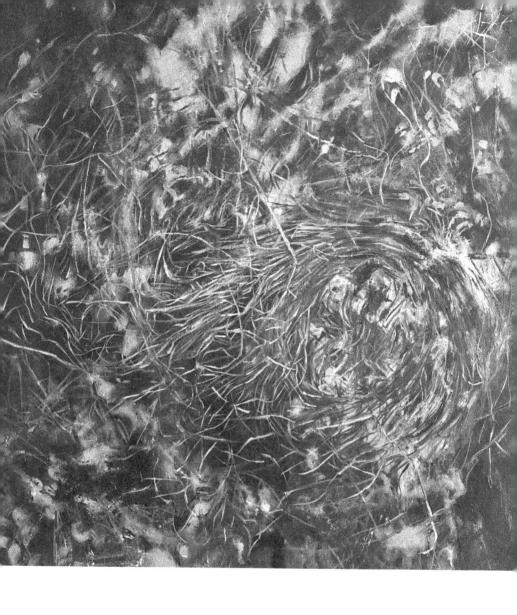

Part I

Mothering in the Face of Austerity

Chapter One

But I'm Hungry

Tara Kainer

Poverty, Mahatma Gandhi said,
is the worst form of violence.
She didn't understand
until tight in its grip her world shrunk
to this tiny, dark box where crushed
together with her two small children
every which way she turns
there is something to block her, every time
she raises herself up, someone
knocks her back down. The first time
she slapped her toddler hard
he reached for the milk
tipping it over, all they had left
until the next cheque day—nothing
to do but cry over spilt milk,
huddled together she wailed and he howled,
heads hanging, two blue figures in a fixed
landscape, her stomach churning at the thought
of going to the food bank or drop-in for more.
She can't face their questions—that look—
pity or condemnation—both
cause her hands to sweat,

a collapsing of her innards, the loss of her voice.
In the beginning
she expected kindness, actually waited for a call.
Are your kids okay? they'd ask, *How are you coping?*
would acknowledge what she's going through
instead of justifying their own impotence
by pointing a finger at her, recognize who she is,
not equate her with her diminished circumstances.
Now she shuts herself and her kids up in their cramped,
hot apartment, puts the bicycle lock on the fridge door.
Even when her son cries, *But I'm hungry, mummy!*
she tells him to wait for his supper, calculates
how long the food will last, sits still and cold as stone.

"We're a Package Deal Now:" Young Mothers from Government Care in Saskatchewan Assess their Social Welfare Experiences

Marie Lovrod, Stephanie Bustamante, and Darlene Domshy

"Who do you trust when you're from [government] care?"
—Youth participant

This chapter presents the perspectives of twelve young mothers in and from government care and custody, who have been steeped from childhood in the disciplinary practices of neo-liberal care regimes. All have experienced out-of-home care or been held in the youth justice system for a year or more. As current or former systems youth,[1] all have been temporary or permanent provincial wards in Saskatchewan, where benefits end at eighteen, with possible extension to twenty-one for eligible care agreements. All have lived with extended family, in foster or group homes, youth detention centers, or some combination thereof. All have been held in custodial relation by the neoliberal welfare state, as both children and mothers.

As present or former state wards, systems mothers have "care experiences" (Butler and Benoit 25) that may vary considerably from societal expectations of good care. Yet they can be held to higher standards of care for their children than they received from their state-sponsored guardians. This paradoxical situation reflects neoliberal logics, which reproduce, via contemporary public services structures, aggressive patriarchal and colonial biases that are organized through persistent notions of deserving and undeserving service recipients (see Race and Stefanick, this volume) as measured by market forces.

Caroline MacDonald-Harker argues that the demands of intensive mothering have grown as women have joined the paid labour market (3-4). At the same time, neoliberal democracies commodify and externalize caring responsibilities, squeezing public welfare programs and intensifying pressures on individuals and families. Patricia Hill Collins argues that Western governments use mainstream nostalgia for heteropatriarchal family values (63) to legitimize such approaches. In conjunction with strategic budget cuts that exploit unpaid reproductive labour, reduced investments in what Joan Tronto calls a "public ethic of caring with one another" constitute a failure to ensure that social service providers are well informed and able to meet the broadest spectrum of needs (11). Young mothers in and from care endure the contradictions of the state claiming to be responsive to their lived realities while it remains, in fact, blind to them, even with advocates supporting their efforts (see Labman, this volume).

Targeted along intersecting axes of race, class, gender, and young parenthood, participating mothers emphasize the harsh realities that characterize neoliberal social welfare schemes, identify supportive people and resources they have encountered along the way, celebrate their own vigorous resilience, and bring their practical knowhow to the task of making meaningful service improvements. Emphasizing emergent themes through section headings framed in the mothers' own words, this chapter outlines participant experiences of social welfare systems—from their exposure (or lack thereof) to public health and sex education, to the processes of discovering and delivering their babies, to the challenges of raising their children under often adverse economic circumstances and punitive state surveillance. Participants argue that their desire to be better mothers to their children than the state was for them reveals how state emphasis on cost obstructs more effective practices of placing mutual care "at the center of democratic political agendas" (Tronto ix).

This study was conducted in partnership with the Saskatchewan Youth in Care and Custody Network (SYICCN)—a nonprofit community-based service organization (and member of Youth in Care Canada), designed to operate in contexts led by, for, and about youth (ages fourteen to twenty-four) in and from government care. For over twenty years, SYICCN members have co-created knowledge to improve care experiences and transitions to adult citizenship as well as to inform public education about care systems. SYICCN supports peer connections through social gatherings where alumni and adult supporters reinforce youth aspirations towards solution building. Local networks across the province create spaces where systems youth can develop self-advocacy and leadership skills. Learning that they are not alone in their care experiences is vital to surviving child welfare systems, with their uneven delivery of care.

Our project team consists of: a former youth justice worker, now SYICCN director (and mother); the research coordinator (former SYICCN director), a healthcare professional with considerable network leadership experience (also a mother); the provincial outreach coord-inator; and an academic researcher (and grandmother) who has been developing collaborative research projects with SYICCN staff, youth, and alumni for more than a decade. SYICCN's board—with half youth members and half adult supports—served as supervisory stakeholders for this project.

Methodology: "Getting Together with Other Mothers from Care Would Be Good"

SYICCN has adopted a set of guiding principles to ensure that all research projects are youth driven and centred; age appropriate with meaningful consent processes; and subject to youth input on study design, data analysis, recommendations, project evaluation, and outcomes. The network also has ownership of the research results. Across several previous research initiatives—including a longitudinal study of the role of networking in the lives of participating youth (Lovrod and Domshy), a transition-supports project, (Lovrod, Busta-mante, and Domshy) and the participatory development of youth-friendly online tools for success—young parents have expressed interest in holding critical discussions about the challenges of parenting while living in or transitioning from government care, and beyond. Since mothers in and from care are more likely to have custody of their

MARIE LOVROD, STEPHANIE BUSTAMANTE, AND DARLENE DOMSHY

children (Dworsky and Courtney 1351)—that is, to be systematically produced as lone mothers (see Bergen and Hunter, this volume)—the network decided to begin by considering their perspectives and needs.

Because young mothers are busy people, we set out to develop this line of inquiry based on two focus group discussions designed to outline and evaluate the issues, which were scheduled several months apart. Participants could get to know one another while following simple narrative prompts to describe their journeys as mothers, with ongoing opportunities to elaborate upon resulting themes and outputs. Ethics approval was obtained through the University of Saskatchewan. Participants had the opportunity to review the project objectives and ask questions before providing written consent. As agreed, focus group prompts were loosely organized around the processes of obtaining sexual health education, discovering pregnancy, giving birth, becoming young mothers, and then parenting or coparenting in the context of relationships with social welfare workers and agencies. Participants were invited to collaborate in data analysis and to review and revise evolving versions of this paper.

Participants: "You Never Escape Your Care Experience"

On a sweltering day in July 2017, a group of young mothers—now in their late teens and early twenties—gathered at SYICCN offices in Regina with their children (aged three months to eight years) to discuss their unique relationships with social services as systems youth who became parents while in care or custody. The following December, the group convened again, with two new members, who had heard about the project through the provincial network. They trudged through winter snows, often with babes in arms or preschoolers in strollers, to gather at the Regina Public Library, with its well-appointed selection of children's books and toys. Both times, the women met to share reflections on mothering during and after state guardianship.

One of the women who joined the second gathering was in care when her children were born, but she aged out more than a decade ago; she is now raising thriving teenagers. Another had aged out and then gave birth to two children, still preteens. Five participants are Indigenous or Métis; the rest are settler descended. Though invited, recent immigrants and queer-identified youth did not attend, owing to the often challenging circumstances associated with their respective social positions. One former systems youth with a visible disability, who identifies as queer and works in early childhood education, was among the paid child-minders. All of the participants were recruited as SYICCN members currently in or recently from care (except the two alumni who participated as mentoring mothers). The December gathering reviewed and elaborated upon the summary analyses of the July results.

Adjusting the Critical Lens: "I Was Considered High Risk"

Young mothers with care experiences provide a powerful critical lens on neoliberal care regimes, which function as much to decline eligibility for services as to provide access to them (Rutman et al. 150). Historical and contemporary child welfare schemes have been shaped by colonialist and market-based ideologies that exacerbate disparities (Blackstock 285; Strong-Boag 69; see Bergen, this volume). Systems mothers differ from their peers, as they rely on busy social workers or foster parents to help navigate child welfare, educational, healthcare and justice systems. As such, they may struggle to explain their experiences as state wards to publics who may not fully appreciate how the barriers they face affect their efforts to actualize as caring adults (Nybell 1233).

Unbeknownst to the organizers, an antichoice demonstration was taking place outside the building (which also houses physician's offices) on that first July afternoon. In a spirited discussion, participants recalled their own or others' past pregnancies and terminations; they noted how the demonstrators' use of graphic images could force parents to explain the startling pictures to children or might retrigger birth trauma flashbacks. The demonstration recontextualized our discussions of participants' past decisions and their systems-informed perspectives on uneven access to reproductive choice.

Many factors may contribute to a mother from care confronting an unplanned pregnancy. Given that Saskatchewan has the highest provincial teen pregnancy rate (Statistics Canada), she would not be alone. However, due to the often chaotic conditions endured by systems youth, including multiple moves amid shifting social workers, schools, and communities (Lovrod, Bustamante, and Domshy 221), young mothers from care may have fewer interpersonal supports than most.

They will almost certainly face stigma in their interactions with health-care professionals as well as in educational and social service systems. They may experience coercion regarding pregnancy and adoption decisions, if they carry to term. There will be surveillance—including by child welfare—if they choose to raise their child. If a young mother is Indigenous, racialized, a recent immigrant, queer, or has a disability, these issues are compounded.

Although numerous studies engage systems perspectives on young parents or offer social insights on intensive, empowered, and empowering mothering (McDonald-Harker; O'Reilly), Melissa Radey et al. suggest that despite "high rates of pregnancies, births, and repeat births among young women aging out of foster care, few studies have examined the day-to-day experiences of parents aging out, their strengths, and their needs" (2). Deborah Rutman et al., meanwhile, point out that "the construction of adolescent pregnancy as inherently 'bad,' with negative consequences for both mother and child, comes from predominantly white, middle class definitions of what is acceptable mothering, and ignore the positive functions of adolescent pregnancy and mothering in marginalized racial, class and ethnic communities" (150), as these young mothers work to develop constructive life plans for themselves and their children.

Findings: "There's Not Even a Policy—Something Should Be Written in for Young Moms"

Sexual Health Education—"Anything Can Happen"

Comprehensive sexual health education enables reproductive choice and respectful sexual expression. However, sexual health and parenting education practices are complicated by child welfare experiences. One young mother said, "If you're in kinship care with your grandmother or an uncle, they're not going to tell you anything about sex. How do you make sure people in care know about their sexual health? My foster mom brought the health nurse to show me a video." A First Nations participant responded that "My grandma told me about the birds and bees at four, so I knew the differences between girl and boy bodies, in a healthy way. In first grade, we had the lesson on good touch/bad touch." But a settler-descended participant's grandmother "gave me the old-fashioned version: Don't do it or you're going to hell." One foster mother had admonished a participant: "'You should ask the doctor about birth control.' It was more like being accused of having sex and then learning about other uses for contraception." Another participant commented: "Nothing was discussed in my foster homes. Even getting your period was hush hush." "My learning about birth control," one mother remarked, "was being yelled at by a social worker, with my boyfriend outside the wall." Misinformation, harsh judgments, and neglect are not sound preparation for informed consent.

Nevertheless, participants gave thoughtful assessments of best practices in sexual health education. One commented that "Kids are not getting sex ed at the appropriate time. Sixth grade is too late. Why isn't it being taught before puberty? In grade five, I was scared to change in the bathroom because I was already wearing a bra, and there had been no discussion at all." "It's true," another added. "My preschool step-daughter overheard a conversation and asked me what 'sex' was, so even at a young age, children can have questions."

For youth removed from their families of origin for sexual interference, sex education can be a loaded topic. One mother whose son attends a progressive community school said their curriculum is quite open and begins early. However, she was uncomfortable with "good touch/bad touch" training, because it implies that children should initially try to resist inappropriate behaviour on their own. Several mothers wanted to ensure good sexual health training at home. One said that "I ask my children to show me what they learn in school. We have a lot of body positivity in our house and use very open language so they know that every relationship is not heterosexual."

Some participants reported receiving some parental training, whereas others had none. One carried a raw egg around for a week at school, while another signed out a mechanical baby with a wind-up key to learn about babies' needs. In a community-based parenting class, one mother was advised that to care for her child, she must care for herself because "everything you get, your child gets." Banding together as mothers was a valued strategy, although participants had few opportunities to discuss mothering with others from government care. One commented insightfully: "Given that foster parents receive training, why wouldn't parents from care also receive parental training? It's obvious!" All wanted to do better by their own children.

Being Pregnant: "Nobody Would Understand Unless They Have Been in Your Position"

Child welfare systems seldom communicate confidence in youth success. Eve Tuck calls the practice of treating targeted individuals, groups, and communities as predictably defeated and broken, "designating damage" (412). "Damage stories" attribute the effects of broad social forces to individuals. For example, American research shows that early pregnancy and child birth are two to three times higher among youth from government care than nonsystems youth (Shpiegel and Cascardi 278). Such statistics could be used to label systems youth as prone to poor decisions rather than recognizing how being in care may deprive youth of support in making life decisions. Another plausible interpretation may recognize that since foster parents, institutional staff, and social workers rarely become long-term mentors—although some maintain informal connections beyond youth transitions out of the system (Sulimani-Aiden 43)—young mothers who raise children from socially vulnerable positions may be taking steps towards relational empowerment by choosing to become mothers.

Several participants felt positive about caring for their children, even under challenging circumstances. Unfortunately, neoliberal welfare regimes measure system success through the removal of youth from state dependency, stressing their market-based employability. Young people aging out of care, therefore, face pressures associated with adult independence sooner than "non-foster youth whose parents are likely to extend support to their children throughout the transition to adulthood and beyond" (Radey et al. 2). This dynamic offloads responsibility for job readiness onto systems youth, whether or not their care experiences make that outcome even marginally realistic. Given that "the demands of early parenting may compromise employment, social, and educational opportunities" (Radey et al. 2), failure to address systemic barriers to successful adult transitioning, and parenting, undermines optimal futures for young mothers and their children (Hunter, this volume).

The tension between the expectations placed upon youth within the care system and participants' own understanding of meaningful care was palpable as mothers described discovering their pregnancies. One was "overwhelmed and wondered, how will I tell the adults? Even they were crying" when she told them. Another asked her worker whether she had children and was told, "No, but I have two dogs!" as if the differences in privilege or caring commitments could be so glibly compared. One participant emphasized the difficulty in finding placements for mothers with children: "If I got pregnant in my foster home, I would have been kicked out. My foster mother wouldn't take babies under sixteen months." Similarly, a mother who gave birth in her early teens faced a panel of social workers, "four against one," who decided the fate of her daughter: "They wanted me to give her up for adoption. It was intimidating. Thankfully, my [foster] mom was there to speak up for me." Because she was supported to keep her first baby while finishing high school in care, this mother retains custody of both of her children. One married mother with two healthy children who were born after she transitioned from care, felt intimidated well into her second pregnancy: "When they say that your kid may be special needs halfway through and people are asking if you are going to abort, I literally wanted to cry." Another reported, "Only one friend stayed in touch. You really find out who your true friends are the moment you get pregnant." A round of nods greeted a participant's aspiration to defeat the odds: "I want to be someone positive."

Quantitative research suggests that empowered mothering may provide a pathway out of intergenerational systems involvement. In a recent study of 576 Manitoba mothers who gave birth while in care between 1998 and 2013, as compared with 5,366 adolescent mothers not in care when they gave birth, Elizabeth Wall-Wieler et al. found that systems mothers were significantly more likely to have a child removed within the first two years of life. They argue for better programs to keep mothers and children together, wherever possible. Phyllis Cohen et al. show that "enhancing empathy, reflection, connection and support" (125) produces attachment, attunement, and future-orientation through better practices of caring with mothers from government care. Connective practices that emphasize "understanding and accepting—rather than criticizing, correcting, or repairing" (125) offer a necessary departure from neoliberal logics and inequities.

Prenatal Care: "Hell No; I Did Not Need to Be Gawked at as an Eighteen-Year-Old in Those Classes"

Participation in prenatal programs was inconsistent. One mother's family disowned her, "so it was less likely to have adults advocating for prenatal programs in care." Another was in a group home for her pregnancy but would run away: "It was really a jail for kids, very depressing." Flight could so easily be read as noncompliance rather than as a life-affirming impulse.

One mother's worker was her "go-to person," who got her "to and from appointments," whereas another "had no support." When one mother advised that "They should talk more about breastfeeding in prenatal care," another replied, "I would have loved that!" One participant who had graduated high school but was dealing with addictions when she became pregnant "quit cold turkey" when she found out she was pregnant. Another was moved into a rural foster home at fourteen, when she became pregnant. "The mother in that family was the only person there for me; I went through three different workers during my pregnancy ... so felt like I was placed and then forgotten." Another found the "healthy mother/healthy baby" program as well as her social worker and doctor to be sensitive and helpful. Social services provided milk cards, food vouchers, and prenatal vitamins to several expectant mothers, ensuring healthy prenatal diets.

Social workers and healthcare providers pressed participants to clarify their pregnancy decisions. The doctor of one participant was especially "judgmental," since she hadn't talked to her family yet, "so it was scary to be questioned right up front." Another "asked about adoption right away" because she was sixteen. Another participant's social worker asked if she was going through with her pregnancy and looked into adoption options for her. Another mother said that "Once I had made my decision, my doctor was pretty good." All wanted access to doulas or midwives to support them giving birth. Doulas decrease labour duration and Caesarian sections, enhance maternal-infant attachment and breastfeeding, and reduce postpartum depression (Phillips and Kelly 118).

Birth: "You Have a Belly and Then a Baby; It's the Best Moment but the Weirdest Moment"

In her study of transitions to parenthood among heterosexual Canadian couples, Bonnie Fox argues that having agency in birthing decisions can improve maternal experiences (75). Without social supports, mothers lack the knowledge to help them prepare for mothering; they feel overwhelmed by responsibility and isolation, especially in the baby's first year, making empowered mothering difficult to achieve (115). The problematic neoliberal claim that "everyone has an equal opportunity to get ahead" (Luxton 216) is even less convincing under parenting conditions in contemporary Canadian child welfare.

Healthcare professionals trained to engage primarily with mainstream mothers during childbirth and postpartum may be woefully unaware of how little an expectant mother from care may know about giving birth; they may also offer unhelpful commentary they might otherwise avoid with older patients (Fox 76). One participant noted, "They should read your file. As a first-time mom, I was only comfortable with family there." All agreed that there should be more training about young mothers, particularly from child welfare, to help prepare them for parenting. One waited alone, without explanation or support, in an emergency room: "Young moms don't necessarily know what is going on; they have just no idea." One participant's baby came in the ambulance, and others were in labour for long hours. One said, "I didn't know what the mucous plug was; people don't explain the process of birthing."

At the same time, as one participant said, "People don't have a filter, or think about what they are saying." She continued: "While I was there to give birth, they started asking me about some of my scars. How could they ask me that at such a time?" One mother spent her first night in the hospital alone: "The doctors and nurses expected me to know what to do." A mother who gave birth at fourteen "had a long labour, complications, forceps, and required a blood transfusion." Another with a good hospitalization experience pointed out that even though her worker was supportive, she still had communications issues: "I went into labour on a Friday evening and workers are nine to five, Monday through Friday. We're not supposed to share personal information, so she had no idea." In another case, "The social worker from the hospital came because if you've been in care, social services will be keeping an eye on you." One worker "actually came into the delivery room after forty-two hours of labour, talking about taking my daughter. Luckily, my [foster] mom was there to support me."

On a survey about her hospital experience, one mother noted how little follow up is available for young mothers. Another said that she got in "trouble for procedures like burping and was treated badly for falling asleep when breastfeeding." All agreed there is a great need to challenge the discrimination that surrounds young mothers from care and minority backgrounds of all ages. Yvonne Boyer, for example, documents two recent cases of racism in Saskatchewan healthcare, one targeting Indigenous women for involuntary sterilization and another citing egregious neglect at the intersections of race and poverty (1408). In

"Sexual and Reproductive Health, Rights, Realities and Access to Services for First Nations, Inuit and Métis in Canada," Jessica Yee et al. argue that combatting these forms of discrimination requires implementing culturally safe services, fighting queerphobia, and supporting people with disabilities (634).

After hospitalization, several mothers made use of urban schools with daycare and other support services; others were expected to leave familiar school settings once they became mothers, while the same did not apply for young fathers. Many felt pressured to return to class mere days after giving birth, with their milk coming in, often in class. Muscling through recovery in school in order to meet care eligibility requirements meant that they experienced unnecessary suffering.

Despite these challenges, participating mothers made efforts to care for one another. One participant with a sister from care declared, "We've always been there for each other." When a participant indicated she was still breast feeding her two-year-old, another said, "I wish I could have done that longer." One sought advice from her peers: "In my postnatal group, there are a couple of moms who lost their babies. What do you say to them, without being hurtful?" A participant, whose best friend is from care, noted that their two families trade childminding duties because there is no "grandma to come and grab one of them." Similarly, another mother still in touch with her biological family explained that her cousin and his wife help now with her son, even though they did not get along when they were young.

Surveillance: "Being from Care Gives Us Perspective on the System"

Care experiences may leave young mothers wary of social service providers. One participant said the following: "We don't want to put our kids through that. We didn't have daily routines or a strong sense of family. We weren't taught how to parent, haven't had a reliable parent. When we got in trouble, we didn't have that support." Another elaborated, "Caregivers were always worried we would become young moms; it becomes a self-fulfilling prophecy." "Being Aboriginal," one mother explained, "I felt even more uncomfortable with the statistics and the stereotypes, like, 'Everyone saw that coming.'" One young mother testified that "No foster parent expressed love for me; in a group home, it's inappropriate for them to even comfort you in any way." Another quoted a sibling, who used to tell her to love herself "because nobody else will."

SYICCN members have often described being "burned" when seeking help to cope with complicated life situations. If mothers request support to deal with anxiety or addictions, their children are likely to be apprehended. Funding is maternally channelled in order to nudge young fathers out of the picture. Providing child support could threaten the father's financial situation and affect their longer-term earning power, which serves no one: "Social services can use the relationship with him to reduce their costs by expecting him to cover them. There are racist attitudes too."

Familial abuse or neglect, including within child welfare systems, makes it difficult for some young mothers to trust childminders and respite workers. "Providing stability for my kids was hard because I've been in so many foster homes since I was a baby. When my baby was two months old, my foster family was pushing me to get back into sports; but I didn't trust anybody with my daughter." Another confirmed, "Even having a sitter is hard for me; I've been bothered by my closest relatives, so trust is really hard."[2]

Fear of social service surveillance was common. One mother stated: "When I was in the hospital and they told me a worker was coming, I thought they were going to take my child right then. My family wasn't there for me. I actually had my child's dad call in on me a few times, vindictively." Another confirmed the following: "There's a lot of pressure because anything could lead to them taking your child. It's hard to be open with social workers. I'm very selective in what I share. So you can't even create a relationship with social workers." One mother shared how systemic neglect affected her parenting:

> I noticed right after I had my son, child protection was in my life. Pregnancy led me to sobriety. But within two months, they took him; I was struggling and didn't have reliable babysitters, so he was neglected. I felt a lot of pressure even before anything happened. They didn't suggest programs. I got the baby blues because I didn't know how to cope. I wanted support around addictions because I didn't want to go down that road, and right away, my child was taken. I wanted him home, so I found the necessary resources myself. Fortunately, my sister became a foster parent and took care of him until I was stable enough to bring him home.

Some mothers have benefited from "extended supports [to age twenty-one]" and compassionate workers. However, even good worker connections can by undermined by the rules: "I've just amazed my worker so much, but when I turned eighteen, I suddenly got a new one. The last worker was with me the longest, and then I got switched. It might have been better to just stay with my previous worker. But I'm also extremely independent. I don't go to my worker for much." Resisting reliance on overburdened workers becomes a necessary strategy: "I didn't keep in touch with my workers, just did my own thing ... still don't." One mother talked about the lack of stability in the system: "I wasn't in care for very long, more living with family and relatives, but there is a lack of stability, still. I was in a foster home briefly, but I don't think I even had a worker. How much support is there for kinship care? Services are really lacking that way." Disproportionate numbers of Indigenous children are placed in kinship care, often with grandmothers, who are not as well supported as foster parents from settler communities.

Conclusion: "I Still struggle, but at the End of the Day, My Kids are My Happiness"

Despite tremendous challenges, participants were growing as empowered and empowering mothers. One, who was recently accepted into a youth worker training program, read her application statement. She described pregnancy as "a beautiful opportunity to change my life" and disclosed her past struggles with addictions and sex work, noting that she was ... a child of abuse, raised in group and foster homes as a high risk child:

> I attended and completed a parenting group and got a counsellor there. I really enjoyed connecting with other parents, so joined other parenting and women's groups. One is called Parents as Teachers, essentially training parents how to be early childhood educators. I got involved with Youth in Care and am now a board member. I started to recognize my strengths and accomplishments, learning about myself and how to care for my child. I've been clean and sober for more than a year and graduated with the class of 2017. I truly am grateful to have such awesome care providers. Without their dedication to me and my family's development, I don't know where I would be. I'm excited to see how far I will go; I did this all for my sons.

Participants had several suggestions for their systems peers: "Stay confident and ask questions"; "Always have a support person"; "Attend a prenatal class if you can and educate yourself on the process of birth, so you know what you want and what to expect"; "You need a backup plan to natural birth; there's a small window for an epidural and the anaesthesiologist has to be available"; "Requisition vouchers from your worker are a good way to learn about budgeting. Then, when you are ready, you can move on"; "Having other moms from care to talk with helps. There are groups online for expectant mothers and parents"; "See whether your worker can treat your addiction as a disability"; "If you are serious about school, you can get your supports extended"; and "Take care of yourself. Being a mom is tiring; we all need a break now and then."

Young mothers with care experiences must develop resilience and optimism in the face of systemic pessimism about their futures. To illustrate, a recent SYICCN leadership conference was undersubscribed (with fewer participants than usual), because social workers could not imagine their wards as potential leaders. Similarly, a proposal for a participatory design project for online networking tools was critiqued by education and social work professionals as too optimistic about the capacities of systems youth who requested web-based resources in a province without rural transportation services. However, in our experience, when network youth are supported to examine systemic conditions together, they begin to recognize their circumstances as potentially surmountable. For young systems mothers, activists and researchers invested in caring with one another, informed hope is a renewable resource for empowered mothering; it rebuilds connections strained by social hierarchies that exploit reproductive labour through narrowly conceived and overdetermined neoliberal policies, practices, and processes.

Endnotes

1. We use the term "systems youth" to describe young people who grow up in care or custody with the state as parent (Lovrod, Bustamante, and Domshy 211).

2. Being "bothered" is a prairie euphemism for being molested or sexually abused as a child.

Works Cited

Blackstock, Cindy. "The Complainant: The Canadian Human Rights Case on First Nations Child Welfare." *McGill Law Journal*, vol. 62, no. 2, 2016, pp. 285-328.

Boyer, Yvonne. "Healing Racism in Canadian Health Care." *Canadian Medical Association Journal*, vol. 189, no. 46, 2017, pp. 1408-9.

Butler, Kate, and Cecilia Benoit. "Citizenship Practices among Youth who have Experienced Government Care." *Canadian Journal of Sociology*, vol. 40, no. 1, 2015, pp. 25-49.

Cohen, Phyllis, et al. "Promoting Attachment and Mentalization for Parents and Young Children in the Foster Care System: Implementing a New Training and Treatment Approach in an Agency." *Journal of Infant, Child and Adolescent Psychotherapy*, vol.15, no. 2, 2016, pp. 124-34.

Collins, Patricia Hill. "It's All in the Family: Intersections of Gender, Race, and Nation." *Hypatia*, vol. 13, no. 3, 1998, pp. 62–82.

Dworsky, Amy, and Mark E. Courtney. "The Risk of Teenage Pregnancy among Transitioning Foster Youth." *Children and Youth Services Review*, vol. 32, no. 10, 2010, pp. 1351-56.

Fox, Bonnie. *When Couples Become Parents: The Creation of Gender in the Transition to Parenthood*. University of Toronto Press, 2009.

Lovrod, Marie, and Darlene Domshy. *Our Dream, Our Right, Our Future: Voices from Saskatchewan's Youth in Care and Custody Network*. SYICCN, 2011.

Lovrod, Marie, Stephanie Bustamante, and Darlene Domshy. "Pathways: Community-Engaged Research with Youth Transitioning to Adult In(ter)dependence from Government Care." *Celebrating Child Welfare Transformations*, edited by H. M. Montgomery, et al., University of Regina Press, 2016, pp. 211-239.

Luxton, Meg. "Feminist Scholarship and Family Sociology." *Canadian Review of Sociology*, vol. 52, no. 2, May, 2015, pp. 212-221.

McDonald-Harker, Caroline. *Mothering in Marginalized Contexts: Narratives of Women Who Mother in and through Domestic Violence*. Demeter Press, 2016.

Nybell, Lynn M. "Locating 'Youth Voice': Considering the Contexts of Speaking in Foster Care." *Children and Youth Services Review*, vol. 35, no. 8, 2013, pp. 1227-35.

O'Reilly, Andrea. "Outlaw(ing) Motherhood: A Theory and Politics of Maternal Empowerment for the Twenty-First Century." *Hecate*, vol. 36, no. 1/2, 2010, pp. 17-29.

Phillips, Deborah Lee, and Crystal Kelly. "Social Work Should Embrace Doulas." *Health & Social Work*, vol. 39, no. 2, 2014, pp. 117-20.

Radey, Melissa et al. "'It's Really Overwhelming': Parent and Service Provider Perspectives of Parents Aging out of Foster Care." *Child and Youth Services Review*, vol. 67, 2016, pp. 1-10.

Rutman, Deborah et al. "Undeserving Mothers? Practitioners' Experiences Working with Young Mothers In/From Care". *Child & Family Social Work*, vol. 7, 2002, pp. 149-59.

Shpiegel, Svetlana, and Michelle Cascardi. "Adolescent Parents in the First Wave of the National Youth in Transition Database." *Journal of Public Child Welfare*, vol. 9, no. 3, 2015, pp. 277-98.

Statistics Canada. Table 13-10-0416-01; *Live Births, by Age of Mother*, doi.org/10.25318/1310041601-eng.

Sulimani-Aiden, Yafit. "In Between Formal and Informal: Staff and Youth Relationships in Care and After Leaving Care." *Child and Youth Services Review*, vol. 67, 2016, pp. 43-49.

Strong-Boag, Veronica. *Fostering Nation? Canada Confronts its History of Childhood Disadvantage*. Wilfred Laurier University Press, 2011.

Tronto, Joan C. *Caring Democracy: Markets, Equality, and Justice*. New York University Press, 2013.

Tuck, Eve. "Suspending Damage: A Letter to Communities." *Harvard Educational Review*, vol. 79, no. 3, 2009, pp. 409-28.

Wall-Wieler, Elizabeth et al. "The Cycle of Child Protection Services Involvement: A Cohort Study of Adolescent Mothers." *Pediatrics*, vol. 141, no. 6, 2018, pp. 1-8.

Yee, Jessica et al. "Sexual and Reproductive Health, Rights, and Realities and Access to Services for First Nations, Inuit and Métis in Canada." *Journal of Obstetrics and Gynaecology Canada*, vol. 33, no. 6, 2011, 633-37.

Chapter Three

Mother-Child Programs in Prison: Disciplining the Unworthy Mother

Lynsey Race and Lorna Stefanick

S tate welfare support has traditionally been premised on the notion of the worthy and the unworthy recipient. This characterization is especially true for mothers, who are often subjected to the disciplinary power of the state to enforce patriarchal notions of what constitutes good mothering behaviour (Cantillon and Hutton, this volume). What comprises appropriate mothering behaviour varies over time and among cultures; however, "liberal capitalist states have long contemplated and supported a particular family form—heterosexual, patriarchal, and nuclear—with a breadwinner husband, a stay-at-home wife, and 'legitimate' children" (Gavigan and Chunn 742). In Canada's early years, provincial support in the form of mothers' allowances was uneven, as it was denied to First Nations women in some provinces and restricted to British subjects in others (Gavigan and Chunn 743). Generally speaking, the most worthy recipient of state income support was a Caucasian, stay-at-home mother whose husband died, which through no fault of her own temporarily left her with no income until she was able to remarry. Today, a widow may not be expected to remarry, but she is expected to join the workforce to support herself and her children. A racialized working mother whose husband cannot, or refuses to, support his family continues to be seen as a less deserving recipient of income support because of her poor life choices. The least deserving recipients are young, unmarried mothers who use drugs or alcohol. Mothers who do not identify as heterosexual or cisgender, or who have a physical, intellectual, or mental impairment, are additionally burdened with negative assessments. These concept-ualizations of worthiness have shown remarkable resilience; as mothers move further away from traditional mothering stereotypes, state supp-ort morphs into state control.

State actors have provided a variety of supports for families with children, such as tax benefits, mothers' allowances, medical benefits, and subsidies for rent and childcare. Mothers receiving welfare, however, are subjected to various types of surveillance and are punished for nonconforming behaviour in a way that other mothers are not. Poor and racialized women feel these gender-based structural penalties most acutely, which are exacerbated by the austerity politics associated with neoliberalism. One frequently overlooked group in discussions of marginalization is incarcerated mothers, even though these women embody the concept of "the unworthy mother" who needs to be dis-ciplined and often requires income support upon release from prison. This chapter examines prison mother-child programs (MCPs), in which mothers can reside with their children during their incarceration to mitigate the harm of maternal separation. We ask the following question: Do these programs represent a meaningful response to the needs of marginalized mothers who need support during and after their incarceration, or do these programs represent another method of control, surveillance, and punishment of mothers in need of discipline?

This question is particularly salient because prisoner populations worldwide are increasing and are disproportionately affecting women and marginalized communities. In Canada, for example, Indigenous people are imprisoned at seven to eight times the rate of non-Indigenous Canadians (Nichols 435).[1] Between 2005 and 2015, there was more than a 50 per cent increase in incarcerated women in federal penitentiaries, compared to less than a 10 per cent increase for men. Aboriginal woman make up the fastest growing population of Canadian prisoners; between 2005 and 2010, their rate of incarceration almost doubled (Government of Canada, Office of the Correctional Investigator 2). More than 70 per cent of imprisoned women are mothers to children under the age of eighteen and are more likely to be supporting children on the outside than men (Canada Office of the Correctional Investigator 50). Federally sentenced women offenders are twice as likely as men to have mental health issues and to be serving time for drug-related offenses. As the narrative of the worthy and unworthy poor is propagated by neoliberal discourse in a retracting state, motherhood becomes increasingly precarious; women are held criminally responsible for situations that are socially constructed, such as living in poverty. Mothers who are incarcerated because of substance use, sex work, or theft related to poverty are vilified as opposed to understood as victims of gendered and structural violence. Deemed unworthy, these mothers are subject to punitive measures from neoliberal states, such as having their children taken away. Mothers who are the targets for state interventions are rarely white or middle class (Golden 3). Their children also suffer; in Canada, Aboriginal children are grossly overrepresented in state care (Turner 6). The outcomes for children in care are dismal; among other things, these children have an increased likelihood of being incarcerated themselves.

The establishment of MCPs seeks to reduce harm caused to children and families due to the imprisonment of mothers. We argue, however, that these programs are ultimately another mode of state surveillance and control of marginalized women. Moreover, MCPs are only available to a small minority of women who pass an extensive vetting process, which deepens the chasm between worthy and unworthy mothers. Although MCPs prevent the separation of children from their mothers, they are only a quick fix to deeper societal inequalities (Haney 120-21), which are exacerbated by the morphing of the welfare state into the carceral state. As such, MCPs can be seen as an extension of a punitive, surveillance state that criminalizes those who are victims of structural violence, further relegating some women to the bottom of the unworthy mother's group.

Neoliberalism and the Criminalization of Poverty and Motherhood

It is commonly accepted that neoliberalism's focus on individual responsibility, combined with the disappearance of various types of state support, has feminized poverty, since mothers caring for children are particularly vulnerable to austerity measures (Brodie 94; Ross 56; Allen et al. 920). But neoliberalism has also criminalized poverty. Rather than seeing poverty as the result of complex social and economic factors—and, most recently, the disappearance of the social safety net—poverty is reduced to being the product of moral failing in need of correction (Wacquant 41). Those who engage in antisocial behaviour linked to being poor are seen as being the most in need of correction, which takes the form of punishment through the criminal justice system, as opposed to being given support to overcome economic, social, and health barriers.

Janine Brodie argues that neoliberal governance has resulted in the "institutionalization of insecurity," which has the largest impact on society's most vulnerable (93). Across all societies, women, and in particular women with children, are the least able "to go it alone" and to be the "entrepreneurial self who takes personal responsibility for her successes and her failures" (Brodie 103). Although technology will eventually make biology less relevant to reproduction in the future, currently, those who give birth to children and those who identify as female will bear the brunt of domestic tasks within families. These tasks include childrearing and elder care, which limit their ability to be economically self-sufficient by pursuing paid employment and educational opportunities. Economic dependence on partners is the root cause of the gendered nature of poverty; the year that women become single mothers, they are the most likely of any group to become impoverished (Ross 81). Because children typically live with their mothers in the absence of a dual-parent household, gendered poverty extends to children. Linda Ross argues that neoliberal political ideology has resulted in "relegating poverty to the private rather than the public domain. The social welfare programs and the taxation systems needed to eliminate poverty are given low priority" (67). Moreover, greater welfare conditionality creates new social risks that fall heavily on women and, in particular, mothers (Allen et al. 909). As income precarity increases, so too does the rate of imprisonment of women. The most common reason women are imprisoned in Canada is theft; 66 per cent of female convictions for theft relate to shoplifting (Kong and AuCoin 4). Because austerity measures emphasize the obligations of individuals to be responsible for their own wellbeing and require "individuals to conduct themselves according to sensibilities of enterprise, resilience, thrift, and hard work" (Allen et al. 909), living in poverty is viewed increasingly as the result of personal failing, instead of the result of systemic structural inequalities or the retraction of welfare state.

Poor mothers who use substances are particularly vulnerable to negative judgments about their suitability to raise children; they are conceived as immoral and, thus, unworthy of income support. The war on drugs in the United States took aim at poor and racialized neighbourhoods and was particularly harmful for women in these communities (Levi et al. 10). In Canada, the 2012 introduction of the Safe Streets and Communities Act intensified the criminalization and subsequent legal consequences of minor drug offenses stemming from nonhabitual drug use. Tougher laws punish drug users in order to protect public tax dollars from providing social assistance to people with supposedly poor moral standing, even though their substance use may be an attempt to self-medicate because of overwhelming situational and health issues exacerbated by poverty. Punishing poverty-related drug use with incarceration is an expensive strategy. The costs of an expanding prisoner population far exceed the costs associated with maintaining basic social supports, such as low-income housing (Wacquant 51). Moreover, the gendered nature of childrearing makes it much more likely that children will be relinquished to state care and familial ties will be broken when mothers as opposed to fathers are incarcerated. An inadequate or absent loving parental attachment in childhood, particularly maternal deprivation, is a strong predictor of difficulty in forming intimate relationships later in life (*Inglis v British Columbia* 83; Monchalin 166) and/or substance use issues resulting from the reliance on a "social lubricant" (Monchalin 166). Moreover, "Separation of incarcerated mothers from their infants has been associated with depression and suicidal ideation, increased use of alcohol and drugs and increased criminal activity" (*Inglis v British Columbia* 84). Substance use is the result of unmet needs—be it trauma, emotional/physical pain, or simply not having enough food or a secure place to live. The poor, and in particular the racialized poor, are criminalized as opposed to rehabilitated as a result of these unmet needs. The dismantling of families when children are removed from their incarcerated mothers produces more trauma and unmet needs, resulting in a circular effect of criminalization.

Although the retraction of state social supports affects all women, women with physical, intellectual or mental impairments, LGBTQ women, and racialized women are particularly vulnerable to social marginalization and negative assessments of their ability to mother. One study focusing on women with intellectual and cognitive impairments in conflict with the law notes that these "incarcerated women are between 77-90% more likely to report extensive histories of emotional, physical and sexual abuse than the general population" (Levine, Proulx, and Schwartz 249). They have experienced childhood trauma, substance use, and/or intimate partner violence, which can be the result of deprivation in early childhood, fetal alcohol spectrum disorder, and brain injuries due to physical assault. These issues continue to remain "invisible" because a diagnosis requires a "comprehensive individual, family and social assessment," which may be inaccessible to them because of their physical location or their economic situation (250).

Those women whose physical, cognitive, and mental impairments are visible face barriers to motherhood that are socially constructed. Because mothering for them is conceived as an impossible social role, their parenting abilities are intensely scrutinized. Lars Grue and Kristin Laerum observe that these women "are often looked upon as passive receivers of help and social services, and not as women themselves capable of caring" (673). The most violent manifestations of this thinking are eugenic practices, such as forced sterilization, which Linda Steel and Leanne Dowse refer to as "lawful medical violence" (187). Less intrusive barriers to motherhood also are disabling. A mother who has a physical impairment is not disabled because she uses a tool for mobility; she is disabled because the toilets on the maternity ward are wheelchair inaccessible. Similarly, a woman with mental health issues who cannot afford therapy or medications similarly is disabled. Because women with impairments are not expected to become mothers, when they do have children "close attention is given to the way in which they perform in their role as mother" (Grue and Laerum 674).

Socially constructed barriers include cisnormative frameworks for assigning gender that create systems that are extremely difficult to navigate for those whose gender does not align with their biological sex (Bassichis et al. 15-19). Pathologized as psychologically unstable and deviant, transgender people face extreme forms of social exclusion and violence which "pushes trans people to the margins of society where they are more likely to become involved in crime—often for survival— or have their mere presence criminalised (in the case of the criminalisation of homelessness). This places them at greater risk of criminalisation and imprisonment due to homelessness, drug and alcohol use, sex work participation, and mental health issues" (Rodgers, Asquity, and Dwyer

4). As with women with physical, cognitive, and mental impairments, the complex needs of trans women are not met prior to, during, or after their incarceration. Their social exclusion and their inability to go it alone feeds into the stereotype that transgender women, along with women with impairments, are unable to properly mother. As such, they are the least worthy mothers in the unworthy group, and are the last in line for the diminishing pool of state supports, particularly if they are racialized.

The impact of neoliberal austerity measures and the focus on creating safer communities has had a profound impact on racialized Canadians and, in particular, Indigenous peoples. The latter account for about 3 per cent of Canada's adult population in 2015 and 2016, yet they comprise 26 per cent of provincial and federal custodial admissions. Aboriginal women are overrepresented compared to Aboriginal men with respect to admissions; they comprise 38 per cent of provincial and federally sentenced women in Canada (Reitano 5). Incarcerated women are typically young, single mothers, poor, unemployed, and have less than a grade nine education (Finn et al. 6). At both the provincial and federal levels, they are more likely to have needs due to emotional and vocational instability and a lack of familial support (Finn et al. 8; Blanchette and Dowden 2). Although women are less likely than men to be sent to jail upon conviction for an offense overall because they are more frequently one time offenders, they are more likely than men to be sentenced to jail when they are convicted for sex work or drug offences (Kong and AuCoin 11). The severity of crimes does not escalate for most repeat female offenders (Kong and AuCoin 5); after theft, the most common violation for federally sentenced repeat offenders has to do with offences against the administration of justice, such as bail violations, breach of probation, or failure to appear in court. Within the provincial penal system, drug use is the most common offence, followed closely by theft (Finn et al. 1).

Marginalized mothers with few social supports in punitive states are persecuted for their presumed failings as opposed to being understood as victims of oppressive institutional structures that create economic and social barriers (Wallace, this volume). Their children are also victimized by these structures. In Canada, the racialization of so-called bad mothers is a continuation of ongoing colonial projects that violently intervene in the family and social structures of Indigenous peoples (De Leeuw, Greenwood, and Emilie Cameron, 282). The enduring trope of the "lazy Indian" easily graphs onto the neoliberal narrative of the unproductive citizen who is unworthy of state social assistance (Taylor-Neu et al. 78-79). A hundred years ago, the poverty, high infant mortality rates, and high tuberculosis rates among Indigenous children was not viewed as a by-product of colonialism but rather as an unfortunate by-product of addressing inadequate parenting. Today's high rates of poverty, suicide, homelessness, and school leaving are viewed in a similar fashion. The solution to these problems continues to be "saving" Indigenous children through state intervention (Government of Canada, Truth and Reconciliation Commission 69).

One of the most notorious state interventions in Indigenous families was the residential school system. Indigenous children were forcibly removed from their families and communities and placed in state-run schools to integrate them into colonial Canadian society (De Leeuw, Greenwood, and Cameron 289). In 1907, the chief medical officer of the Department of Indian Affairs documented the schools' inadequate diets, poor hygiene, and overcrowding in substandard buildings (Bryce 15-18). The Truth and Reconciliation Commission explored these problems in depth over a century later. The sexual and physical abuse residential school survivors suffered at the hands of their colonial caretakers was known as early as 1868 and is well documented (The Government of Canada, The Truth and Reconciliation Commission 7; Monachlin 126-28). In some schools, the death rate of pupils was as high as 69 per cent (Bryce 18). The legacy of this violence is intergenerational trauma, which is both a product and a reproducer of negative social determinants, such as poverty, which result in poorer health for Indigenous families (De Leeuw, Greenwood, and Cameron 285). Moreover, poverty in the twenty-first-century neoliberal state is increasingly becoming a predictor of penal incarceration.

Although the last residential school closed in Canada in 1996, state intervention in Indigenous families has continued through contemporary child welfare policies. In 2011, Indigenous children made up almost half of children in the state care even though they represent only 7 per cent of children in Canada (Turner 6). Despite this overrepresentation, Lisa Monchalin notes that "First Nations Child and Family Service agencies receive 22 per cent less funding than provincial agencies" (169). Most Indigenous children are removed from their parents for structural reasons as opposed to abuse. Cindy Blackstock provides insight into this reality:

A detailed analysis of the primary type of child maltreatment indicates that Aboriginal children are less likely than non-Aboriginal children to be reported to child welfare authorities for physical, sexual and emotional abuse, and exposure to domestic violence, but were twice as likely to be reported for neglect. When researchers unpacked the neglect, the only factors that accounted for the overrepresentation were caregiver poverty, poor housing, and substance abuse. (75-76)

The strategy of removing children from their family because of substandard housing is counterproductive. The grim prospects for children separated from their families, and in particular Indigenous children, are well known. One study of Indigenous homeless youth reveals that 65 per cent had been in state care at some point (Gaetz et al. 49). These young adults face almost insurmountable barriers in entering the workforce and living independently due to their lack of social and economic supports. Unsurprisingly, homeless youth have a greater likelihood of involvement with the criminal justice system (Gaetz et al. 57). As noted by the Truth and Reconciliation Commission, "In establishing residential schools, the Canadian government essentially declared Aboriginal people to be unfit parents.... Child neglect was institutionalized, and the lack of supervision created situations where students were prey to sexual and physical abusers" (7).

Although the negative effects of state interventions in families are particularly obvious with respect to Indigenous peoples, they are felt by all families who lose their children to state care. The children bear the brunt of these impacts. Naomi Nichols et al. note that "youth in—and leaving—state care experience disproportionately negative outcomes in several domains, including: housing, education, employment, criminal-legal system involvement, and overall health and wellness" (5). They further note that children in state care are 193% more likely to end up homeless than children who have no history of involvement with the child welfare system (4). Marie Lovrod, Stephanie Bustamante, and Darlene Domshy (this volume) argue that young women who have grown up in the child welfare system are both stigmatized and held to a higher mothering standard than other mothers, increasing the likelihood that they will lose their children to state care. Laws vary by province in Canada and by state in the United States, but in both countries, mothers will lose parenting rights permanently after a prescribed amount of time.

In the United States, parenting rights are lost after a child has been in state care for about fifteen months (Levi et al. 55). This is due in part to the 1997 Safe Families Act, which dictates that foster care agencies must begin adoption proceedings for children who have been in care for fifteen months out of the previous twenty-two, and provides bonuses for states that increase adoptions (Halter 555-56). In comparison to intact families, children taken into state care are more likely to have substance use issues and/or to be imprisoned themselves as youth or adults, and their mothers more likely to have substance use issues and reoffend after separation. By dramatically increasingly the incarceration of women due to the criminalization of poverty, the Canadian government is continuing to perpetuate a cycle of violent familial intervention. The removal of children from their mothers into state care reproduces itself in the form of incarceration in prison when the children become adults. The next section focuses on MCPs as a way to break the cycle of intergenerational incarceration.

Mother-Child Programs: Innovative Solution or Disciplining the Unworthy?

MCPs seek to lessen the impact of maternal incarceration on children; however, practices vary widely between countries and between prisons. As women overwhelmingly remain the primary caregiver, programs that allow fathers to remain with their children are practically nonexistent; only in Finland may children reside in prison with either parent (Pösö et al. 517). MCPs remain rare and understudied. Tarja Pösö, Rosi Enroos, and Tarja Vierula argue that a lack of data renders children admitted to the prison system with an incarcerated parent institutionally invisible. Even basic information, such as statistical data regarding the number of children living in prisons, has not been consistently documented; children are not considered prisoners and are commonly excluded from prison databases (Pösö et al. 517). The shortage of empirical studies notwithstanding, the studies of MCPs globally suggest that they serve to increase the surveillance and control of marginalized mothers. Importantly, they do not address the gendered nature of raising children and the economic disadvantages of being a mother. They also do not address structural disadvantages that increase the risk of engagement in the antisocial behaviour that results in maternal incarceration.

American studies of prison nurseries outline many positive outcomes for children, such as the health benefits of being breastfed (Elmalak 1089). Even if newborns only remain with their mother until they are a year old, they will exhibit lower rates of depression and anxiety as preschoolers when compared to children who were separated from their incarcerated mothers at birth (Covington 131). Infants who form a strong bond with a primary caregiver (usually the mother) have a greater chance of healthy development in childhood and develop greater resiliency than those without such a bond, who are much less likely to use substances, such as alcohol, as an adolescent or as an adult (Elmalak 1090). Resiliency is significant, given that children of incarcerated mothers are more likely to be incarcerated themselves (Covington 131). MCPs have the additional benefit of lessening the possibility that the child will be relinquished to state care (Elmalak 1091).

Proponents of MCPs argue that another advantage of prison nurseries is improved maternal behaviour. These programs require inmates to have a low security rating, remain in good standing, and be compliant with prison rules, such as maintaining drug-free urine (Elmalak 1091). After release, inmates who have been allowed to keep their infants with them in prison have low rates of recidivism (Elmalak 1089, Goshin, Byrne, and Henninger 117). Pösö et al. report that some incarcerated parents living with their children in parent-child programs in Finland felt that they were more present in their parenting while in prison due to the elimination of substance use, since the prison required parents to remain clean and afforded them supports to do so (520).

MCPs are not without their problems, however. To participate, incarcerated mothers are subject to increased surveillance and control, which perpetuate the labelling of mothers as either worthy or unworthy. In her study of an MCP run by a nongovernmental organization in California (given the pseudonym "Visions"), Lynne Haney observes that the facility began "as a promising alternative to punishment" but quickly morphed into an institution with its own unique method of power (106). Referencing the work of Stanley Cohen, she warns "that systems of control can expand as they become centralized and defused" and implores us "to think seriously about how penal reforms can quickly become symptoms of gendered and racialized injustices" (106). Haney concludes that without an in-depth analysis of MCPs and other related prison reforms to reduce incarceration rates, California prisons may be deinstitutionalized in a similar manner to mental hospitals in the 1970s: "carelessly and irresponsibly" (106).

Haney's study is particularly insightful in that it analyzes how motherhood is conceptualized and practiced within a prison setting. Despite successfully passing an extensive vetting process that probed prisoners' backgrounds for histories of child abuse, neglect, and other dangerous parental behaviour, prisoners were stripped of their parental authority upon entering Visions. Controlling autonomy is an essential part of all penal institutions; however, self-autonomy is an important aspect of parental authority. At Visions, parental authority ultimately rested with the institution. Inmates were denied basic authority over their children's lives and were under constant surveillance, particularly when it came to scrutiny of their mothering capabilities. Women were unable to assert any of their parental preferences—for example, when children could snack outside of mealtimes, what type of food their children could eat, when their children could watch television, and what they could watch (Haney 114). As a result, many inmates felt that their children not only recognized their mothers' lack of authority but also used Visions's rules as a means of manipulating them. The complete lack of privacy was equally problematic, resulting in every aspect of mothering being analyzed by guards, counsellors, and other prisoners (Haney 115). Prisoners who expressed defiance or resistance (either real or perceived) to institutional rules had access to their children curtailed, even if this defiance had little or nothing to do with their mothering (Haney 123). Children, thus, become a disciplinary tool of the prison system (and later the state) to enforce particular conceptions of motherhood, submission, and good behaviour.

Haney argues that Visions became an extension of the cultural controls exacted on poor and racialized mothers that make motherhood private for privileged mothers and forcibly public for others. In Visions, motherhood was not a right of imprisoned women, as envisioned by feminist prison reformists. Instead, prisoners were assumed to be deficient in parenting capabilities and in need of correction by those who knew what it meant to be a good mother (Haney 117). Ultimately, Visions still operated as a prison that prescribed a certain type of mothering fraught with gendered assumptions and harmful beliefs surrounding race and class. It assumed that good mothering must be intensive and fulfilling (Cantillon and Hutton, this volume), and those mothers who were indifferent or not completely fulfilled by the privilege of mothering their children were in defiance of the Visions's mandate (Haney 118). Moreover, there was no effort to keep the children connected with their fathers; fathers rarely visited their children, and staff did not acknowledge the frustrations women had regarding the lack of involvement of the fathers. Mothers were expected "to deal with their own issues first" (Haney 119). Once women were released from prison, they were on their own; no information was provided on how to access social supports for themselves or their children upon reentry into the outside community.

Irma Eloff and Melanie Moen's study of an MCP in South Africa's Pretoria Female Prison (PFP) makes similar conclusions: autonomous action, privacy, and spontaneous interaction between mothers and their children were not possible, given the continuous surveillance of prisoners and enforcement of prison rules (716). As in the Visions model (Haney 121), incarcerated PFP mothers had to simultaneously navigate two complex roles: one as prisoner and the other as mother (Eloff and Moen 715). In PFP, children under the age of two were not allowed to leave the prison to see family members or attend preschool; they had very little interaction with the outside world. While prison was not an ideal place for children, many were still better off in Visions and in PFP as the institutions provided regular meals and healthcare (Eloff and Moen 717; Haney 120).

In Canada, women sentenced to prison terms of two years or more serve time in federal institutions, whereas those sentenced to fewer than two years do so in provincial institutions. As elsewhere, Canadian data on MCPs are collected inconsistently and are difficult to access. Data collection is further complicated by the fact that in addition to the federal system, each province has its own prison system. With the exception of British Columbia, MCPs are not available at provincial institutions. British Columbia's first MCP began in 1973, and over a hundred incarcerated mothers participated in the program (*Inglis v British Columbia*, 13). That province's most recent MCP began in 2004 with the opening of the Allouette Correction Centre for Women; it was used by nine of the thirteen women who gave birth in prison between 2005 and 2008 (McCormick et al. 21). In 2008, the British Columbia Corrections cancelled the program, announcing that providing care for children was not within its mandate. In 2013, the Supreme Court of British Columbia in *Inglis v British Columbia* ruled that this decision violated the Charter of

Rights and Freedoms, specifically Section 7 (the right to security of person and liberty) and Section 15 (the right to equality). As of 2017, the Alouette Correctional Centre for Women remains the only provincial-level prison institution that offers a mother-child unit; children can live with their mothers up until the age of four (Stone).

The 1990 task force report, *Creating Choices*, made recommendations to improve the plight of federally incarcerated women and, specifically, to address the notoriously overcrowded and poor conditions in Canada's only federal women's prison in Kingston, Ontario. The report emphasizes the importance of allowing mothers and children to remain together and recommends building regional facilities that would allow women to remain closer to home (Government of Canada, Correctional Services, Chapter IX). Corrections Canada piloted its first MCP at the Okimaw Ohci Healing Lodge in Saskatchewan in 1996 (Stone); five years later, all of the newly constructed federal regional prisons for women had programs.

Participation rates in federal MCPS have been low to nonexistent. In 2001, there were twelve mothers participating in the Okimaw Ohci Healing Lodge program; between 2005 and 2010, there were no participants. Across Canada, there were only ten mothers and their children participating in MCPs in 2008 (McCormick et al. 20-21), which was the same year that eligibility criteria for mothers were made more stringent and the age limit for participating children dropped from twelve to five. Between 2008 and 2014, only eight children lived fulltime with their mothers in federal prisons; another six lived with their mothers part time. Indigenous women are routinely given higher security designations than other women, resulting in more intensive forms of incarceration, such as segregation and maximum security (Nichols 436). Because participation in an MCP requires a minimum or medium security rating (Brennan 14), the MCP program actually deepens the chasm between worthy and unworthy incarcerated mothers. Ultimately, however, low participation rates are the result of "policies and decisions that view female offenders as unfit mothers and correctional institutions as unconducive [sic] for children" (Brennan 28).

For those mothers who are able to participate in MCP programs, studies show that poverty, sexism, and racism intersect in powerful ways, rendering some unworthy mothers virtually powerless to exercise autonomy with respect to parenting decisions. Autonomy is further compromised when mothering is performed within a prison setting, where rules are enforced through continuous surveillance. Making changes to increase participation in MCPs is, therefore, counterproductive, given that these programs do not critically interrogate the reasons why women are incarcerated in the first place; instead, they serve to reinforce the levers by which the state surveils and disciplines marginalized mothers.

Motherhood Incarcerated

MCPs attempt to mitigate harm caused to families when mothers are imprisoned. Maternal imprisonment has a greater impact on families than the imprisonment of fathers; it is particularly detrimental to the health and development of children. But upon examination, these programs can be seen as an extension of neoliberal austerity programs that serve to increase the marginalization of those populations that the state has determined to be undesirable. The unprecedented expansion in prison populations is deeply disturbing, particularly as it disproportionately affects racialized communities. Most troubling is that the imprisonment of women is significantly outpacing that of men and that most imprisoned women are mothers. Increasingly, the failure to perform motherhood in a socially acceptable way is a potential criminal offense, as opposed to being conceptualized as a medical or societal problem—problems that are exacerbated by neoliberal austerity politics. Motherhood becomes increasingly precarious, as the state and the public categorize poor women as worthy or unworthy and, subsequently, as good or bad mothers.

More research into the effects of MCPs is sorely needed, particularly in Canada, given the escalating rate of the incarceration of Indigenous women. The limited empirical data available, however, suggest that MCPs end up being another mode of social control; they have become an extension of the state's enforcement of gendered labour and surveillance of poor, racialized, and unworthy mothers. Despite the 2013 British Columbia Supreme Court decision that closing the province's only MCP was a Charter violation, it is clear that Canadian prison systems consider MCPs a privilege that should only be available to worthy mothers. Those who object to allowing children to remain with their incarcerated mothers argue prison is no place for a child. If this is an accurate assessment, however, Rebecca Covington is correct in asserting that it also extends to the child's mother (132). The incarceration of mothers has profound consequences for their dependent children, who often are apprehended by the state and are, subsequently, at high risk of incarceration themselves. In Canada, the cyclical pattern of state intervention is eerily similar to the residential school system, which divested Indigenous parents of responsibility for their children. The result is intergenerational trauma and dysfunction. Alternatives to imprisonment, such as preventative justice and restorative justice in community-based residential systems, should be considered, particularly for pregnant women and mothers with dependent children. These programs are more cost effective and do a better job protecting public safety than prisons (Van den Bergh et al. 691).

Changing the narrative of the worthy and unworthy mother requires addressing the structural reasons for the increasing interaction between women and the justice system. Robust systems of social support that ensure that women and their children have adequate housing, food, medical care (including addictions and mental health treatment), and other necessities of life should be at the forefront of reducing deviant behaviours because they would prevent imprisonment in the first place (Van den Bergh et al. 691). Allowing incarcerated mothers to keep their children with them in prison reproduces gender-based control and dependency on partners, families, or the state, as opposed to addressing the exploitative nature of gendered labour that is at the root of neoliberal austerity policies. Educational and vocational opportunities combined with affordable daycare would assist poor mothers to break the cycle of poverty and incarceration. For women with heath issues, interrogating the assumptions around substance use and the social construction of gender and disability would also be useful in encouraging self-sufficiency. Community-based rehabilitation and support as opposed to incarceration of mothers would help to keep their children out of state care. For Indigenous women in Canada, policies recognizing the intersection of race, gender, and colonization are crucial. Although prison reform could reduce the immediate neglect of incarcerated women, addressing the shrinkage of state social supports associated with austerity politics and the gendered expectations of women would be the most effective ways to begin to dismantle the good and bad mother narratives that result in the increasing criminalization of particular types of mothers.

Endnotes

1. In this chapter, "Aboriginal" refers to Indian, Inuit, and Metis peoples who are recognized in Section 35(2) of the Canadian *Constitution Act 1982*. We use the less specific term "Indigenous peoples" because it recognizes the imposition of state definitions of Aboriginal status. We use the term "Aboriginal" when cited authors use it.

Works Cited

Allen, Kim, et al. "Welfare Queens, Thrifty Housewives, and Do-It-All-Mums." *Feminist Media Studies*, vol. 15, no. 6, 2015, pp. 907-25, doi:10.1080/14680777.2015.1062992.

Bassichis, Morgan, et al. "Building an Abolitionist Trans and Queer Movement with Everything We've Got." *Captive Genders: Trans Embodiment and the Prison Industrial Complex,* edited by Eric A. Stanley and Nat Smith, AK Press, 2011, pp. 15-40.

Blackstock, Cindy. "Residential Schools: Did They Really Close or Just Morph into Child Welfare?" *Indigenous Law Journal,* vol. 6, no. 1, 2007, pp. 71-78.

Blanchette, Kelley, and Craig Dowden. "A Profile of Federally Sentenced Women in the Community: Addressing Needs for Successful Reintegration." *Correction Service of Canada Research Branch*, vol. 10, no. 1, 1998, www.csc-scc.gc.ca/research/forum/e101/101i_e.pdf. Accessed 16 July 2018.

Brennan, Sarah. "Canada's Mother-child Program: Imagining Emergence, Usage and Current State." *Canadian Graduate Journal of Sociology and Criminology*, vol. 3, no. 1, 2014, pp. 11-33.

Brodie, Janine. "Reforming Social Justice in Neoliberal Times," *Studies in Social Justice*, vol. 1, no 2, 2007, pp. 93-107.

Bryce, Peter. *Report on the Indian Schools of Manitoba and the North West Territories. Canada.* Department of Indian Affairs, 1907. *Educate Yourself,* educate-yourself.org/cn/Report-on-the-Indian-Schools-1907-Dr-Peter-Bryce-2.pdf. Accessed 16 July 2020.

Covington, Rebecca. "Incarcerated Mother, Invisible Child," *Emory International Law Review.* vol. 31, 2016, pp. 99-134.

De Leeuw, Sarah, Margo Greenwood, and Emilie Cameron. "Deviant Constructions: How Governments Preserve Colonial Narratives of Addictions and Poor Mental Health to Intervene into the Lives of Indigenous Children and Families in Canada," *International Journal of Mental Health and Addiction*, vol. 8, no. 2, 2010, pp. 282-95, doi.10.1007/s11469-009-9225-1.

Elmalak, Seham. "Babies Behind Bars: An Evaluation of Prison Nurseries in American Female Prisons and Their Potential Constitutional Challenges," *Pace Law Review*, vol. 35, no. 3, 2015, pp. 1080-1106, digitalcommons.pace.edu/plr/vol35/iss3/8. Accessed 2 August 2018.

Eloff, Irma, and Melanie Moen. "An Analysis of Mother-Child Interaction Patterns in Prison." *Early Child Development and Care*, vol. 173, no. 6, 2003, pp. 711-720, doi: 10.1080/0300443032000103070.

Finn, Anne et al. "Female Inmates, Aboriginal Inmates, and Inmates Serving Life Sentences: A One Day Snapshot." *Centre for Justice Statistics, Statistics Canada*, vol. 19, no. 5, 1999, www.statcan.gc.ca/pub/85-002-x/85-002-x1999005-eng.pdf. Accessed 16 July 2020.

Gaetz, Stephen, et al. "Without a Home: The National Youth Homelessness Survey." *Canadian Observatory on Homelessness Press*, 2016, homelesshub.ca/sites/default/files/WithoutAHome-final.pdf. Accessed 16 July 2020.

Gavigan, Shelley A.M., and Doroth E. Chunn. "From Mothers' Allowance to Mothers Need Not Apply: Canadian Welfare Law as Liberal and Neo-Liberal Reforms." *Osgoode Hall Law Journal* vol. 45 no. 4, 2007: 733-71, digitalcommons.osgoode.yorku.ca/ohlj/vol45/iss4/5. Accessed 16 July 2020.

Golden, R. *War on the Family: Mothers in Prison and the Families They Leave Behind*. Routledge, 2005.

Goshin, Lorie S., Mary W. Byrne, and Alana M. Henninger. "Recidivism after Release from a Prison Nursery Program," *Public Health Nursing*, vol. 31, no. 2, 2014, pp. 109-117.

Government of Canada. Office of the Correctional Investigator. *Annual Report 2014-2015*, 2015, www.oci-bec.gc.ca/cnt/rpt/pdf/annrpt/annrpt20142015-eng.pdf. Accessed 7 July 2018.

Government of Canada. The Truth and Reconciliation Commission. *What We Have Learned. Principles of Truth and Reconciliation.* McGill-Queen's University Press, 2015, publications.gc.ca/site/archivee-archived.html?url=http://publications.gc.ca/collections/collection _2015/trc/IR4-9-1-1-2015-eng.pdf. Accessed 16 July 2018.

Government of Canada. Correctional Services Canada. "Creating Choices: The Report of the Task for of Federally Incarcerated Women," *Correctional Services*, 1990, www.csc-scc.gc.ca/women/ toce-eng.shtml. Accessed 16 July 2020.

Grue, Lars, and Kristin Tafjord Laerum. "'Doing Motherhood': Some Experiences of Mother with Physical Disabilities." *Disability and Society*, vol. 17, no.6, 2002, pp. 671-83, doi: 10.1080/09687590220 00010443.

Halter, Emily. "Parental Prisoners: The Incarcerated Mother's Constitutional Right to Parent" *Journal of Criminal Law and Criminology*, vol. 108, no. 3. pp. 539-67.

Haney, Lynne. "Motherhood as Punishment," *Journal of Woman in Culture and Society*, vol. 39, no. 1, 2013, pp. 105-30, doi: 10.1086/ 670815.

Inglis v. British Columbia. (Minister of Public Safety). BCSC2309. Docket No. S087858, 16 Dec. 2013, ifls.osgoode.yorku.ca/wp-content/uploads/2013/12/Judge-Ross-re-Inglis-v.-British-Columbia -Minister-of-Public-Safety-12-16.pdf. Accessed 16 July 2020.

Kong, Rebecca, and Kathy AuCoin. "Female Offenders in Canada." *Canadian Centre for Justice Studies, Statistics Canada*, vol. 28. no. 1, 2008, www.statcan.gc.ca/pub/85-002-x/2008001/article/10509-eng.htm. Accessed 16 July 2020.

Levi, Robin, et al. "Creating the 'Bad Mother': How the U.S. Approach to Pregnancy in Prison Violates the Right to Be a Mother." *UCLA's Women's Law Journal*, vol. 18, no. 1, 2010, pp. 1-77.

Levine, Kathryn Ann, Jocelyn Proulx and Karen Schwartz. "Disconnected Lives: Women with Intellectual Disabilities in Conflict with the Law." *Journal of Applied Research in Intellectual Disabilities*, vol. 31, 2018, pp. 249-58, doi: 10.1111/jar.12387

McCormick, Amanda V. et al. *In the Best Interests of the Child: Strategies for Recognizing and Supporting Canada's At-Risk Population of Children with Incarcerated Parents*. University of the Fraser Valley, Centre for Safe Schools and Communities, 2014.

Monchalin, Lisa. *The Colonial Problem: An Indigenous Perspective on Crime and Injustice in Canada*. University of Toronto Press, 2016.

Nichols, Naomi et al. "Child Welfare and Youth Homelessness in Canada: A Proposal for Action." Canadian Observatory on Homelessness Press, 2017, homelesshub.ca/childwelfare. Accessed 16 July 2020.

Nichols, Robert. "The Colonialism of Incarceration," *Radical Philosophy Review*, vol. 17, no. 2, 2014, pp. 435-55, doi: 10.5840/radphilrev 201491622.

Pösö, Tarja., Rosi Enroos, and Tarja Vierula. "Children Residing in Prison with their Parents: An Example of Institutional Invisibility," *The Prison Journal*, vol. 90, no. 4, 2010, pp. 516-533.

Reitano, Julie. "Adult Correctional Statistics in Canada." *Canadian Centre for Justice Statistics, Statistics Canada*, 2017. www.statcan.gc.ca/pub/85-002-x/2017001/article/14700-eng.pdf. Accessed 16 July 2020.

Rodgers, Jess, Nicole Asquity, and Angela Dwyer. "Cisnormativity, Criminalisation, Vulnerability: Transgender People in Prisons." Tasmanian Institute of Law and Enforcement Studies. Briefing Paper no. 12, February 2017.

Ross, Linda. *Interrogating Motherhood*. Athabasca University Press, 2016.

Stone, Laura. "Women Behind Bars: A Baby's Home behind the Barbed Wire." *Calgary Herald*, 25 May 2012, www.calgaryherald.com/news/alberta/women+behind+bars+baby+home+behind+barbed+wire/5540938/story.html. Accessed 16 July 2020.

Steel, Linda, and Leanne Dowse. "Gender, Disability Rights and Violence Against Medical Bodies." *Australian Feminist Studies*, vol 38, no. 88, 2018, pp. 187-202.

Taylor-Neu, Robyn et al. "(De)Constructing the 'Lazy Indian': An Historical Analysis of Welfare Reform in Canada." *Aboriginal Policy Studies* vol. 7, no. 2, 2019, pp. 65-87.

Turner, Annie. "Living Arrangements of Aboriginal Children 14 Years and Under." *Statistics Canada Insights on Canadian Society*, 13 Apr.

2016, hwww.statcan.gc.ca/pub/75-006-x/2016001/article/14547-eng.pdf. Accessed 16 July 2020.

Van den Bergh, Brenda J. et al. "Imprisonment and Women's Health: Concerns about Gender Sensitivity, Human Rights and Public Health," *Bulletin of the World Health Organization*, vol. 89, no. 9, 2011, pp. 689-94, doi: 10.2471/BLT.10.082842.

Wacquant, Loïc. *Punishing the Poor: The Neoliberal Government of Social Insecurity*. Duke University Press, 2009.

Chapter Four

"Making America Great Again"? Neoliberal Politics, Poverty, and Women's Health

Lynda Ross and Shauna Wilton

There's nobody better than me on the military.... I think women
really like that. I think they want to be safe at home. I have
tremendous respect for women. No, I wouldn't say I'm a feminist.
I mean, I think that would be, maybe, going too far. I'm for
women. I'm for men. I'm for everyone.
—President Trump (qtd. in Farrer)

The election of President Donald Trump in 2016 symbolized the
success of a new form of populism, a "volcanic eruption of a
new and even angrier brand" (Nash 11), distinct from both
historic left-wing populism as a movement aimed against "Big Money"
and right-wing populism's attacks on "Big Government" (Nash 10).
Whereas left-wing populism directs resentment and anger at social
injustice, inequality, precariousness, and the political structures
responsible for them, right-wing populism focuses its ire on those
individuals cared for by the state and on minority groups perceived to
be different from "us" (Salmela and von Scheve 440). In response to
economic difficulties resulting from neoliberal globalization, left-wing

populism draws attention to the impact of income inequality, whereas right-wing populism blames open borders, immigration, and liberal ideologies for low wages and unemployment as well as focusing on solutions that disenfranchise the "other" (Moghadam and Kaftan 1). Trumpism shares the same core ideals of neoliberalism and right-wing populism, two ideologies "closely bound together" (Hendrikse 171). But Trumpism also differentiates itself from both ideologies through President Trump's way of governing, including his almost complete disregard for political principles (Cohen). While acknowledging Trump's antiestablishment, antiglobalist, and economic nationalist agenda, Trumpism could be interpreted as neither a political nor an ideological movement but instead as a psychological phenomenon—not a "break with conservatism but the apotheosis of it" (Goldberg). The current success of right-wing populism, and by extension, Trumpism, is not, however, simply a consequence of Trump's personality or his agenda. Instead, it can be defined by the sociopolitical dynamic that has provided fertile ground for right-wing populist ideologies (Wodak and Krzyżanowski 472). Thus, although Trumpism is not a new pheno-menon, it "bares painfully naked deep-seated and historically powerful fears of 'white decline' and threatened borders that have animated politics and policies in the U.S. for as long as its history" (Gökariksel and Smith 639). Mediatization, the volume of presidential lies, the embrace of white nationalism, chaos in the White House staffing, as well as Trump's attempts at undermining the integrity of the judicial system in the United States (U.S.), all contribute to Trumpism feeling more dangerous than the right-wing populism of the past. As Cas Mudde points out "Trump doesn't control 'Trumpism.' He is merely the current voice of the radicalised base."

Neoliberalism has had a negative effect on the lives of middle- and working-class Americans, with marginalized women faring demon-strably worse. The "relationship between an increasingly crisis-ridden neoliberal capitalism and the politics of the far-right" (Davidson and Saull 707) has given way to the anger and resentment of those in the West who find themselves economically dislocated by the factors—privatization, financial deregulation, free trade, and globalization—that define neoliberalism. The election of President Trump on an antigovernment, right-wing populist platform heralded the beginning of a new gender politics in the U.S. And one of Trump's most egregious attempts at policy reform has been his attack on universal healthcare ("Obamacare"). His vision of American society, shaped without the pretext of a universal healthcare system, will result in more women and children put at risk of living in impoverished circumstances, all but guaranteeing their poorer health outcomes.

In this chapter, we argue that although the political situation in the U.S. is dire, it is not without hope. Hope stems from the fact that Trump has struggled and ultimately failed to get support from Congress for his vision of dismantling the Affordable Care Act (ACA) as part of his agenda to make America great again. The women who organized in opposition to President Trump's policies are a major source of hope for positive change, as they continue to mobilize in great numbers to promote the interests of all Americans. In the sections of this chapter that follow, we continue our discussions of neoliberalism, right-wing populism, and the ways in which they inform income inequality. We further discuss the relationship between poverty and health and the role of healthcare in alleviating the potential suffering of the most vulnerable. We conclude our chapter on a hopeful note by highlighting the broad grassroots mobilization against Trump's policies and his administration.

Neoliberalism, Right-Wing Populism, Trumpism, and Healthcare

The current success of Trumpism, as noted earlier, is not simply a consequence of Trump's personality or agenda but is deeply engrained in a history of white privilege and a constitution that favours individual rights and freedoms over the needs of society as a whole. Ruth Wodak and Michał Krzyyżanowski suggest, following from the work of Hans-George Betz and Stefan Immerfall, that right-wing populism can best be defined in the following way:

[It is] a hybrid political ideology that rejects the post-war political consensus and usually, though not always, combines laissez-faire liberalism and anti-elitism with other, often profoundly different and contradictory ideologies. This ideology is considered as populism because of its appeal to the "common man/woman," as to a quasi-homogenous people, defined in an ethno-nationalist way. (475)

Since the 1980s, neoliberal ideology has dominated the politics of Anglo-Saxon countries, including the U.S., with its existing political culture rooted in the liberal tenets of small government and individual freedom (Wilson). Suspicious of big government and government interference in the lives of citizens, the U.S. has been slower than other countries to adopt welfare state measures, which has resulted in one of the weakest welfare states among all Western democracies. This fact is particularly relevant to discussions about poverty and health—two areas that have a disproportionate impact on the lives of women.

Neoliberalism represented a backlash against the welfare state of the postwar period and argued for more market freedom and less government and state interference (both in markets and in the lives of individuals). Whereas the Keynesian welfare state of the postwar period advocated for the political control of markets, neoliberalism aimed for the market control of politics (Fraser). The assumption underpinning neoliberal ideology is that states are inefficient distributors of social goods; markets can do it better and more cheaply, without creating intergenerational dependence on social programs. Not only does neoliberal ideology promote the benefits of market over state control, but it does so in opposition to institutions that are interpreted as placing constraints on the economic freedoms of individuals. These institutions include, for example, "trade unions, professional associations, social housing and socialized medicine, in fact any institution or regulation seen as somehow impinging on the right of individuals to exercise their individual economic freedom and autonomy" (Bruce 46). The pairing of a general distaste for, and distrust of, government control, as well as privileging individual economic rights and freedoms over the wellbeing of all citizens, is clearly not a new ideology in the U.S. or in other Western democratic states. However, the historical political culture of the U.S., with its focus on individualism, makes it particularly fertile ground for neoliberal and antistate rhetoric and policy as well as, ultimately, for right-wing populist ideology.

The fact that Trump, during the 2016 presidential campaign, could gain support for his bid for the presidency through using antiestablishment slogans such as "drain the swamp" and promises of "deregulation" to remove government's interference in business interests is testament to neoliberalism's deep entrenchment in American consciousness. Although Trump's popularity has waned during his time in office, he has managed through numerous executive orders to diminish government interference in business interests in the U.S., without regard for the potentially catastrophic environmental, climate, and human outcomes of this deregulation. During his campaign and tenure in office, Trump repeatedly promised to "repeal and replace Obamacare" (the Affordable Care Act). In the second presidential debate in October 2016, in keeping with neoliberal ideology and right-wing politics, he stated:

> Obamacare is a disaster. You know it. We all know it. It's going up at numbers that nobody's ever seen, worldwide.... Nobody has ever seen numbers like this for health care. It's only getting worse.... We have to repeal it and replace it with something absolutely much less expensive. And something that works, where your plan can actually be tailored. We have to get rid of the lines around the state, artificial lines, where we stop insurance companies from coming in and competing. (Politico Staff)

In November of 2017, after almost a full year in office, President Trump tweeted: "Obamacare is OWNED by the Democrats, and it is a disaster. But do not worry. Even though the Dems want to Obstruct, we will Repeal & Replace right after Tax Cuts!" (qtd. in Thomsen).

President Trump has been largely unsuccessful in gaining the congressional support that he needs to make these changes, and, to date, he has managed only to repeal the individual mandate (Qui). Neoliberalism partially helps to explain why there might be some support to abandon notions of universal healthcare. Trumpism pushes the neoliberal agenda further through what is widely acknowledged to be Trump's position against "all things Obama" (Cillizza). This factor, paired with the distaste by right-wing populists for government interference with healthcare, helps us to understand Trump's interests in repealing the ACA—legislation that is regarded by many as Obama's "greatest domestic achievement" (Millward).

Neoliberalism and Income Inequality

The income disparity between rich and poor in the United States is remarkable, not only in regards to its magnitude but also for the way it portrays the bleak state of economic inequality (Amadeo; Buckley and Barua; Bunyan 492; Ferguson and Lavalette 4). In addition to contributing to income inequality, the same neoliberal rhetoric "has violently and grievously *severed* conceptualizations of race, gender, sexuality and other oppressions from class" (Battacharya 114), which serves to reinforce income inequalities through wealth allocations that closely parallel racial and ethnic distributions in the U.S. For example, today, the median family wealth for the non-Hispanic white population is ten times that of Hispanics and more than twelve times that of African Americans (Dickman, Himmelstein, and Woolhandler 1432).

Top incomes have risen to unprecedented levels in the U.S. but so has extreme poverty, as it has more than doubled over the past three decades and has most severely affected ethnic minorities and women. In 2016, more than one in eight American women lived in poverty, which translated into more than sixteen million women, with the highest poverty rates for Black, Latina, and Native American women (National Women's Law Centre [NWLC]). Moreover, "more than 1.6 million households in the USA, including 3.5 million children, survive on incomes of less than $2 per person per day—WHO's definition of extreme poverty" (Dickman, Himmelstein, and Woolhandler 1432). Families headed by single mothers were five times more likely than married couple families to live in poverty; as many as six in ten poor children lived in female-headed families in 2016 (NWLC). Although these conditions cannot be attributed to President Trump, his lack of concern is evidenced by his inattention to policies that could improve the lives of those living in poverty.

The reality of poverty is often disputed or dismissed by the political leaders of the right, as "Margaret Thatcher once called poverty 'a personality defect'" (Bregman). President Trump recently proclaimed to a cheering crowd in Iowa that he "love[s] all people, rich or poor, but in [cabinet] positions I just don't want a poor person" (qtd. in Russell), and Ben Carson, as head of the Department of Housing and Urban Development, called poverty "a state of mind" (qtd. in Peck). More than ever, this sort of populism, driven by a neoliberal ethos, treats poverty as a personal issue, devoid of race, class, gender, and social contexts.

Individuals living in poverty suffer not only the hardships that go hand in hand with trying to exist in a nation where others are seen to reap the benefits of wealth; they are also forced to deal with the stigma associated with being poor.

Poverty and Women's Health

The rise in income inequality in the U.S. from the 1980s to the present coincides with widening inequalities in the physical and mental health between the rich and the poor (Wilkinson and Pickett). Living in poverty has tangible and negative physical health consequences (Bor, Cohen, and Galea). Chronic health conditions, including stroke and heart disease, follow a predictable pattern of rising prevalence with declining income. Poverty's relationship to poor health is also realized in the widening life expectancy gap between rich and poor Americans, with the richest 1 per cent living ten to fifteen years longer than the poorest 1 per cent (Dickman, Himmelstein, and Woolhandler 1431; Gaffney and McCormick 1442; Sanders). Not only does poor health increase the chances of early death, it also threatens the economic stability of families through limiting their economic productivity, bankrupting households, and, ultimately, impoverishing families (Bor, Cohen, and Galea 1476)—all conditions that are exacerbated in the absence of universal healthcare coverage.

The adverse consequences of living in poverty for mothers and children are undebatable. Poverty can severely compromise pregnancy outcomes (Nagahawatte and Goldenberg; Phipps), and without health insurance and proper obstetric care during and following pregnancy, the risks of negative maternal health and poor infant outcomes increase (Flenady et al.). Women living in poverty, whether pregnant or not, are much more prone to suffer from anxiety and depression as well as to engage in risky licit and illicit drug use and to be targets of interpersonal and sexual violence (Al-Sahab et al; Beeber, Perreira, and Swartz; Bombard et al; Goldenberg et al.). These situations, alone or in combination, place pregnant women living in poverty at greater risk for negative maternal and infant outcomes (Khalifeh et al; Nagawatte and Goldenberg).

Food and housing insecurity present additional grave threats to the health and wellbeing of many pregnant women, mothers, and children

LYNDA ROSS AND SHAUNA WILTON

living in poverty. Women's nutritional status both before and during pregnancy plays a key role in their reproductive health and in the health of their unborn children. Food insecurity translates into an inability of individuals to provide adequate food for themselves and their families. Low infant birth weight and preterm births are associated with perinatal and infant mortality that results from malnutrition during pregnancy (Glinianaia et al.). For children, nutritional deprivation is linked to an increased risk of hospitalization, poor health, and developmental delays (Cutts et al.). Housing status is another strong social determinant of health for both mothers and children (Cutts et al.; Taylor and Edwards). Although housing and food insecurity present major challenges for mothers and for their children, homelessness is an exponentially worse situation in terms of children's physical, cognitive, and emotional health (Moore, McArthur, and Noble-Carr). Shortages in affordable housing combined with increasing rates of poverty have contributed to an increase in the number of homeless individuals. In the U.S., there are an estimated 3.5 million people who are homeless; 17 per cent are women, and almost one-third are families with children (Finfgeld-Connett). The weakening of the social welfare system, combined with insufficient healthcare coverage, exacerbates the vicious cycle of poverty in the U.S.

Trump's campaign against Obamacare and his attacks on the limited American welfare state, along with his controversial position on many gender issues, place American women and their health in a precarious position, with the dysfunctional healthcare system in the U.S. contributing in significant ways to inequality (Sanders 1376). According to Merrill Goozner "the Republican Party has consistently opposed universal coverage—the idea of health care as a right—since at least the 1930s" (123). Although the ACA was passed by Congress in 2010 without a single Republican vote, it did signal universal health insurance coverage as a policy goal for the first time in U.S. history (Goozner 122). The ACA, fully implemented in 2014, was an attempt to increase the number of people receiving health insurance and to improve coverage for all. Access to Medicaid was increased; subsidies were provided to those who could not otherwise afford private insurance; and the healthcare categories designated as essential were expanded (e.g., preexisting conditions, paediatric care, chiropractic care, and autism treatment) (Willison and Singer 1225).

If President Trump's threats to "repeal and replace" were successful, the numbers of inadequately and uninsured individuals would sig-nificantly increase, further burdening the poor while leaving the wealthy relatively unscathed. Currently, with the market controlling healthcare, "Americans pay the highest prices in the world for health services in a system characterized by tremendous waste" (Goozner 124). This already dire situation, with its disproportionately negative affects on marginalized women, became even more precarious with the election of President Trump.

Many viewed the election of President Trump in 2016 as a serious attack on the social fabric of America and on the lives of marginalized Americans. Although the decades prior to his election witnessed only negligible gains for poor people, and for women in particular, and saw levels of poverty increase, Trump's erratic and ideological populist policies represent a significant threat to advocates for the poor, ill, and disenfranchised. However, three years into President Trump's first term there may be some signs for hope.

Room for Hope: Pushing Back

During the first year of Donald Trump's presidency, between ten and fifteen million Americans protested against Trump, his government, and his policies (Kauffman). Since Trump's election, more people have joined political protests and demonstrations than at any other time in American history, including during the Vietnam War (Kauffman). Many of the organized political anti-Trump activities have been initi-ated by women, and although not all protests are specifically directed at the issue of healthcare, they represent a broad-based, intersectional, and grassroots movement that offers hope for the future of American democracy. The demonstrations reflect a changing political climate in which mobilization is driven by social media and funded through small individual donations, as organizations endeavour to ensure broad rep-resentation of different ethnic, class, gender, sexual, and religious mi-norities within their policies and structure. We are witnessing a new wave of movements that are broad coalitions of antifascist, profeminist, and pro-LGBTQ emerging in response to the populist right-wing movements, which tend to be racist, heterosexist, and homophobic, engage in othering, and emphasize traditional gender roles (S. Roth).

In the year after Trump came to office, several notable protests took form, including the Poor People's Campaign, the Women's March on Washington, Indivisible, and various sports protests. The Poor People's Campaign, though not a gender-based or women-centred organization, specifically addresses healthcare in its intersectional platform, noting on its website that 32 million Americans lack health insurance, 40 per cent of Americans have taken on debt because of medical issues, and that healthcare-related debt is the number one cause of bankruptcy in the U.S. ("Poor People's Campaign"). The Women's March on Washington received an extraordinary amount of media coverage with their first march held in January of 2017. The march brought together "people of all backgrounds—women and men and gender nonconforming people, young and old, of diverse faiths, differently abled, immigrants and indigenous" ("Women's March"). Despite beginning as a largely white and middle-class women's group organized through the informal social networks of Facebook, the organization now deliberately works to become more representative and diverse (Gökariksel and Smith 633).

Indivisible emerged immediately following Trump's election in 2016 when two ex-Congressional workers posted an online guide based on the methods of the Tea Party to oppose Trump through targeted activism aimed at congressional representatives (B. Roth). The organization is now affiliated with over six thousand grassroots local chapters. The initiative was largely adopted by white, middle-class, and middle-aged women, who feel threatened in a way they did not before (Graff). Indivisible is also gradually expanding its base to include more diverse and marginalized groups.

Although none of these organizations focus primarily on healthcare or the health concerns of women, they do represent hope for women through the intersectional and multi-issue approach they take to political activism. In fact, the lack of specific movements aimed only at healthcare reform in the U.S. is indicative of the current forms of political mobilization, which have moved from single issue organizations dominated by one identity based group to become broad based, diverse, and prepared to shift their attention to a range of issues as they arise. A number of shared characteristics point to these changes within the organizations mentioned above. First, although Indivisible and the Women's March were started by white, middle-class women, and the Poor People's Campaign emerged from the Black rights movement, they have all deliberately expanded their support base to include diverse representatives of marginalized groups in America. Second, none of these movements focus on a single political issue; instead, they advocate on a wide range of issues spanning economics, poverty, gender and sexual rights, equality, racism, healthcare, and the environment. Furthermore, they seek to explicitly draw out the linkages between diverse but interrelated issues, including, for example, illuminating the relationship between gender, poverty, and healthcare. Finally, these groups all reflect the importance of the Internet and social media for organizing and fundraising in the twenty-first century. Both Indivisible and the Women's March began on social media and used the existing social networks of individuals to launch their movements. All three groups use social media to organize events, recruit, and fundraise. The day of the vote repealing Obamacare, "A rallying cry went out on Twitter: Want revenge on the lawmakers who voted yes? Click here to give $5 to defeat them in next year's midterms" (Kroll 36). That day anti-Trump groups raised over $4.2 million in small dollar amounts using the online tool ActBlue (Kroll). Their success represents the importance of social media, not only for getting the message out and organizing resistance but also for funding organizations in ways distinct from traditional political sponsorship.

Three years into Trump's term as American president, however, organized opposition to his reign and protests appear to be in decline. The mobilization appears to have peaked with the midterm elections in 2018, which saw record numbers of women and minorities running for and winning office (Cooney). Despite the mistakes and controversies, Trump's popularity is increasing, and the urgency behind the protests and mobilization for the midterm elections is diminishing (Pollitt). In an editorial for *The Nation*, Katha Pollitt considers whether the decline is due to "Trump Fatigue" or a sense of resignation. As America moves into the 2020 election cycle, renewed opposition and energy will hopefully emerge, as another term of Trump politics and attacks on healthcare will have an increasingly negative impact on American women.

Conclusion

Banu Gökariksel and Sara Smith argue that "if there is one thing to be optimistic about now, it is the energized grassroots resistance movement that is reaching out to all 'Others' of the white masculinity that the current administration is enshrining as the essence of 'America'" (629). Through unprecedentedly large demonstrations in the U.S., millions of women allied with other marginalized groups have made their disapproval of Trump and his political ideals, including his attacks on Obamacare, clear. The fact that public support for healthcare legislation in the U.S. is gendered provides hope that women will be successful in lobbying for positive change. Women are more likely than men to support government involvement in the provision of healthcare generally and the ACA more specifically (Lizotte). Mary-KateLizotte suggests that "Women are not only more supportive than men of an activist government in the abstract but also on specific, concrete policies like the Affordable Care Act" (216), which translates into the fact that "women are more likely than men to support government initiatives to help the poor" (Lizotte 216).

The ACA's Medicaid—a plan that provides essential health services to millions of Americans—is currently under threat: "Cuts would have devastating consequences for millions of Americans, including the nearly 40 million women who rely on Medicaid" (Katch, Schubel, and Broaddus). For women who are mothers or for those imagining motherhood in the future, cuts to Medicaid will mean a reduction in their access to, among other medical services, family planning, maternity care, and treatment for substance use disorders. Already a disproportionate number of women in the U.S., particularly those from minority and Indigenous groups, have incomes falling well below the poverty line (NWLC). For mothers who live in poverty, it will mean making more compromises, which will affect their own, as well as their children's, physical and mental health.

In looking to other countries as positive role models for state controlled healthcare systems, it is clear that there are workable solutions. Although positive change to the current healthcare system in the U.S. is possible, such change can only happen in an environment where materialist and consumerist values are replaced with an ethos of care and compassion as well as a realization by government that "Maximizing GDP is not the same as maximizing wellbeing" (Khan 55). With economic inequality in the U.S. at a historical high and higher than in any other industrialized country in the world, the consequence for a large proportion of the population, including disproportionate numbers of women and children, is poverty. Philip Alston, United Nations special rapporteur and watchdog on extreme poverty, warned in June of 2018 that "If food stamps and access to Medicaid are removed, and housing subsidies cut, then the effect on people living on the margins will be drastic" (qtd. in Pilkington). Prioritizing "economic growth over and sometimes at the cost of social, moral and environmental nourishing of societies" (Khan 59) will not stem the negative impact of neoliberalism on women (Dobrowolsky), nor will it decrease the feminization of poverty (Goldberg and Kremen 2). The remarkable activism we have witnessed in the protests and women's marches happening in the U.S. since the 2016 election provides the most tangible, if limited, hope that positive change is possible. Demands from this movement suggest a desire for a welfare state that values social programs, including universal healthcare, and a rejection of neoliberal policies that have for too long placed the burden of responsibility on individuals for their own economic success, security, and health outcomes.

Works Cited

Al-Sahab B., et al. "Prevalence of Smoking during Pregnancy and Associated Risk Factors among Canadian Women: A National Survey." *BMC Pregnancy & Childbirth,* vol.10, no. 1, 2010, pp. 24-32.

Alston, Philip. "Extreme Poverty in America: Read the UN Special Report." *The Guardian,* 15 December 2017, www.theguardian.com/world/2017/dec/15/extreme-poverty-america-un-special-monitor-report. Accessed 17 July 2020.

Amadeo, Kimberly. "Income Inequality in America." *The Balance,* 25 Aug. 2017, www.thebalance.com/income-inequality-in-america-3306190/. Accessed 17 July 2020.

Battacharya, Tithi. "Donald Trump: The Unanticipated Apothesosis of Neoliberalism." *Cultural Dynamics,* vol. 29, no. 1-2, 2017, pp. 108-116.

Beeber, Linda, Krista Perreira, and Todd Swartz. "Supporting the Mental Health of Mothers Raising Children in Poverty: How Do We Target Them For Intervention Studies?" *Annals of the New York Academy of Science,* vol. 1136, no. 1, 2008, pp. 86-100.

Bombard, Jennifer et al. "Chronic Disease and Related Risk Factors among Low-Income Mothers." *Maternal and Child Health Journal,* vol. 16, no.1, 2012, pp. 60-71.

Bor, J., G. Cohen, and S. Galea. "Population Health in an Era of Rising Income Inequality: USA, 1980-2015." *The Lancet,* vol. 389, 2017, pp. 1475-1490.

Bregman, Rutger. "Utopian Thinking: The Easy Way to Eradicate Poverty." *The Guardian,* 6 Mar. 2017, www.theguardian.com/commentisfree/2017/mar/06/utopian-thinking-poverty-universal-basic-income. Accessed 17 July 2020.

Bruce, Ian. "Resisting Neoliberalism through Political and Social Critique: The Guardian Column of Polly Toynbee." *Discourse, Context and Media,* vol. 10, 2015, pp. 45-53.

Buckley, Patricia, and Akrur Barua. "Are We Headed for a Poorer United States: Growing Wealth Inequality by Age puts Younger Households Behind." *Deloitte Insights,* 12 Mar. 2018, www2.deloitte.com/content/dam/insights/us/articles/4423_Issues-by-the-numbers_article/DI_Issues-by-the-numbers_3.18.pdf. Accessed 17 July 2020.

Bunyan, Paul. "The Role of Civil Society in Reducing Poverty: A Case Study of the Living Wage Campaign in the UK." *Local Economy,* vol. 31, no. 4, 2016, pp. 489-501.

Cillizza, Chris. "The Real Reason Trump Is So Dead Set on Crushing Obamacare." *The Point,* 13 Oct. 2017, www.cnn.com/2017/10/13/politics/trump-obamacare-subsidies/index.html. Accessed 17 July 2020.

Cohen, Richard. "Defining Trumpism: Ideology of Our Age." *New York Daily News,* 30 Apr. 2018, www.nydailynews.com/opinion/defining-trumpism-ideology-age-article-1.3964276. Accessed 17 July 2020.

Cooney, Samantha. "Here Are Some of the Women Who Made History in the Midterm Election." *Time Magazine.* 19 Nov. 2018, time.com/5323592/2018-elections-women-history-records/. Accessed 17 July 2020.

Cutts, Diana, et al. "US Housing Insecurity and the Health of Very Young Children." *American Journal of Public Health,* vol. 101, no. 8, 2011, pp. 1508-14.

Dickman, Samuel, et al. "Inequality and the Health-Care System in the USA." *The Lancet,* vol. 389, no. 10077, 2017, pp. 1431-41.

Dobrowolsky, Alexandra, editor. *Women & Public Policy in Canada: Neo-Liberalism and After?* Oxford University Press, 2009.

Farrer, Martin. "Trump Interview: 'I'm Very Popular in Britain. I Get a lot of Fan Mail.'" *The Guardian*, 2018, www.theguardian.com/us-news/2018/jan/29/donald-trump-interview-piers-morgan-im-very-popular-in-britain-get-a-lot-of-fan-mail. Accessed 17 July 2020.

Ferguson, Ian, and Michael Lavalette. "Looking Back on 2016." *Critical and Radical Social Work*, vol. 5, no. 1, 2017, pp. 3-6.

Finfgeld-Connett, Deborah. "Becoming Homeless, Being Homeless, and Resolving Homelessness among Women." *Issues in Mental Health Nursing*, vol. 31, no. 7, 2010, pp. 461-69.

Flenady, Vicky et al. "Stillbirths: The Way Forward in High-Income Countries." *The Lancet*, vol. 377, no. 9778, 2011, pp. 1703-17.

Fraser, Nancy. "Feminism, Capitalism and the Cunning of History." *New Left Review*, no. 56, March-April, 2009, pp. 97-117.

Gaffney, Adam, and Danny McCormick. "The Affordable Care Act: Implications for Health-Care Equity." *The Lancet*, vol. 389, no. 10077, 2017, pp. 1442-52.

Glinianaia, Svetlana, et al. "No Improvement in Socioeconomic Inequalities in Birth Weight and Preterm Birth over Four Decades: A Population-Based Cohort Study." *BMC Public Health*, vol. 13, no. 1, 2013, pp. 345-53.

Gökarıksel, Banu, and Sara Smith. "Intersectional Feminism beyond U.S. Flag Hijab and Pussy Hats in Trump's America." *Gender, Place and Culture*, vol. 24, no. 5, 2017, pp. 628-44.

Goldberg, Gertrude S., and Eleanor Kremen. "The Feminization of Poverty: Discovered in America." *The Feminization of Poverty*, edited by Gertrude Schaffner Goldberg and Eleanor Kremen, Greenwood Press, 1990, pp. 1-16.

Goldberg, Jonah. "Trumpism Is a Psychology, Not an Ideology." *National Review*, 7 Mar. 2018, www.nationalreview.com/2018/03/donald-trump-movement-psychology-not-ideology/. Accessed 17 July 2020.

Goldenberg, Robert et al. "Epidemiology and Causes of Preterm Birth." *The Lancet*, vol. 371, no. 9606, 2008, pp. 75-84.

Goozner, Merrill. "The Many Consequences of Repealing Obamacare." *Challenge*, vol. 60, no. 2, 2017, pp. 122-40.

Graff, E. J. "They Persisted: The Women of Indivisible." *Mother Jones*, vol. 42, no. 4, 2017, pp. 34-63.

Hendrikse, Reijer. "Neo-illiberalism." *Geoforum*, vol. 95, 2018, pp. 169-172.

Katch, Hanna, Jessica Schubel, and Matt Broaddus. "Medicaid Works for Women—But Proposed Cuts Would Have Harsh, Dispro-portionate Impact." *Center on Budget and Policy Priorities*, 2017, www.cbpp.org/research/health/medicaid-works-for-women-but-proposed-cuts-would-have-harsh-disproportionate-impact. Accessed 17 July 2020.

Kauffman, L.A. "We Are Living through a Golden Age of Protest." *The Guardian*. 6 May 2018, www.theguardian.com/commentisfree/2018/may/06/protest-trump-direct-action-activism. Accessed 6 Aug. 2020.

Khalifeh, Hina, et al. "Intimate Partner Violence and Socioeconomic Deprivation in England: Findings from a National Cross-Sectional Survey." *American Journal of Public Health*, vol. 103, no. 3, 2013, pp. 462-72.

Khan, Mohammed. "Putting 'Good Society' Ahead of the Economy: Overcoming Neoliberalism's Growth Trap and its Costly Con-sequences." *Sustainable Development*, vol. 23, no. 2, 2015, pp. 65-73.

Kroll, Andy. "Checks and Balances: ActBlue's Fundraising Wizards." *Mother Jones*, vol. 42 no. 4, 2017, pp. 36-37.

Lizotte, Mary-Kate. "Investigating Women's Greater Support of the Affordable Care Act." *The Social Science Journal*, vol. 53, no. 2, 2016, pp. 207-17.

Millward, David. "What Is Obamacare and Why Does Donald Trump Want to Repeal the Affordable Care Act?" *The Telegraph*, 31 July 2017, www.telegraph.co.uk/news/0/obamacare-does-donald-trump-want-repeal-affordable-care-act/. Accessed 17 July 2020.

Moghadam, Valentine, and Gizem Kaftan. "Right-Wing Populisms North and South: Varieties and Gender Dynamics." *Women's Studies International Forum*, vol. 75, July-August, 2019, pp. 1-9.

Moore, Tim, Morag McArthur, and Debbie Noble-Carr. "Stuff You'd Never Think of: Children Talk about Homelessness and How They'd

Like to Be Supported." *Family Matters,* vol. 78, 2008, pp. 36-43.

Mudde, Cas. "Trumpism Is Ingrained in White America. When He Goes, It Will Remain." *The Guardian,* 28 Dec. 2017, www.theguardian.com/commentisfree/2017/dec/28/donald-trump-white-america-republican-party. Accessed 17 July 2020.

Nagahawatte, N. Tanya, and Robert Goldenberg. "Poverty, Maternal Health, and Adverse Pregnancy Outcomes." *Annals of New York Academy of Science,* vol. 1136, no. 1, 2008, pp. 80-85.

Nash, George. "American Conservatism & the Problem of Populism." *The New Criterion,* September, 2016, vol. 35, no. 1, pp. 4-14.

National Women's Law Centre (NWLC). "Women and Poverty, State by State," 14 Sept. 2017, *NWLC,* nwlc.org/resources/women-and-poverty-state-state/. Accessed 17 July 2020.

Peck, Jamie. "Poverty? Oh, That's Just a 'State of Mind' for the Trump Administration." *The Guardian,* 26 May 2017, www.theguardian.com/commentisfree/2017/may/26/poverty-state-of-mind-ben-carson-trump-administration. Accessed 17 July 2020.

Phipps, Shelley. "The Impact of Poverty on Health: A Scan of Research Literature, Canadian Institute for Health Information," 2013, *Secure,* secure.cihi.ca/free_products/CPHIImpactonPoverty_e.pdf. Accessed 17 July 2020.

Pilkington, Ed. "Trump's 'Cruel' Measures Pushing US Inequality to Dangerous Levels, UN Warns." *The Guardian,* 1 June 2018, www.theguardian.com/us-news/2018/jun/01/us-inequality-donald-trump-cruel-measures-un. Accessed 17 July 2020.

Politico Staff. "Full Transcript: Second 2016 Presidential Debate." *Politico,* 2016, www.politico.com/story/2016/10/2016-presidential-debate-transcript-229519. Accessed 17 July 2020.

Pollitt, Katha. "Take Back the Streets! It's 2019. Where have all the protesters gone?" *Nation.* vol. 308, no. 1. 29 July 2019.

Poor People's Campaign. www.poorpeoplescampaign.org/. Accessed 17 July 2020.

Qui, Linda. "Trump Falsely Claims to Have 'Repealed Obamacare.'" *New York Times,* 2017, www.nytimes.com/2017/12/20/us/politics/factcheck-trump-tax-repeal-health-care.html. Accessed 2 Feb. 2018.

Roth, Benita. "Learning from the Tea Party: The US Indivisible

Movement as Countermovement in the Era of Trump." *Sociological Research Online*, vol. 23, no. 2, 2018, pp. 539-46.

Roth, Silke. "Contemporary Counter-Movements in the Age of Brexit and Trump: Changing Perspectives on Social Movements Introduction to Rapid Response." *Sociological Research Online*, vol. 23, no. 2, 2018, pp. 496-506.

Russell, Graham. "Trump Says He Doesn't Want a 'Poor Person' in Cabinet Roles." *The Guardian,* 22 June 2017, www.theguardian.com/us-news/2017/jun/22/donald-trump-says-he-doesnt-want-a-poor-person-in-cabinet-roles. Accessed 17 July 2020.

Salmela, Mikko, and Christian von Scheve. "Emotional Dynamics of Right- and Left-Wing Political Populism." *Humanity & Society,* vol. 42, no. 4, 2018, pp. 434-54.

Sanders, Bernie. "An Agenda to Fight Inequality." *The Lancet,* vol. 389, no. 10077, 2017, pp. 1376-77.

Taylor, Matthew, and Ben Edwards. "Housing and Children's Well-being and Development: Evidence from a National Longitudinal Study." *Family Matters,* no. 91, 2012, pp. 47-61.

Thomsen, Jacqueline. "Trump Vows to Repeal and Replace ObamaCare 'Disaster.'" *The Hill,* 23 Nov. 2017, thehill.com/homenews/administration/361693-trump-vows-to-repeal-and-replace-obamacare-disaster. Accessed 17 July 2020.

Wilkinson, Richard, and Kate Pickett. *The Spirit Level: Why Greater Equality Makes Societies Stronger.* Bloomsbury Press, 2010.

Willison, Charley E., and Phillip M. Singer. "Repealing the Affordable Care Act Essential Health Benefits: Threats and obstacles." *AJPH Perspectives,* vol. 107, no. 8, 2017, pp. 1225-26.

Wilson, Richard W. "American Political Culture in Comparative Perspective." *Political Psychology,* vol. 18, no. 2, 1997, pp. 483-502.

Wodak, Ruth, and Michał Krzyżanowski. "Right-Wing Populism in Europe & USA: Contesting Politics and Discourse beyond 'Orbanism' and 'Trumpism.'" *Journal of Language and Politics,* vol.16, no. 4, 2017, pp. 471-84.

Women's March. *Mission.* www.womensmarch.com/mission/. Accessed 17 July 2020.

Chapter 5

Stratified Motherhoods: Gaps and Contradictions in Social Protection of Mothers and Their Children in Brazil

Nathalie Reis Itaboraí

Brazil owes a social debt to its citizens who have been marginalized based on gender, race, social class, and regional geography through much of its history, and access to maternal rights is similarly stratified. For example, women in formal paid employment can access four to six months of maternity leave, but poor women who work in the informal sectors are only eligible for a social assistance program known as the Bolsa Familia Program (BFP), which provides support at a level below 20 per cent of the minimum wage. Looking specifically at such inequalities, this chapter will review a range of inequalities among mothers in their access to social supports; it will demonstrate mothers' unequal citizenship in Brazil and highlight the consequences for mothers' welfare and opportunities as well as the effects of this stratification on the (re)production of inequality. In reviewing Brazil's current social security system, maternity leave program, and other social supports for mothers and their children, it is apparent that there are significant gaps between benefits, beneficiaries, and the budgets of maternity social protection policies. The political, material, and moral economies (such as stigmatizing discourses about the poor) that are used to legitimize inequality and conceal the stratified nature of the policies must also be exposed in order to develop analyses and budgets that meet the needs of all mothers.

Stratified Citizenships and the Role of State in the (Re) production of Social Inequalities

To understand the social protection of motherhood, it is necessary to consider the larger debate about social security in Brazil and Latin America relating to the role of the state in reducing social inequalities throughout their citizens' lives. There have been many advances in social security programs in Brazil since its most recent Constitution was implemented in 1988 (Delgado, Jaccoud, and Nogueira 35-36). A national health system has been established, and it serves about 75 per cent of the Brazilian population. Progressive reforms have increased retirement benefits for urban workers and, importantly, in rural areas through noncontributory protection for rural workers. Finally, social assistance programs—such as the BFP and the Benefício de Prestação Continuada (BPC, or "continuous cash benefit," which guarantees a minimum income for poor elderly people and people with disabilities)— have contributed to poverty reduction through income transfers. The inclusion of social assistance programs in public policy is seen as a step forwards as compared to the prior tradition of charitable and philanthropic private actions. The universalistic approach of the Brazilian Constitution (1988), which brought together different social movements in its formulation, is inseparable from redemocratization within the country after two decades of dictatorship (1964-1985).

Despite these advances, Brazil has faced difficulties in the regulation and financing of its social security programs. In addition, since its enactment, there have been fundamental challenges to the rights contained within the Constitution. Guilherme Delgado, Luciana Jaccoud, and Roberto Passos Nogueira suggest that the Constitution was created from several paradigms. Thus, the regulation of social security combines different criteria: universalistic (health and rural retirement); contributory (urban retirement); and selective (social assistance). They emphasize that in Brazil, as in Latin America in general, the contributory format, rather than the universal Beveridgian basic benefit, is the dominant approach, which leaves significant segments of the population without social protection.

According to Melissa Campana Alabarce, since the goods and services needed for living can be acquired from one's family, the market, and the state, welfare regimes can be seen as a set of diverse practices that allow welfare to be decommodified and defamilialized. The welfare system, thus, reduces poverty and improves the distribution of resources between groups and across the lifecycle (29). However, the stratified character of social security (where eligibility depends on contributions or workforce participation) hinders the redistributive effect of state welfare systems, which is why Campana Alabarce advocates that social protection should be conditional only on citizenship.

Fernando Filgueira has endeavoured to classify the different models of the welfare state in Latin America and highlights the stratified character of available social protection: "Such policies presented a limited development that was strongly biased to the urban sectors and with preferential coverage for those incorporated into the formal labor market.... In addition, the sectors actually protected clearly showed a marked stratification regarding access, coverage and quality of the benefits" (10). He defines Brazil, along with Mexico, as "Dual Regimes" that co-opt the elites and repress the popular sectors (20). In this context, the "State apparatus [is] less bent towards redistributing for popular support and more oriented towards redistributing for elite accommodation and popular control" (25).

Where social protection is so stratified, basic welfare needs are met through families, particularly women. In Brazil, the family is an important source of social protection (Goldani). Thus, with unequal social protection from the state, families assume social risks (such as the costs related to unemployment and the absence of public care) according to their private resources, usually damaging the poorest who are the most unprotected. Therefore, "familism" is an expression that can be read as "an indicator to measure the extent to which families absorb social risks in social welfare regimes" (Campos and Teixeira 23). In this context, gender is an often forgotten dimension of stratification. There are inequalities between men and women in how they access social security: more men access retirement benefits and more women access social assistance. Additionally, social protection systems have historically been constructed to protect the male provider and generally rest upon gendered family responsibilities.

Social protection is also stratified by age. Public policy is, in general, made by older adults who may prioritize their own needs and provide less protection to children. On top of this, inequalities accumulate across the lifecycle. One can imagine a map of social protection that represents the distribution and the amount of benefits according to the identity of the beneficiaries and the types of benefits. For each benefit, it is possible to see who is excluded and included across the lifecycle—from being born to a mother under social protection to accessing retirement in old age. Public policies, historically, reward the top classes, victimize vulnerable people, and reaffirm social polarities through the corporatism of the strongest groups and the political fragility of the weakest, which is in contrast to the idea that the state must correct social inequalities created by the market. Often, only those who are "economically citizens" have access to the stratified citizenship (Filgueira 27), precisely because a good part of social protection is based on formal workforce attachment.

Although some universal services no longer dependent on workforce participation began to be offered under the new Constitution, inequality continues to follow lines of class, gender, race, age, rural/urban location, and regional development. Poverty is racialized, gendered, and youthful. Just over half of the Brazilian population (54 per cent) are of mixed race or African descent, but they are three quarters of the poorest decile (IBGE 96). Women are also overrepresented among the poor (Medeiros and Costa). The incidence of poverty is also much higher among children because economic protection (such as pensions and the BPC) is available to the elderly and persons with disabilities in poor families but not for poor children in general. However, between 2005 and 2015, the percentage of children and adolescents living in poor households (households where monthly income per capita was less than 25 per cent of the minimum wage) decreased from 22.4 per cent to 17.6 per cent for children aged zero to four years and from 20.7 per cent to 18.0 per cent for those aged five to fourteen years old (IBGE).

From 2004 to 2013 in Brazil, poverty fell from more than 20 per cent to about 9 per cent of the population, whereas extreme poverty fell from about 7 percent to 4 percent (Soares et al). This decline was due to the expansion of the labour market and significant increases in transfers to the poor through the BFP and other social security measures. However, in terms of geographic distribution, the profile of poverty has not changed much, remaining concentrated in the north and northeast regions as well as in rural areas.

Poverty is worse for many because some social security programs—including maternity leave, disability leave, and unemployment insurance—depend on formal workforce attachment. The labour market is characterized by a significant percentage of informal work, with the percentage of workers in formal jobs varying from 46.2 to 58.2 between 2005 and 2015 (IBGE). Yet the unemployment rate (people aged sixteen and over) was 9.4 per cent in 2015, and higher for young people (22.8 per cent) and women (11.6 per cent).

Brazilians remain unaware of these inequalities, blaming lower-class families and women for their poverty. This symbolic class struggle was evident in the public reactions to the BFP (Lavinas et al.), the first national Brazilian strategy to combat poverty. Any study of poverty must take account of both material and symbolic inequalities: the first includes capital, resources, and social provisions, and the second relates to the production of meanings used to justify poverty and inequalities. Within this context, we examine the proportion of citizens covered and the relative generosity of the benefits offered to support mothers and their children as well as some aspects of inequalities concerning the legitimacy (or stigmatization) of social protection modalities.

Inequalities in Access to Maternity Leave in Brazil

Maternity and paternity leave are intended to allow a parent to care for a child in the first months of life while keeping parents' salaries for the duration of the leave. Maternity leave was first established in Brazil in 1943, with the Consolidation of Labour Laws (CLT). The leave was eighty-four days to the mother and had to be paid by the employer, which motivated discrimination against female workers. In 1974, under Law 6.136, maternity leave was included among social security benefits. The 1988 Constitution increased the period of leave to 120 days. Rural and domestic workers were included in 1991 (Law 8.213) and temporary workers in 2012 (Súmula 244 TST). Despite these additions, access to leave is unequal and stratified, since it is available for women in formal work when half of the labour force is in informal work. Maternity leave is paid at full salary, and for some public sector workers and workers in some private companies extended maternity and paternity leaves (adding sixty and fifteen days, respectively) are now allowed (Law 11.770, 2008).

Maternity protection policies are important for the social wellbeing of children and families and also for gender equality. Perhaps reflecting the perception in Brazilian society of the responsibilities of mothers and fathers for childcare, fathers only became entitled to leave with the new Constitution, and they are only entitled to five days. Paternity leave is only available to men in the formal market and can be extended up to twenty days for some workers, similar to maternity leave.

Although gender equality supposes parental leave (maternity and paternity) and other care policies are equally available to men and women, I will focus this analysis on the available information on maternity leave. In Latin America, the International Labour Office (ILO) and United Nations Development Program (UNDP) consider that workers' family responsibilities (provided for in ILO Convention 156, which was not signed by Brazil) are generally not present in Latin American legislation. Maternity protection is the only measure of family and work reconciliation.

The ILO through its Maternity Protection Convention no. 183 (2000) seeks to regulate maternity protection: "The absence of income security during the final stages of pregnancy and after childbirth forces many women, especially those in the informal economy, to return to work prematurely, thereby putting at risk their own and their children's health" (ILO 1). Maternity protection is considered a human right of women, children, and families as well as a mechanism for promoting gender equality in work, preventing workplace discrimination, and supporting healthcare and income security for mothers and newborn children (xi). The ILO recognizes the importance of protecting mothers and children independently of contributions, as the organization proposes universal cash benefits, which are open to all, including the unemployed and informal workers.

However, in Brazil, despite regional and labour market inequalities in the protection of motherhood, there has also been an increase in access to maternity leave due to the growth in the number of women working in the formal sector (between 2004 and 2015, the number of maternity leaves granted by companies increased almost 2.5 times) and to changes in legislation to include rural and domestic workers (Ansiliero and Rodrigues). Even so, less than a quarter of Brazilian children were born to a mother with maternity leave protection in 2010. The percentage is higher in the most developed federal states of the southeast and south regions, where there are more formal jobs for women (In Graph 1, from Espírito Santo to Rio Grande do Sul).

Therefore, Brazil is far from providing universal coverage. Many poor mothers who are employed in the informal market or are unable to work because of a lack of job qualifications or insufficient childcare services[1] cannot access maternity leave (Hunter, this volume). Cash transfer programs (such as the BFP) to poor mothers do not meet their needs. They are of much lower value and were introduced much later than other indirect transfers, which benefit privileged mothers more. These differentials show that the family policies for motherhood and early childhood fail to counter the starting point of deep inequality.

Public Policies for Mothers in a Comparative Perspective

A significant limitation of maternity protection is that it is available only to women in formal employment. Those who are not covered are eligible only for the BFP, which "has been affirming itself as an initiative that expands the income guarantee system of Brazilian social protection, serving a previously excluded public and fulfilling a specific and complementary role in Social Security" (Delgado, Jaccoud, and Nogueira 28-29). The racialized profile of poverty is reflected in social assistance, where people of mixed race and African descent (72.8 per cent) and Indigenous people (0.7 per cent) are overrepresented.[2]

However, a comparison between the BFP and maternity leave shows that they reach different women, with the BFP covering most of the households in the poorer states of the north and northeast regions (In Graph 1, from Rondônia to Bahia). Maternity leave is part of labour rights, whereas the BFP is a social assistance program, implying different levels of social protection—a Brazilian reflection of the "contract vs. charity dilemma" (Gordon and Fraser) for inequalities among women.

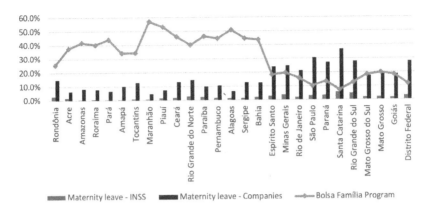

Graph 1: Number of maternity benefits granted as a percentage of the number of live births per federal state (2010) and percentage of households receiving BFP per federal state (2013)[3]

The BFP was established in 2003 to benefit families living in poverty or extreme poverty (defined as those with monthly income per capita between R$ 60.01 and R$ 120.00, and below R$ 60.00, respectively).[4] The small budget of the program (less than 0.5 per cent of Brazil's GDP) has been criticized, especially when contrasted with the bigger budget of other public programs. From a moral economy perspective (Fassin), recipients are stigmatized. Although the BFP is praised for its focus on poor people (Soares and Sátyro), as Sônia Rocha reminds us, media coverage is full of prejudices and stereotypes about lazy and dependent poor families, echoing public opinion, and often highlights misuse of the program (Wallace, this volume). Lena Lavinas et al. have shown that the conditions for accessing the program (children must be vaccinated and attend school) are less about ensuring the effectiveness of the BFP and more about contenting public opinion expectations of a moralizing role in order to supposedly induce good manners and practices among recipients. Themes related to motherhood and childcare—including the constant suspicion that poor, and especially younger, women have too many children—feed these moral judgments even though young women's fertility rates have been declining since 2000 and women's autonomy has increased across social classes with many of the policy changes (Itaboraí). Thus, although there is not necessarily a feminization of poverty in Brazil, there is a feminization of social assistance, which is, perhaps, the reason there is no feminization of poverty. Feminist criticism usually points out that the state invokes women's role in protecting the vulnerable, which mobilize conservative femininity logics that reiterate their role as mother (Mariano and Carloto; Cantillon and Hutton, this volume). In this sense, mothers are beneficiaries of temporary and stratified protection while also providing continuous and free protection in a context of limited public care policies.

Structural inequalities remain firmly anchored in unequal social protections and an unfair tax system (Lustig) by stratifying rights and benefits depending on group membership. For example, income tax deductions (an indirect income) for dependent children are more valuable on average than the BFP (benefits for children in poverty and extremely poverty were R$ 32.00 and R$ 102.00 respectively in 2012, and the tax deduction was R$164.56). These gaps remained relatively stable in the period between 2004 and 2018 (Graph 2). Higher income families receive greater state support and have had access to it since 1924, almost eighty years before the BFP was introduced to support lower income families. They also benefit from this support without any of the stigma attached to BFP mothers. Additionally, the tax deduction is available until a child turns twenty-one (or twenty-four if in postsecondary education), whereas BFP only covers the child until age eighteen.

Public opinion in Brazil tends to be moralistic, legitimizing both the privileges of upper income earners and the countless requirements and conditions imposed upon the poor. The benefits provided to upper income earners, such as exemptions, deductions, and lower proportional taxation, are not recognized as forms of state support and are, thus, enjoyed without any of the stigma attached to receipt of benefits like the BFP. It is crucial that conversations about benefits to support families take account of the structural dimensions of social inequalities in order to overcome the traditional point of view of blaming the lower classes for their poverty based on moral conceptions of their family behaviour.

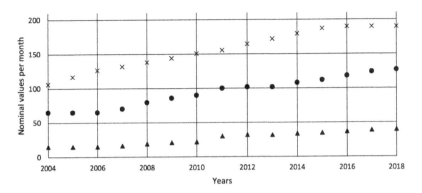

x Tax deductions per dependent ● BFP for families living in extreme poverty ▲ BFP for families living in poverty

Graph 2: Differentials between income transferred directly and indirectly in Brazil between 2004 and 2018—nominal values, average per month legally defined increases, and currency unit is Brazilian Real[5]

Final Considerations

Since maternity leaves were usually segmented in their coverage, reflecting inequalities within the labour market, it was a conditional cash transfer program (BFP) that finally began to extend protection to the poorest Brazilian families. Paradoxically, the criticisms of the limits and the small budget of the BFP show that closing the gaps that separate the living conditions of mothers and their children in Brazil is not expensive[6] and that the benefits multiply across generations. The importance of protecting mothers and young children (Mays, this volume) is increasingly recognized in the face of overwhelming evidence that quality care is essential to children's emotional, cognitive, and physical development (Black et al)—care that, if absent, can hardly be recovered at other stages of life.

Meanwhile the prospects in current Brazil are not optimistic. The BFP, implemented during the Lula and Dilma Rousseff governments, expanded access to social protection for poor mothers and children, but after the impeachment of Rousseff, the Temer government began reducing the BFP. In 2016, Congress approved a Constitutional Amendment (EC n. 95) that restricts investments in new generations for two decades. With the ascension to power of a far-right extremist in 2019, the prospects for social protection are worse, perhaps setting Brazil on a path similar to the United States (Ross and Wilton, this volume).

Even in advanced economies, children and young people are often the main victims of austerity policies (Richardson). With the new political reality in Brazil, an already stratified and nonuniversal protection system risks further reducing children's meagre protection against poverty. Hope for a better social security system that effectively protects mothers and children lies in the political struggle to lay bare the unequal shares of public spending on richer and poorer families and challenging the moral economy that continues to legitimize such inequalities.

Acknowledgment

The author acknowledges the contributions of Lorna A. Turnbull in re-writing this chapter to meet the English language standards of the other chapters in the volume.

Endnotes

1. Childcare policies—that can enable families (especially mothers) to work and earn more—are insufficient and stratified in their access in Brazil (Itaboraí).

2. According to Rogério Nagamine Costanzi and Flávio Fagundes (263) the profile of the beneficiaries by the program in April 2010 (according to the unified system of information and registry of social programs—Cadastro Único) was 7.5 per cent Black, 65.3 per cent Brown, and 0.7 per cent Indigenous. However, the population composition in 2010 was 7.6% Black, 43.1% Brown, and 0.4 Indigenous.

3. Sources: Number of benefits granted (INSS or companies) in 2010—Statistics of Brazilian government MPAS (retrieved from: www3.dataprev.gov.br/infologo/); Number of live births in 2010—Statistics of Brazilian government MS/SINASC (Datasus); Percentage of households receiving BFP—Campello and Neri (163)

4. The currency unit is the Brazilian Real. In October of 2003, when the program was launched, one US dollar was equivalent to three reals.

5. Sources: Osorio and Souza (3) and Brazilian government data.

6. Especially if we consider that Brazil is not a poor country, the GDP per capita was US $ 8,717.2 in 2019 (World Bank). But it is an

incredibly unequal country, with an extremely high *concentration* of *income* at the top of the distribution. Recognizing that in several countries, maternity benefits cover only women in formal employment, the ILO estimated the cost of universal maternity cash benefits in low and lower middle-income countries and found that it would require less than 0.5 percent of GDP for the majority of these countries.

Works Cited

Ansiliero, Graziela and Rodrigues, Eva Batista de Oliveira. "Histórico e evolução recente da concessão de salários-maternidade no Brasil." *Informe da Previdência Social*, vol. 19, no. 2, 2007, pp. 1-9.

Base de dados históricos da Previdência Social. www3.dataprev.gov.br/infologo/. Accessed 18 July 2020.

Black, M. M. et al. "Early Childhood Development Coming of Age: Science throughout the Life Course." *The Lancet*, vol. 389, no. 10064, 2017, pp. 77-90.

Campana Alabarce, Melissa. "Regímenes de Bienestar en América Latina y el Caribe: notas para pensar lo contemporáneo." *Trabajo Social Global: Revista de Investigación en Intervención Social*, vol. 5, no. 8, 2015, pp. 26-46.

Campello, Tereza and Neri, Marcelo. *Programa Bolsa Família: uma década da inclusão*. Ipea, 2013.

Campos, Marta Silva, and Solange Maria Teixeira. Gênero, família e proteção social: as desigualdades fomentadas pela política social. *Revista Katálisis*, Florianópolis vol. 13 no. 1, 2010, pp. 20-28.

DATASUS. tabnet.datasus.gov.br/cgi/tabcgi.exe?sinasc/cnv/nvuf.def . Accessed 18 July 2020.

Decreto nº 8.232, de 30 de abril de 2014. www.planalto.gov.br/ccivil_03/_ato2011-2014/2014/Decreto/D8232.htm. Accessed 18 July 2020.

Decreto nº 8.794, de 29 de junho de 2016. www.planalto.gov.br/ccivil_03/_Ato2015-2018/2016/Decreto/D8794.htm. Accessed 18 July 2020.

Delgado, Guilherme, Luciana Jaccoud, and Roberto Passos Nogueira. *Seguridade social: redefinindo o alcance da cidadania*. Ipea, 2009.

Fassin, Didier. "Compaixão e repressão: a economia moral das políticas de imigração na França." *Ponto Urbe: Revista do núcleo de antropologia urbana da USP*, vol. 15, 2014, pp. 1-26.

Filgueira, Fernando. *Welfare and Democracy in Latin America: The Development, Crises and Aftermath of Universal, Dual and Exclusionary Social States*. United Nations Research Institute for Social Development (UNRISD), 2005.

Fraser, Nancy, and Linda Gordon. "Contrato versus caridade: porque não existe cidadania social nos Estados Unidos?" Traslated by Angela Maria Moreira, *Revista Crítica de Ciências Sociais*, no. 42, May 1995, pp. 27-52.

"GDP per capita (current US$)." *World Bank National Accounts Data, and OECD National Accounts Data Files*. data.worldbank.org/indicator/NY.GDP.PCAP.CD . Accessed 18 July 2020.

Goldani, Ana Maria. "Las familias brasileñas y sus desafíos como factor de protección al final del siglo XX." *Processos sociales, pobración y familia: alternativas teóricas y empíricas en las investigaciones sobre vida doméstica*, edited by Cristina Gomes, FLACSO, 200, pp. 279-98.

IBGE. *Síntese de indicadores sociais: uma análise das condições de vida da população brasileira*. IBGE, 2016.

ILO and UNDP. *Trabajo y familia: hasta nuevas formas de conciliación con corresponsabilidad social*. Santiago, 2009.

ILO. Social Protection for Maternity: Key Policy Trends and Statistics. Social Protection Policy Papers, paper 15, 2015.

IRPF (Imposto sobre a renda das pessoas físicas). idg.receita.fazenda.gov.br/acesso-rapido/tributos/irpf-imposto-de-renda-pessoa-fisica#dedu--o-mensal-por-dependente . Accessed 18 July 2020.

Itaboraí, Nathalie Reis. *Mudanças nas famílias brasileiras (1976-2012): uma perspectiva de classe e gênero*. Garamond, 2017.

Lavinas, Lena, et al. *Projeto: medindo o grau de aversão à desigualdade da população brasileira através dos resultados do Bolsa-Família*. Rio de Janeiro, 2012.

Legislação do Imposto de Renda Pessoa Física de 1843 a 2015. receita.economia.gov.br/sobre/institucional/memoria/imposto-de-renda/legislacao/legislacao-do-imposto-de-renda-pessoa-fisica-de-1843-a-2013 . Accessed 18 July 2020.

Lustig, Nora. *Fiscal policy, Income Redistribution and Poverty in Low and Middle Income Countries*. CEQ Institute Commitment to Equity, Working paper 54, January 2017.

Mariano, Silvana Aparecida, and Cássia Maria Carloto. "Gênero e combate à pobreza no Programa Bolsa Família" *Faces da desigualdade de gênero e raça no Brasil*, edited by Alinne Bonetti and Maria Aparecida Abreu, IPEA, 2011. p. 61-78.

Medeiros, Marcelo, and Joana Simões Costa. Poverty among Women in Latin America: Feminization or Over-representation? Anpec, 2005.

Osorio, R. G. and P. H. G. F Souza *O Bolsa Família depois do Brasil Carinhoso: uma análise do potencial de redução da pobreza extrema*, Ipea, 2012, Nota Técnica, n. 14, ipea.gov.br/agencia/images/stories/PDFs/nota_tecnica/121221_notatecnica14_disoc.pdf. Accessed 18 July 2020.

Richardson, D. "Child Poverty and Family Policies in the OECD." *Revue Belge de Securite Sociale*, 2015, socialsecurity.belgium.be/sites/default/files/rbss-1-2015-richardson-fr.pdf. Accesed 18 July 2020.

Rocha, Sônia. "O Programa Bolsa Família: evolução e efeitos sobre a pobreza." *Economia e Sociedade*, vol. 20, no, 1, 2011, pp. 113-39.

Rogério, Nagamine Costanzi, and Flávio Fagundes. "Perfil dos beneficiários do Programa Bolsa Família." *Bolsa família 2003-2010: avanços e desafios*, edited by J.A. Castro and L. Modesto, Ipea, 2010, pp. 249-70.

Soares, Sergei, and Natália Sátyro. *O Programa Bolsa Família: desenho institucional, impactos e possibilidades futuras*. Ipea, 2009.

Soares, Serguei et al. *Perfil da pobreza: Norte e Nordeste rurais*, IPC-IG, 2016, www.ipc-undp.org/pub/port/Perfil_da_pobreza_Norte_e_Nordeste_rurais.pdf. Accessed 18 July 2020.

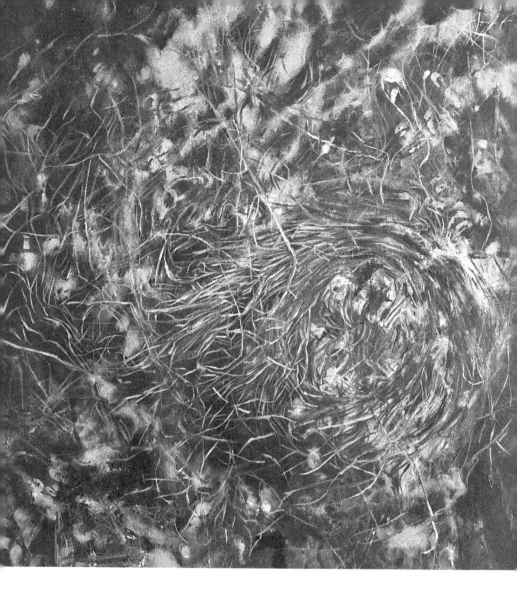

Part II

Images of Mothering

Chapter Six

Austerity Culture and the Myth of the Mumpreneur

Roberta Garrett

The cultural circulation of the term "mumpreneur" encompasses a number of different and often contradictory attitudes towards female employment in the early twentieth-first century. This chapter unpacks the various ideological fantasies projected onto and perpetuated by mumpreneurs using feminist, sociological and historical perspectives; it also analyzes the construction of the mumpreneur identity in various online and print sources in relation to the cluster of socioeconomic circumstances that gave rise to her existence. The chapter considers the mumpreneur in relation to the longer history of women's employment, thereby highlighting the limitations of this concept in terms of its economic viability as well as in terms of gender, race, and class equality.

Neoliberalism and Women's Employment Patterns since the 1980s

Maternal participation in the labour force in Western countries has grown steadily from the 1950s onwards but continues to be heavily concentrated in the areas "of the five 'Cs'—caring, catering, cashiering, cleaning and clerical" (*Trades Union Congress* 2). In the United Kingdom (UK), women currently make up 65 per cent of public sector workers, with an even higher percentage in such areas as local government, teaching, and nursing; black and minority ethnic women, meanwhile, are particularly concentrated in lower skilled and lower paid areas of both the public and private sector, such as cleaning and unskilled care work (*Trades Union Congress* 2). Women's participation patterns reflect the extension of the "separate spheres" ideology into employment, in which women's entry in the workplace, particularly at a more skilled level, was historically legitimated by an ethos of public service and self-sacrifice. Although levels of female employment continued to rise from the 1960s onwards, the association of female employment with either low-level retail and service sector jobs or higher-level caring professions, such as those in education and health-care, remained fairly static from the postwar period until the 1980s. It was at this point that a minority of educated, generally white middle-class women moved into a wider range of occupations. The increase in the number of women entering higher education led to a (limited) expansion of professional women in such areas as law, business, and finance, which received much media attention in terms of a perceived shift in gender roles and emergence of the fantasy of the sexy but masculine career woman. But this increase also reflected the changing political and economic landscape (Tasker 89-115).

In the 1980s, neoliberalism began its first serious assault on social democratic systems. Associated with the New Right in the United States and Thatcherism in the UK, neoliberal social, political, and economic theory was presented as an antidote to the recession of the 1970s—a crisis that right-wing governments attributed to intransigent unions and collectivism rather than the inherent contradictions and boom and bust cycles of capitalist production. The assent of a neoliberal doxa of individualism, choice, and competition was accompanied by the aggressive promotion of privatization, the scaling back of public services and state housing provision, and the gradual erosion of hard-won workers' rights and protection (Gamble; Harvey). It also promoted what Wendy Brown describes as "a more generalised practice of 'economising' spheres and activities heretofore governed by other tables of value" (21), such as health and education. As many have pointed out, neoliberal policies have had a marked impact on gender roles and the material conditions of women's lives as workers and mothers in Western countries. Female participation in paid employment has continued to rise steadily since the 1980s, but the dominant areas in which working-class and ethnic minorities are more likely to be employed—"caring, catering, cashiering, cleaning and clerical"—have been those hit hardest by neoliberal policies in terms of suppressing workers' rights, falling wages, and increasing levels of job insecurity. This situation has tipped many British working-class women and ethnic minority women, along with their families, into poverty and has increased the dual burden, particularly felt by poor and ethnic minority women, by reducing state support for families (e.g., care for the elderly and state childcare). However, the picture for white, middle-class women has been more complex and is strongly associated with the discursive and ideological construction of the "mumpreneur" label.

Neoliberalism and Female Aspiration

The New Right ideology of the 1980s tended to promote highly polarized, traditional gender norms and viewed feminism as threat to the stability of the family. However, various authors have demonstrated that in the last decade or so, neoliberal ideology has sought to incorporate and harness certain aspects of feminist thought (McRobbie, The Aftermath; Fraser; Scharff; Rottenberg). Many female British conservative politicians, including the former Prime Minister Teresa May (who was photographed wearing a "This Is What a Feminist Looks Like" t-shirt) are now keen to be associated with women's issues in a manner that would have been unthinkable during the Thatcher-Reagan era. As the number of women entering higher education has equaled or exceeded that of men, recent neoliberal governments have shifted towards applauding and encouraging female ambition and economic self-sufficiency rather than endorsing early or stay-at-home motherhood and economic dependency on an assumed male breadwinner.

Although the majority of current right-wing politicians have far more progressive views on gender equality than their twentieth-century predecessors, the right-wing endorsement of female employment and a general ethos of female self-sufficiency is, of course, strongly related to the desire to reduce state support for single mothers. It has also been fueled by economic policies (such as a reduction in public sector wages and pensions and the introduction of university fees) that have made it less and less possible for all but the very wealthiest of families to thrive on one income. However, the endorsement of female ambition and the expansion of acceptable careers for women have not been accompanied by a gendered redistribution of traditional domestic and caring duties.

Indeed, as many feminist critics have noted—from the somewhat tongue-in-cheek (and, therefore, optional) revival and celebration of traditional female craft and domestic skills (Negra) to the more serious and unavoidable business of steering children through an ever more hierarchical, monetized, and privatized neoliberal early childcare and education system—the range of duties assigned to the maternal role has expanded rather than contracted in line with higher levels of maternal employment. Despite this, paternal involvement in childcare and household tasks has remained relatively static (BBC News).

The cultural investment in what Sharon Hays and others have dubbed "intensive mothering" or "new momism" (Douglas and Michaels) from the mid-1990s onwards has also incorporated child psychology and development theories focusing almost exclusively on the mother-child relationship (Hays). This change has led to a greater emphasis on maternal bonding alongside the popularization of all-consuming modes of motherhood, such as the attachment parenting movement. Of course, as has been the case since the growth of childcare advice, the preferred mode of parenting covertly favours white, middle-class mothers who are less likely to be in fulltime employment than white working class or ethnic minority mothers. Tracey Reynolds argues in the introduction to her study of Caribbean mothers in the UK that mothering is revealed to be as equally racialized as it is gendered. Contemporary discourses generally overlook this factor and universalistic claims of mothering are based on white, middle-class and heterosexual practices. In the UK, media scare stories concerning the damaging effects of daycare for young children have not been confined to such publications as the notoriously right-wing and woman-hating *Daily Mail* or the staunchly old-school and sexist *Telegraph*; instead, they appeared regularly in the lifestyle sections of left-leaning, progressive sources, such as *The Guardian*, in opinion columns written by popular psychologists, such as Olivier James and Sue Gerhart. As Sara Cantillon and Martina Hutton argue in their contribution to this volume:

This idea of total self-sacrifice for your child (and its implicit message of emotional fulfilment) has been widely criticized as being too white and middle-class focused; too frivolous and excessive for its negative impact on maternal psychological wellbeing; and too physically and emotionally draining for mothers while not even necessarily being in the best interests of the child (Gunderson and Barrett). The ideal of intensive mothering requires women not only to put their child's needs before their own in every respect but to be able to display this to others through their everyday practices, such as consumption and food preparation.

Angela McRobbie points out that within neoliberal culture, the prior emphasis on collective state childcare as a positive innovation that would enhance the lives of young children through inculcating social skills has become "unthinkable, for the reasons of its socialist, communist and welfare-ist heritage, and thus its cost to the state" ("Feminism" 128). As the project to expand state childcare was abandoned (even by nominally leftist governments, such as New Labour in the 1990s and early 2000s), "banal phrases such as the 'work/life' balance, came to replace more sustained debate about how motherhood and work could be realistically combined without women jeopardising their opportunities in the workplace" (128).

It is within the context of the neoliberal absorption of certain aspects of popular feminism (understood by most feminist critics as the ideology of aspirational postfeminism)—as well as a renewed cultural belief in neotraditional, mother-centred postwar child development concepts, a media emphasis on the potentially damaging effects of nonmother childcare, rising housing costs, and a shrinking public sector—that the concept, if not the term, "mumpreneur" first emerges. For example, the heroines of popular domestic fiction and "mum's lit" comic fiction of the early 2000s are presented as capturing the zeitgeist of what it means to be a contemporary working mother. Although many of the protagonists are freelance writers specializing in family-orientated lifestyle journalism, mum's lit novels are also peopled by mothers who turn towards small-scale business ventures linked to traditional feminine domestic skills and interests. A typical example of this plotline occurs in the best-known mum's lit novel from this period, journalist Allison Pearson's *I Don't Know How She Does it*. After struggling to maintain her duel commitments to family and a high-powered career in finance, heroine Kate Reddy chooses to resolve her work-life conflicts by abandoning her city job, moving to the countryside, and assisting a struggling local business that specializes in the production of handmade dolls houses. Significantly, in mum's lit, few of the female characters work in the traditional spheres of employment associated with respected female professionals, such as education or healthcare.

Mum's lit fiction, thus, captured a distinct ideological shift taking place by the early 2000s in terms of aspirational career goals for middle-class mothers. The dominant narrative justifying middle-class women's employment from the 1960s to the 1990s was one that sanctioned female professionals in the labour force by acknowledging their ability to enhance the public realm by making a contribution to caring occupations. This narrative has gradually been replaced by one in which women are encouraged to avoid what are euphemistically described as "work-life" balance issues (i.e., childcare problems) by retreating into the domestic realm and transforming their existing feminine skills and interests into commercial transactions that benefit their individual families rather than society as a whole. The cultural endorsement of maternal self-employment in female-orientated popular cultural forms thus complies with a more general ideological thrust towards the prioritization of the private over public sector and the state's desire to unleash the entrepreneurial spirit in ordinary citizens. For example, in 2014, the conservative-dominated coalition government established a scheme to offer mentoring and seed funding specifically to female-led small businesses in the UK. The then-minister for women and equalities, Jo Swinton, launched the scheme with the following comments:

> It is vital that we support female entrepreneurs. There are more women-led businesses in the UK than ever before, and we know that if women were setting up and running new businesses at the same rate as men, our economy could benefit from 1 million more entrepreneurs. Mentoring is key to this. It helps to build confidence, develop key business skills and provides a network of contacts for those starting out. That's why we are funding a series of mentoring events across the UK, launching tomorrow on Women's Entrepreneurship Day.

The Self-Presentation of the Mumpreneur

Although the cultural idealization of certain kinds of female-run business ventures has a long history, the circulation of the term "mum-preneur," is much more recent. Most references—typically found in online magazines, forums, social media forums, and newspapers—

have appeared in the last decade. The term is, therefore, either explicitly or implicitly, aligned with the 2007-2008 recession and, in the UK, the imposition of austerity measures, although this is rarely acknowledged directly. There are two British online magazines catering for this community. *The Business Mum's Journal*, sponsored by the mother and baby-related products retail chain, *Mothercare*, was launched in 2008, which was shortly followed by the arrival of *Mumpreneur UK* in 2010. There are also numerous online mumpreneur networks, with both an American and a British Facebook mumpreneurs networking site (both started in 2011), along with numerous advice websites on becoming a mumpreneur. There are also a number of competitions and award schemes for budding mumpreneurs, the most prominent being the *Mumpreneurs UK* and the Natwest/*Daily Mail* Aphrodite Award. In terms of more conventional (print) media sources, *The Telegraph, Independent* and *Daily Mail* have all produced features on the growing 'phenomena' of the mumpreneur over the last decade: "The Rise of the Mumpreneur" and "Want a Lesson in Business Networking? Mumpreneurs Know Best" (*The Telegraph*); "Mums Do the Business" (*The Independent*); and "Meet the Mums Who Are Setting up their Own Business" (*The Guardian*). Not surprisingly, the notoriously right-wing, socially conservative, and female-orientated *Daily Mail* ran several stories: "The School Run Entrepreneurs," "The Rise of the Mumpreneur," and "Who Will Be Crowned Our Mumpreneur of the Year?"

The definition varies according to source, but there are certain key factors that mark out mumpreneurs from the business community or entrepreneurs more generally. First, they are the parents of young children. Second, they are female. There are no "dadpreneurs" or "parentpreneurs," only mumpreneurs, who in the vast majority of tabloid stories and magazine articles are also white. The term thus brings together two apparently opposed terms in an uneasy alliance: the reliability and nonthreatening cuddliness associated with the humdrum and familiar (traditional, white, and middle-class) mum with the risk-taking, wheeler-dealing, traditional, and phallic connotations of entrepreneurship. The tension between these terms results in a number of contradictions and conflicts in mainstream depictions of the mumpreneur figure. As Jo Littler argues, celebrities who rebrand themselves as mumpreneurs—such Myleene Klass, a reality-television-created pop star turned CEO of a women's clothing company, or Annabel Karmel, a writer of successful family cookery books—tend to emphasize their hectic lives and highlight the grit, determination, and passion necessary to combine their ventures with family life, lest they will be regarded as privileged dabblers (320).

In contrast, the mothers whose stories are featured in either mumpreneur magazines or mainstream print media are often depicted as ordinary mums who have chanced upon a niche selling opportunity, which has been triggered by discoveries made through their everyday parenting activities. The noncelebrity mumpreneur's response to the success of her small-scale business venture is more likely to be surprise and gratitude, not protestations over long hours and sleep deprivation. Some so-called inspirational stories of ordinary mums do begin by briefly acknowledging a recession-linked redundancy, but economic need is rarely emphasized as a motivation for starting home-based businesses. Despite the overwhelming evidence that women are passed over for promotion, paid less than their male colleagues, and even manoeuvered out of their jobs after becoming mothers, there is no mention of gender-pay gaps or structural or institutional sexism in the workplace. In keeping with neoliberal ideology, the dominant narrative is one of choice, freedom, and flexibility. The featured mumpreneur's primary motivation is the desire for work-life balance, which is understood in the highly traditional sense that mothers will naturally and inevitably assume the role of primary caregiver and housekeeper, whether they are single or in a relationship, working part or fulltime. The only justification offered outside of personal choice and a desire to fulfil the neotraditionalist, intensive mothering role while remaining economically active is to assist other mothers by providing new products and services, which will enhance children's lives. These are a few examples from *Mumpreneur UK* ("Butterfly Occasions"):

> Sotiria Spantidea, a busy mother of two, decided to turn her back on her successful IT career in the City to start an online children's boutique store.
>
> Why I quit my City career to set up Butterfly Occasions .....
>
> My journey into entrepreneurship started as simply an enjoyable hobby, as I loved to search online for unique and unusual items for my children's bedrooms. I have two little boys aged 3 and

aged 5 years old, and like many mothers, I had ideas of the quality and designs I wanted but often couldn't find them on the high street or from mainstream retailers.

Soon, I realised that I was pretty good at researching and collating ideas, and decided to share them with friends and family. After receiving positive feedback about my choices of toys and furniture, I decided to take the plunge and turn my hobby into a fully-fledged business!

The biggest challenge however for 2015 will be trying to juggle my business and family life! It's not an easy thing to do, but I always try to find time to do the things I love and to be with the people I love. I'm trying not to steal the time I spend with my children to do my business as my family comes first.

Bubble Bum (inflatable car sears) mumpreneur/owner, Grainne Kelly (Mumpreneur UKb).

"How did you come up with the idea for BubbleBum?"

I was travelling with my two kids back and forth to England to visit my mother-in-law who was very poorly at the time and every time I arrived at the car rental desk they didn't have the car booster seats, even though I had pre-booked them. I got into a real strop and asked loads of questions as to why they didn't have them, to be told simply that they didn't have the space. After speaking with friends, I found that this is actually a very common problem faced by parents so I decided that there was a need for an inflatable and portable solution that was lightweight and easy to fit into hand luggage.

In the rare instances in which mumpreneurs become celebrated founders of sizable companies, the rhetoric that surrounds them still emphasizes domesticity and family. For example, the narrative surrounding Julia Deane, founder of The Cambridge Satchell Company (a successful UK brand that sells brightly coloured leather school satchels for adults), highlights her desire to increase her income rather than create a useful product. However, Deane was at pains to point out that this was motivated by the need to send her child to a fee-paying school rather than through a personal desire for wealth or fame. As Louise

Eccles writes in the Daily Mail: "When Deane discovered her daughter was being bullied, she vowed to move her to the £12,000-a-year school down the road. But unable to afford the fees, the housewife sat down at her kitchen table and wrote a list of ten ways to raise money. She says the greatest reward of her venture has been fulfilling her promise to her daughter."

As demonstrated above, the aspirational narrative woven around Deane's not inconsiderable success promotes the belief that self-help, a can-do attitude, and the cultivation of entrepreneurial qualities are more admirable than trying to improve public services and institutions. Deane's narrative assumes the superiority of private over state education and plays on the widespread fear among middle-class British parents that their child will be victimised by feral, underclass children if sent to a standard, nonselective, state-funded school.

The presentation of these ventures, particularly in *Mumpreneur UK* and *Mums in Business*, reproduces the visual style and somewhat patronising tone of personal interest narratives in women's lifestyle publishing. As stated above, the majority of the featured mumpreneurs are white, and the businesses are orientated towards child products and services, with names that are consciously cute and whimsical, such as Little Pickles Marketplace, Coochie Coo Nappies, Corporate Baby, Big Hugs, and Mess Around. Although, surprisingly perhaps, *The Daily Mail* featured a Scottish mumpreneur who had started a successful micro-brewery, most of the companies specialized in either luxury or safety-oriented child products and services (such as *Bubble Bum*). The mumpreneurs descriptions of their products also place heavy emphasis on home crafts and a general ethos of bucolic wholesomeness, as they view their organic, natural, and recycled products as part of a small-scale protest against toxic modern child products on behalf of their offspring. Indeed, the overall visual language of the pieces associates good, responsible mothering with the adoption of an antiurban and antimodern stance that is far removed from the reality of a modern, urban, and multicultural Britain and is covertly, if not overtly, ethnically biased in favour of white, middle-class mothers. Yet despite this wholesome, antimodern, and antitechnological stance, and as with many small start-up businesses, they are largely reliant on internet promotion and sales, using this as a way of directly appealing to customers. Online promotion thus allows female entrepreneurs to avoid many of the discriminatory practices that have historically deterred women from starting small businesses, such as the failure to secure the capital necessary to obtain a shop, although none of the articles mention gender discrimination.

Finally, I want to discuss the specific problems with the concept of the mumpreneur in terms of its blatant reinforcement of certain gender, race, and class positions within the culture of neoliberalism generally and the politics of austerity more specifically. Despite the state and media promotion of competitive individualism, the rise of neoliberal politics has been coterminous with the normalization of a neotraditionalist view of family life and the maternal role in particular (Negra; Ringrose and Walkerdine). As state support for public-funded institutions and services withers, parental anxiety, particularly in relation to the health and education of their offspring, increases. The mumpreneur's stated desire to achieve work-life balance is, thus, more accurately the need to combine this mode of privatized and professionalized mothering with remaining economically productive. As paid childcare is expensive and requires relinquishing the level of control currently required to achieve good mother status, being self-employed and engaged in work that is aligned to motherhood and domesticity seems the obvious way to resolve the perennial work-childcare conundrum without demanding any serious change in work culture or gender roles.

There are other obvious ways in which the mumpreneur feeds into a culture of neoliberal self-determination and austerity measures. First, mumpreneurs are often public sector managers and workers who have either been pushed or opted to take redundancy in the wake of conservative cuts to public services. Second, many of the services they provide—particularly in the area of franchised playgroups with a niche element (such as the "messy" play company Mess Around) or basic advice on children's health and safety (such as Mini First Aid, a privatized service to instruct mums on basic first aid tips for children)—are moving into the space vacated by dwindling public services. As the vast majority of the cited mumpreneurs are white, middle-class, and university-educated women who held down professional jobs prior to becoming mothers, the rise of the mumpreneur raises the disturbing prospect of more wealthy women charging poorer ones for basic services (such as toddler playgroups or healthcare advice), which would, in earlier years, been provided by the state.

These issues reveal a more covert aspect of the celebration of the mumpreneur in terms of both class and gender. The mumpreneur both banishes and evokes the spectre of two abject female folk devils. The most prominent of these is the phallic and avaricious business woman or "career bitch." Although depictions of women working in sectors unrelated to traditional feminine goods and services have become more commonplace since the 1980s, they are, nonetheless. still presented as troubling and incompatible with normative views of gender roles and family life. As feminist critics argued in the early 1990s, the initial cultural representations of such women in film and television frequently presented them as either damaged and cruel (most notoriously in *Fatal Attraction*) or as essentially nice, normal women who eventually eschew the corporate world in favour of more traditional feminine occupations (*Baby Boom*, *Working Girl*). Although the range of professional women featured in popular representations has widened since the 1990s, competitive reality programs, such as *Dragon's Den* and *The Apprentice*, continue to draw on and promote the stereotype of the hard-nosed, antimaternal corporate woman or entrepreneur. The stigma attached to being a business women has lessened along with the emergence of number of outspoken female members of the current Conservative Party, but the underlying media hostility to such women surfaces in gloating stories about the personal lives of women, such as "city superwoman" Nicola Horlick or dot.com millionairess Martha Lane Fox.

In the context of ongoing sociocultural resentment towards women working in traditional male spheres, the mumpreneur's extreme and performative white, middle-class "mumsiness" appears as a screaming disavowal of the phallic attributes projected onto such women. Indeed, it could be argued that the cultural presentation of mumpreneur business practices and motivations are far more closely aligned to a middle-class, feminine, and austerity culture of retro-thrift and "make do and mend" (Jensen; Bramall) than the dirty, unfeminine, and cut-and-thrust world of the male business tycoon. The mumpreneur's thrifty, no-nonsense desire to do her bit for her family rather than expect state or community support is a foil to a second figure of abject femininity, which has also loomed large in the rhetoric of austerity: the scrounging "chav" mum (Tyler; Allen and Osgood). In the UK in particular, the 2006-2007 crash was seized upon by the coalition government as an opportunity to increase the depth and severity of neoliberal cuts to public sector services and welfare provision under the banner of austerity. Many of these cuts had a disproportionally negative effect on women, particularly single mothers, as they were much more likely to work either in the public sector or in the more casual, insecure areas of private sector employment. As poorer mothers were tipped into poverty, using foodbanks to feed their families, the media intensified their attack on benefit cheats, especially through poverty- porn reality programs depicting disadvantaged mothers as fat, feckless, and work shy. Unlike in the United States, where the idea of welfare queens was specifically racialized and associated with poor, Black single mothers (Douglas and Michaels), the demonized British poor single mother was imaged as slovenly and white.

The rhetoric surrounding the mumpreneur (sometimes also referred to as a "kitchen table tycoon") works hard to offset the suspicion that their humble maternal qualities might be tainted by the egotism and unapologetic greed associated with the alpha-male entrepreneur. Nevertheless, mumpreneurs are presented as prudent, self-sufficient individuals whose response to either economic or personal catastrophe (such as redundancy or needing to provide for a disabled child) is to find ingenious ways to support their families rather than expect state handouts. Thus, the enthusiastic promotion of the mumpreneur figure, particularly in the right-wing print media, also functions as a covert indictment of her slovenly shadow sister: the benefit-dependent chav mother.

Conclusion: The Myth of the Mumpreneur

It might seem obvious at this point that the discursive construction of the mumpreneur plays into both traditional views of gender and parenting culture and a "strivers versus skivers" austerity rhetoric, in which the most disadvantaged members of society, such as impoverished single mothers, are made scapegoats for the excesses of neoliberal capitalism. Yet even within the terms of neoliberal ideology, the concept of the "mumpreneur" is highly problematic. If the socioeconomic justification for the endorsement of entrepreneurship is one of long-term economic growth, providing employment and trickle-down wealth creation, the small scale of many of these businesses—and their heavy reliance on a form of self-branding that are wholly wedded to the particular life stage and personal family focus of the mumpreneur herself—precludes long term survival and growth.

Ironically, far from creating jobs, through the stated advantage of flexible working, the majority of small-scale mumpreneur businesses employ few or no other staff while also reducing the need for the childminders, nannies, and nursery staff that the founders might otherwise have employed if they had continued in their prior careers. Unlike the more successful founders of startup businesses, who are often male entrepreneurs working within the booming tech sector, mumpreneurs tend to be relatively privileged white, university-educated mothers who are finding ways to remain economically active while they cope with the onerous task of raising children in neoliberal culture. Terms such as "pin-money" are banished from these life-affirming stories of female freedom self-actualization and achievement. Yet the discourse surrounding them is no less sexist, racist, and classist in its assumption that mothers should be secondary household earners whose economic activity should be both subservient to and aligned with the white, middle-class construction of intensive mothering as good mothering.

Endnotes

1. The UK equivalent of the welfare queen.

Works Cited

Allen, Kim, and Jane Osgood. "Young Women Negotiating Maternal Subjectivities: The Significance of Social Class." *Studies in the Maternal*, vol. 1, no. 2, 2009, pp. 1-17.

BBC News. "Women Still Do More Household Chores Than Men, ONS Finds." *BBC*, 10 Nov. 2016. www.bbc.co.uk/news/uk-37941191. Accessed 18 July 2020.

Bramall, Rebecca. *The Cultural Politics of Austerity: Past and Present in Austere Times.* Palgrave, 2018.

Brown, Wendy. *Undoing the Demos: Neoliberalism's Stealth Revolution.* Zone Books, 2015.

Douglas, Sharon, and Meredith Michaels. *The Mommy Myth: The Idealisation of Motherhood and How It Has Undermined All Women.* Free Press, 2005.

Eccles, Louise. "Mum Who Couldn't Afford Daughter's School Fees Makes £12million a Year Selling Satchels." *Daily Mail*, Dec. 9, 2012, www.dailymail.co.uk/news/article-2245651/Cambridge-Satchel-Company-mum-afford-daughters-school-fees-makes-12m-year.html. Accessed 18 July 2020.

Fraser, Nancy. "Feminism, Capitalism and the Cunning of History." *New Left Review*, vol. 56, 2009, pp. 97-117.

Gamble, Andrew. *The Free Economy and The Strong State*. Routledge, 1994.

Gerhart, Sue. "Democracy Begins at Home: Society Has Become Too Selfish and Materialistic – We Should Listen to Each Other and Especially to Our Children, Psychotherapist Sue Gerhardt Tells Sally Weale." *The Guardian*, 1 May 2010, www.theguardian.com/lifeandstyle/2010/may/01/childcare-sue-gerhardt-psychotherapist. Accessed July 18 2020.

Hays, Sharon. *The Cultural Contradictions of Motherhood*. Yale University Press, 1998.

Harvey, David. *A Brief History of Neoliberalism*. Oxford University Press, 2005.

James, Olivier. "Nursery Feud: Putting Under-Threes in Full-Time Daycare Can Promote aggressive Behaviour, Warns Olivier James." *The Guardian*, 9 Jan. 2005, www.theguardian.com/lifeandstyle/2005/jan/09/healthandwellbeing. Accessed 18 July 2020.

Littler, Jo. *Against Meritocracy*. Routledge, 2018.

McRobbie, Angela. *The Aftermath of Feminism: Gender, Culture and Social Change*. Sage, 2008.

McRobbie, Angela. "Feminism, the Family and the New 'Mediated' Maternalism." *New Formations: A Journal of Culture/Theory/Politics*, vol. 80-81, 2013, pp. 119-37.

Jensen, Tracey. "Riots, Restraint and the New Cultural Politics of Wanting." *Sociological Research Online*, vol. 18, no. 4, 2013, pp. 36–47.

Negra, Diane. *What A Girl Wants? Fantasising the Reclaimation of Self in Postfeminism*. Routledge, 2009.

McGee, Mel. *Supermummy: The Ultimate Mumpreneur's Guide to Online Business Success*. Bookshaker, 2009.

Methven, Charlotte. "Work Life: The School-Run Mumpreneurs." *The Daily Mail*, 18 Jan. 2014, www.dailymail.co.uk/home/you/article -2541308/Work-life-school-run-mumpreneurs.html. Accessed 18 July 2020.

Mumpreneur UK. "Mumpreneur Spotlight: Butterfly Occasions." *Mumpreneur UK*, www.mumpreneuruk.com/mumpreneur-spotlight- butterfly-occasions/. Accessed 18 July 2020.

Mumpreneur UK. "Mumpreneur Spotlight: Garinne Kelly, Bubble Bum." *Mumpreneur UK*, www.mumpreneuruk.com/mumpreneur- spotlight-garinne-kelly-bubble-bum/. Accessed 18 July 2020.

Mutton, Sheree. "The rise of the 'Mumpreneur': Why Educated Women Are Quitting Their Jobs and Starting Their Own Businesses—and Raking in Millions." *The Daily Mail* (Australia), 1 Nov. 2017, www. dailymail.co.uk/femail/article-5037821/Rise-mumpreneur-women- starting-businesses.html. Accessed 18 July 2020.

Reynolds, Tracey. *Caribbean Mothers: Identity and Experience in the UK*. Tufnell Press, 2005.

Ringrose, Jessica, and Valerie Walkerdine. "Regulating the Abject." *Feminist Media Studies*, vol. 8, no. 3, 2008, pp. 227-46.

Rottenberg, Catherine. *The Rise of Neoliberal Feminism*. Oxford University Press. 2018.

Scharff, Christina. "Disarticulating Feminism: Individualization, Neoliberalism and the Othering of Muslim Women." *European Journal of Women's Studies*, vol. 18, no. 2, 2011, pp. 119-34.

Sturgis, India. "Who'll Be Our Mumpreneur of the Year? It's a Major New Trend—The Women Juggling Motherhood with Setting Up Businesses, like These Four. Now We're Looking for YOUR Inspiring Stories." *Daily Mail*, 15 Apr. 2015, www.dailymail.co.uk/femail/ article-3040629/Wholl-Mumpreneur-year-major-new-trend- women-juggling-motherhood-setting-businesses-like-four-looking- inspiring-stories.html. Accessed 18 July 2020.

Trades Union Congress. "Women's Pay and Employment Update: Public/Private Sector Comparison." *TUC*, 2012, www.tuc.org.uk/ research-analysis/reports/womens-pay-and-employment-update- publicprivate-sector-comparison. Accessed 18 July 2020.

Tyler, Imogen. "Chav Mum Chav Scum." *Feminist Media Studies*, vol. 8, no. 1, 2008, pp. 17-34.

Chapter Seven

Support, Subsidies, and Silenced Storylines: The Framing of Mothers on Welfare in Canadian English-Language Print News, 1990-2015

Rebecca Wallace

In an era of retrenchment and pushback against the modern welfare state, news media can play a critical role in both shaping and reflecting public opinion on social programs and those perceived to benefit from them. Throughout the 1990s and early 2000s, amid the deep cuts and changes to eligibility criteria for social assistance programs across Canada, news about welfare served as an important forum for both informing and echoing public sentiment about the purported failures of Canada's social programs. Coinciding with the war on welfare in the United States (U.S.), depictions of the undeserving poor villainized individuals along dimensions of gender, race, and family status; stories of the so-called welfare queen pervaded political debates and brought to question the deservingness of—and policy prescriptions for—mothers on welfare.

With the growing feminization of poverty in Canada, it is increasingly important to attend to the ways in which news outlets project critical images of mothers on welfare that contribute to their continued scrutiny.

This chapter explores the coverage of mothers on welfare in Canadian print media to uncover the central narratives that underlie discussions of social assistance in the news. This project uses automated coding and clustering techniques to extract prominent frames pertaining to mothers on welfare from articles in nine newspapers from January 1, 1990 to December 31, 2015. Principally, this research asks the following questions. 1) What are the central themes or frames that dominate coverage of mothers on welfare in Canadian print media? 2) Do the frames or their prominence change in response to shifts in welfare policy, government, and economic conditions in Canada over the selected timeline? 3) How are the various intersections of mothers' identities— particularly race, citizenship status, family status, and age—covertly and overtly communicated to convey specific ideas about who ought to benefit from social programs?

The results of this analysis capture a number of shifting and contra- dicting themes in conceptualizing the welfare mother as a member of the deserving and undeserving poor. The data suggest that although Canadian news about social assistance and redistribution has not hinged specifically on the welfare queen image that has permeated American political and popular culture, news outlets at the national and regional level play a critical role in politicizing the identity of welfare mothers through the presence and absence of subtle and strategic storylines. The results of the analysis convey that there was not a single narrative that pervaded both news and policy debates; rather, it was a more complex canvas that painted certain welfare mothers as needy, responsible, and hardworking while portraying others as irresponsible, conniving, lazy, and dependent. This chapter explores these contradictions, breaks down the central themes appearing in the coverage of mothers, and speaks directly to the absence of alternative storylines. It concurrently examines the codification of deservingness on dimensions of race, family status, and age as intersecting facets of mothers' identities, highlighting the ways in which these factors are used to characterize and classify certain mothers as more or less worthy than others. The chapter opens by assessing the limited literature on news coverage of welfare in the Canadian context situating this work as part of an important and growing conversation that needs to take place in Canadian research on the politics of deservingness.

Representations of Welfare Mothers in the News

News media serves as an important forum reflecting and shaping public opinion on support for welfare. By selecting "some aspects of a perceived reality to make them more salient in a communicating text, in such a way as to promote a particular problem definition, causal interpretation, moral evaluation, and/or treatment recommendation for the item described" (Entman 52), news stories about poverty are often framed in ways that have the capacity to shape opinions about the root causes of poverty (Iyengar) and support for redistribution more generally (Gilens; Winter). As Martin Gilens asserts in the title of his foundational text on the race coding of media on poverty in the U.S., *Why Americans Hate Welfare*, public support for welfare, or lack thereof, can largely be attributed to media depictions of welfare and those perceived to benefit from it.

Although many researchers of social policy have long remarked that gender is often "written out" of policy analysis, proposals, and prescriptions (Jenson 142), the public image of the welfare mom has been integrally linked to patriarchal perceptions of women's status in the private and public domains and the ways that these views have shifted greatly in the post-World War II era. Mothers' allowance or pension programs were introduced in several countries to support widowed mothers in the inter- and postwar eras, but several factors that emerged in the 1960s and 1970s – including the increase of women in the paid workforce, the increase in rates of divorce and unwed motherhood, and the extension of access to social programs for Black and Latina women – changed ideas about mothers' dependence and deservingness markedly (Fraser and Gordon; Misra, Moller, and Karides; see also Stefanik and Race, this volume). As Joya Misra, Stephanie Moller, and Marina Karides find in their analysis of news coverage of mothers on welfare in the U.S., social assistance programming shifted from labour programs focusing on men's employment to those centred on family. In doing so, policy targets were increasingly perceived as minority women. As policies gradually focused on families and women entered the workforce in higher numbers, news coverage of welfare moms transitioned from sympathetic depictions of white widows to hostile images of uncaring, nonwhite women profiting from the system. Alas, the American welfare queen was born.

The welfare queen was, and continues to be, a political image of the mother on welfare that hinges on racist stereotypes of Black mothers to depict welfare recipients as fraudulent, conniving, irresponsible, and undeserving:

The image of the lazy, licentious, and ultimately un-American Black welfare queen was central to the ideological constructs that justified the War on Welfare.... The image of the welfare queen was a crucial embodiment of the dangers of not entering the wage-labor system. She was represented as a criminal mother who chose welfare over work, was unburdened by restraint, and was physically marked by excess and greed—she was moreover unmistakably Black, obese, part of the under-class and a serious threat to domestic security. (Bezusko 44)

The welfare queen was prominently depicted in news media as someone who put herself before her children (Parker West), and many stories employed racist stereotypes about welfare mothers as immature or "hyperfertile" to support policies that aimed to regulate poor women's reproduction and parenting (Kelly 77). As Laurel Parker West discusses in her media analyses on mothers in American media, the image of the welfare queen also does not rely on overt discussions of race in news coverage. Rather, consistent with Gillens's work, stories on welfare mothers generally employ a race-coded language that implicitly conveys the mother as Black and undeserving (Parker West 332).

Although much of the literature exploring depictions of welfare in news media have focused on the welfare queen and its effects on support for social programming, it is important to note that the literature in this field has been dominated by studies on the American context. Evidence from outside the U.S. could help us better understand the theoretical and practical implications of news media on public opinion towards redistribution, as current findings in the literature may be rooted in context-specific explanations stemming from American political culture, particularly in regard to the politics of race and deservingness. Indeed, as Sylvia Bashevkin has observed in her comparative analysis of welfare policy change in Canada, the U.S., and Britain throughout the 1980s and 1990s, there were distinctly different patterns in the ways that different countries and policy leaders pushed "welfare hot buttons" in debates about policy change. She finds, for example, that politicians in the U.S. readily conveyed the welfare queen image, whereas political leaders in Canada were less likely to evoke divisive language. As such, I turn to the Canadian context to explore the ways in which gender, race, class, and age intersect to produce potentially different depictions of the mother on welfare. There are remarkably few comprehensive studies of welfare in Canadian news media (Lawlor, Mahon, and Soroka), so I look to explore whether there is a comparable figure to the welfare queen in the Canadian context or whether news coverage is perhaps more diverse or fractured. In the sections that follow, I outline the data and methods I employed in examining the central themes of news stories on welfare and delve into the results about competing or contradictory storylines that are commonly featured in Canadian news.

Data and Methods

To conduct a content analysis on Canadian news coverage of mothers on welfare, I acquired a news sample from the Canadian Major Dailies (ProQuest) database. I searched for news stories from January 1, 1990, to December 31, 2015, that referenced mothers on welfare in the headline of the story using the search terms "mom*" or "mother*" and "welfare" or "social assistance." Although mothers on welfare are featured in news stories on welfare more generally, I aimed to acquire a sample that substantively discussed mothers as an identity group to focus exclusively on the ways in which they were stereotyped or analyzed in stories specific to their experiences. Stories were included from Canada's two national newspapers, *The Globe and Mail* and the *National Post*, as well as English-language major dailies from large Canadian cities, including the *Toronto Star, Ottawa Citizen, Montreal Gazette, Calgary Herald, Edmonton Journal, The Province,* and *Vancouver Sun.* The search yielded a total of 368 articles.

I chose to analyze news coverage from 1990 to 2015 in order to assess if the core themes in print media shifted markedly over a period of profound change in Canadian social policy. Mothers on welfare were particularly prominent in the headlines throughout the 1990s when considerable changes to social assistance policies, especially changes to eligibility criteria and the development of workfare programs, came into effect. This twenty-six-year timeline allows us to explore if the framing of mothers on welfare is fixed over time or responsive to changes in the political and economic environment. For the purposes of this analysis, I have broken the timeline down into five- to six-year periods that capture major shifts in welfare policy, outlined in Table 1. Consistent with the major shifts in welfare policies and the political and economic climate over the timeline, the majority of articles about mothers on welfare were written in the 1990s (72 per cent) and early 2000s (22 per cent). News coverage of mothers on welfare drops off markedly around 2005, with news during this most recent decade of the timeline accounting for only 6 per cent of the sample. Further to this, examining the proportion of coverage across the various newspapers, it is clear that most of the coverage of mothers on welfare takes place at the regional or city level, which is, perhaps, consistent with the scope and issue agendas of regional newspapers. The national newspapers together represent only 11.1 per cent of the sample and the *Toronto Star, Edmonton Journal,* and *Montreal Gazette* are the papers with the highest proportions of coverage in this sample (19.6 per cent, 15.5 per cent, and 15.8 per cent, respectively).

Table 1. Welfare Reform Affecting Mothers in Canada, 1990-2015

Time Period	Changes or Events
1990-1994	Economic recession in Canada leads to economic instability and increase in welfare cases. Mulroney government introduces cuts to the Unemployment Insurance program and changes to the Canada Assistance Plan (CAP); federal government adds a ceiling on transfers to the provinces, requiring the provinces to fund more than 50 per cent of the costs for social assistance programming.
1995-1999	CAP is terminated and replaced by the Canada Health and Social Transfer (CHST); by 1998, the Canadian government cuts $6.3 billion in transfers under the CHST. All provincial governments reduce social assistance benefit levels, either overtly, as in Ontario, or covertly by not adjusting benefits levels for inflation for a decade. Modelled after those in the U.S., several provinces introduce Workfare programs and focus on the promotion of employment for welfare recipients;

1995-1999 continued	Ontario Works begins under the Mike Harris government, and mothers on welfare are increasingly scrutinized in his "Common Sense Revolution" campaign.
2000-2004	Given the erosion of federal government funding for social assistance, the provinces exercise their decision-making power over eligibility and administration of benefits. Generally, this leads to a growth in Workfare programs and stricter eligibility criteria for access to welfare. The "spouse in the house" eligibility rules for social assistance are challenged through the courts. In *Falkiner v. Ontario* (2002), the Supreme Court rules that these regulations are discriminatory.
2005-2009	The election of the Harper Conservatives leads to the cancellation of proposed bilateral agreements with provinces pertaining to childcare and Indigenous welfare. The 2008 recession leads to economic hardship across Canada. The federal government temporarily extends eligibility, especially for long-term employees.
2010-2015	Although social assistance policy remains fairly consistent during this period of economic recovery, there is growing attention among social policy researchers to welfare and poverty rates, differences between provincial programs, and concerns about women's experiences with the "welfare trap."

Using this sample, I aimed to address the following questions. 1) What are the central themes that emerge in news coverage of mothers on welfare? 2) Do these themes shift over the selected time periods? 3) How are various intersecting facets of identities—particularly race, age, and family status—conveyed or utilized in news stories about mothers on welfare?

To identify core themes in the news sample through an automated analysis, I used an inductive method of content analysis, specifically employing hierarchal clustering to determine how keywords in the text are used in conjunction with one another. Instead of applying a predetermined set of criteria to the corpus and evaluating the presence or absence of themes that the researcher believes are important, an inductive approach allows the researcher to observe patterns in the covariation of words and identify themes or frames that exist naturally in the corpus. This type of bottom-up approach to analyzing word patterns can signal important information about large themes in the text and their relationship to one another (Pennebaker, Mehl, and Niederhoffer). Utilizing WordStat, a content analysis software program, I explored the most frequent keywords and phrases in the sample and selected those that were substantively related to issues regarding welfare and social assistance for analysis. The objective of this process is to produce a list of terms and phrases that are connected directly to the issue under study and to then assess if and how those terms are used in conjunction with one another in internally coherent frames. Through WordStat's dendrogram function, a feature of the program that uses Jaccard's coefficient to analyze the co-occurrence of selected words and phrases, I was able to derive a series of word clusters and phrases in each of the samples and determine how these clusters were connected to one another. The resulting dendrogram identified six core themes. Given that automated analyses are not perfect and can be subject to error, I followed Andrea Lawlor and Erin Tolley's validation process to ensure that keyword usage in the texts was appropriate in context and accurately reflected the themes.

Although automated analyses are highly effective in identifying core themes of texts and can be calibrated to answer important questions about large bodies of text, there are advantages and drawbacks to this approach. Particularly regarding questions about race, it can be highly valuable to conduct a manual coding or close reading of the text to uncover subtle patterns or covert messages in the text (Tolley). As such, I will discuss each of the core themes identified by the automated analysis and offer qualitative remarks on the ways that these themes convey various facets of mothers' identities—particularly race, citizenship status, age, and family status—to provide a deeper analysis of what is both present and absent in the coverage of mothers on welfare.

Core Themes in English Canadian Coverage

The results of the automated content analysis reveal that there are six core themes in the coverage of mothers on welfare in Canadian news:

1. Work and education—discussions about mothers' pursuit or balancing of childrearing and work or education;

2. Crime and the legal system—discussions of mothers' connections to the criminal justice system, particularly as criminals or frauds;

3. Costs of living—discussions about the costs of living and the struggles of surviving on the welfare budget;

4. Child welfare—discussions of mothers centring on the status of their children's poverty and welfare;

5. Family status and support—discussions about mothers' family/ marital status, reproductive capacity, child custody arrangements, and child support; and

6. Control over need—discussions about mothers' perceived laziness or responsibility in regard to their economic circumstances.

The primary observation here is that unlike much of the coverage of welfare in the U.S., there does not appear to be a singular storyline that is comparable to the welfare queen image in the Canadian coverage. Instead, we see diverse themes emerging that present contradictory depictions of mothers. In some stories, for example, mothers on welfare are depicted as helpless or as lazy or fraudulent in others.

As evident in Figure 1, the work and education theme is by far the most prominent in the news sample. Perhaps surprisingly, discussions about mothers' supposed responsibility for their economic status appears to be the least frequent theme. However, discussions of mothers' connections to crime and the legal system remain the second most common framework in the sample. Once again, this speaks to the apparent paradoxes in news coverage: There is not a monolithic narrative that dominates the coverage of welfare moms in major dailies. However, a number of these themes portray racialized, immigrant, and Indigenous mothers in a markedly different manner. In particular, the crime frame tends to subtly convey nonwhite mothers as fraudulent, covertly signalling that racialized, immigrant, and Indigenous mothers are disreputable and unworthy of social support. These findings underscore the importance of dissecting each frame and analyzing how these themes differently portray nonwhite mothers.

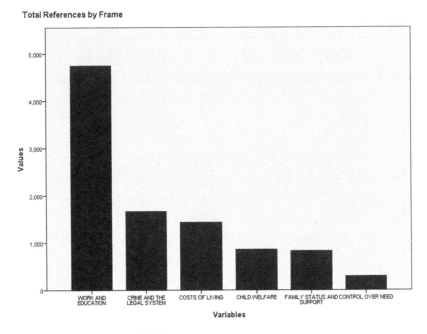

Figure 1. Total References by Frame

Work and Education

The work and education theme focuses prominently on mothers' balancing family responsibilities with their pursuit of work or educational advancement. As evident in Figure 2, the use of this framework importantly shifts and changes over the timeline; it increases throughout the 1990s but drops off markedly in the 2000-2004 period (p<.001). This decrease in attention to work and education may be consistent with some of the policy shifts that we see during this time. As outlined in Table 1, with the rise of Workfare programs in the 1990s, several news stories focused on the challenges that mothers face in balancing work and family responsibilities; however, by the 2000-2004 period, news centred more on issues regarding spouse-in-the-house regulations and challenges regarding the welfare budget.

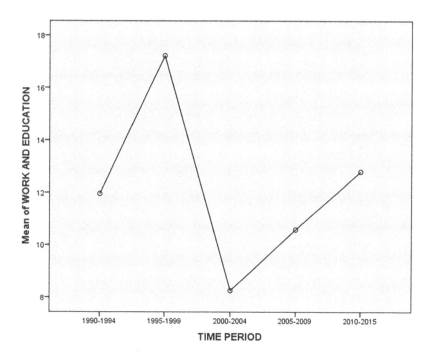

Figure 2. Means Plot, Average References per Story, Work and Education Frame

The work and education theme importantly highlighted some of the challenges around part-time and fulltime work opportunities for women, and the automated analysis revealed that discussions about childcare were inherently linked to this framework. In particular, news coverage focused on the challenges of affordable childcare and accommodations for women employed on a part-time or precarious basis. Some stories also highlighted the challenges that many mothers face in regard to volunteering or unpaid labour. Women are often expected to participate in schools and community organizations, but changes in welfare and Workfare policies rendered this nearly impossible for most. Although this is an important gender gap in terms of welfare politics, few articles actually spoke about the gendered issues underlying this problem. Framed in what Shanto Iyengar (22) would consider an "episodic" manner, stories centred on individual women's experiences and did not speak to larger systemic explanations of poverty, such as the ways that unpaid or care-centred work are generally expected to be performed by women more generally in the

Canadian political economy. Similarly, although some stories high-lighted municipal efforts to employ mothers on welfare in clerical positions with local government agencies and celebrated efforts to assist women in local communities, few news articles interrogated the relegation of women to "pink-collar ghetto" jobs. A lot of the news coverage in this theme importantly highlights many of the challenges that women face in balancing family and work expectations, but there was little critical discussion about the underlying gendered imbalances that facilitate these realities as systemic social issues for mothers.

Crime and the Legal System

This theme was the second most frequent and reflects news that demonstrates women's connections to the criminal justice system, predominantly as perpetrators and partners of perpetrators. Inter-estingly, there are no statistically significant changes in the use of this framework over the timeline. Importantly, this may represent a more common storyline that is grounded in stereotypes about mothers on welfare as guilty and fraudulent, as seen largely in the welfare queen rhetoric from American news content.

An important dimension of this framework is the recipient's race. Although it is highly codified, many of the stories on cases of welfare fraud, theft, or violent crimes note the individual's race. In the case of Indigenous women, this is often done by subtly referencing the reserves on which they live or identifying their connections to Indigenous community organizations. Women who are identified as immigrants are also more often depicted as guilty and taking advantage of the system when it comes to questions of fraud or outstanding debts. For example, a story about a white single mother facing potential charges over an unpaid fine was met with sympathy and public assistance in paying off her debt; conversely, news of a single immigrant mother of five requiring emergency housing was met with letters to the editor about her as a fraud. As one letter reads, "Has she considered becoming a productive member of society? She's been here since 1989. Rather than sitting back and expecting to be supported by the public purse, maybe she should get a job, or at least make plans to better her life" (*Ottawa Citizen*, October 2001). Effectively, although it is codified and often in the form of letters to the editors, Canadian newspapers still commonly convey racialized mothers on welfare as less deserving of assistance through subtle storylines, comparable to much of the coverage that we see on the American welfare queen.

Costs of Living

The cost of living framework centres on the struggles of welfare mothers when it comes to making ends meet. The costs of living theme importantly identifies the many grave challenges of living on a welfare budget and how mothers actively work to cut costs regarding food, shelter, clothing, hygiene, and entertainment.

As evident in Figure 3, coverage of the costs of living drops off markedly in the 2000-2004 era but reenters more prominently into discussion amid the 2008 recession and subsequent economic recovery. A number of stories over the course of the timeline focus on the ways that mothers band together in addressing some of these shortcomings by networking in collective kitchen efforts and sharing resources among one another; other stories praise mothers for their abilities to cut coupons and save on household purchases. This theme also emerges prominently around the Christmas holiday charity campaigns that often showcase a single mother on welfare for the purposes of garnering sympathy for support and donations during the holiday season. Although these stories are often written with the best of intentions, they can present mothers on welfare as helpless and lacking agency. Similarly, focusing on women's efforts to pool resources together and celebrating their thriftiness individualizes the solutions to welfare recipients' budgetary obstacles, instead of challenging the larger systemic policies that render the costs of living as an issue in the first place (Garrett, this volume). Once again, the paradoxes are clear in the ways that some stories seem to revere the cost-saving measures that women make but fail to report on the ways that the welfare programs in all of the provinces do not allow mothers to actually build savings or budget beyond the month's expenses.

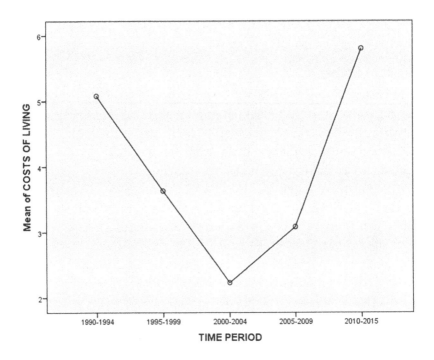

Figure 3. Means Plot, Average References per Story, Costs of Living Framework

Child Welfare

News stories conveying a child welfare theme tend to focus on the ways that being a child of a mother on welfare affects their wellbeing. In particular, stories generally focus on children's health and nutrition as well as the stigma that they face as "welfare kids." This framework was used relatively infrequently in the 1990s, as evident in Figure 4, but it is a more popular storyline in contemporary coverage of mothers on welfare, increasing significantly in the 2010-2015 period (p<.05). This finding is consistent with Canada's shift towards a social investment policy model and a more recent focus on developing policy pertaining to child poverty and welfare that has "sidelined and replaced" women's rights and needs (Dobrowolsky and Jenson 154).

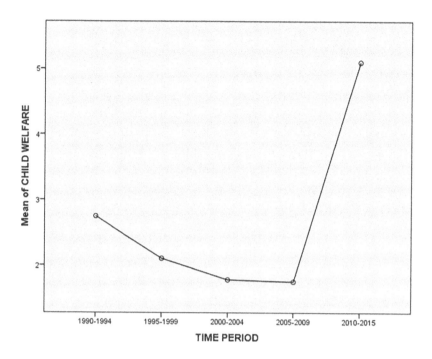

Figure 4. Means Plot, Average References per Story Child Welfare Framework

Although many of these storylines importantly highlight the detrimental effects of poverty on children and the stigma that many face in their communities, it is important to observe the ways that this detracts attention from the larger issues of gendered poverty. As Janine Brodie argues, "the evaluation of the abstract 'poor child' as the focus of social policy reform incorrectly specifies the policy problem" (176). In the social investment era, governments have strategically employed the figure of the child to garner support for limited, targeted investments to reduce child poverty. However, not only did this approach marginalize women who were living in poverty, it also served to sideline other forms of oppression because the figure of the "poor child" typically had no explicit gender or race. This dynamic clearly plays out in the news coverage of children on welfare, as such coverage frequently erases the gendered dimensions of the cycle of poverty for families in Canada. In effect, news stories that centre on the children of mothers on welfare may drive attention away from the root causes of their poverty and stigmatization while failing to address the larger issues regarding the feminization of poverty in Canada.

Family Status and Support

The family status framework focuses on women's marital status, the number of children that they have, and their reproductive capacities. Although most references to this theme focus on the role of fathers—in general, their absence or lack of support—a number of alarming comments also emerge in this framework about curtailing the reproductive freedom of women on welfare. Once again, through letters to the editor, a number of newspapers published commentary that suggests "those who accept welfare must agree to use birth control, and then only until they are economically capable of caring for their children by themselves or with a spouse" (*The Globe and Mail*, December 1990) and that if a woman is "is not married, is not attending school and is not seeking employment, she should have her tubes tied or be put on birth control and not be rewarded with more money with each new baby" (*Montreal Gazette*, June 1991). Perhaps even more concerning is that similar to the crime and legal system framework, there are no statistically significant changes in the frequency of this theme over the timeline. This line of commentary on women's reproduction and marital status is not a relic of the war on welfare; it is a theme that transcends current coverage and continues to play an integral role in evaluations of women's deservingness.

In highlighting some of the challenges that women face as single parents, this framework often depicts women as seeking economic freedom and independence from welfare through marriage. As one mother is quoted as saying, "I'm hoping Prince Charming will come and sweep me away and I'll be rich. I'm sick of the poor life" (*Calgary Herald*, May 1993). A number of these stories also reference mothers' age and are particularly critical of unwed, young, or teenage mothers. Although these storylines are subtle, focusing on mothers' marital and family status may obscure the larger systemic issues that many mothers face as primary caregivers and the economic barriers that substantively affect women's opportunities to advance their social and economic circumstances.

Control over Need

Given the popular rhetoric on welfare recipients, we may anticipate that negative evaluations of welfare mothers' work ethic may be prominent in Canadian news coverage, but this theme is actually the least frequent in the news sample. This framework primarily employs negative stereotypes about welfare recipients and stay-at-home mothers, which facilitate an image of an undeserving recipient of social aid. As exemplified in one article, "We have welfare mothers crying that their children must go without food or that they cannot afford milk for their baby, but they will not give up smoking ... pacifiers are for babies not adults. As for playing bingo—spending on gambling instead of the goods that welfare is intended to buy is the height of irresponsibility" (*Edmonton Journal*, November 1993). Once again, although it represents a small proportion of the coverage, there are no statistically significant changes in the frequency of this framework over the timeline, perhaps reflecting the resilience of these stereotypes over time and across generations.

Conclusions

The evidence in this content analysis points to three primary con-clusions. First, there is not a single storyline or welfare queen equivalent in the Canadian context that appears to dominate this news sample. There are diverse themes that present welfare mothers in contradictory terms as, for example, needy and deserving while also irresponsible and lazy. Whereas certain themes—such as work and education, child welfare, and the costs of living—seem to shift in connection with changes in welfare policies or the political/economic climate, others—such as crime and the legal system, control over need, and family status—appear more fixed in popular depictions of the mother on welfare.

Second, whereas race is a prominent facet of identity in depictions of welfare mothers in the U.S., it appears to be more subtly conveyed through particular storylines in the Canadian context. Race tends to be more covertly codified in news stories of welfare mothers in Canada and coverage often subtly links immigrant, Indigenous, and visible minority mothers to the criminal justice system. This pattern is likely a reflection of the ways that race—and specifically the welfare queen image—did not play into policy debates in the Canadian context as explicitly as they had in the U.S., as Bashevkin observed in her work on "welfare hot buttons."

Lastly, many may anticipate that the coverage of mothers on welfare would be quite hostile in tone, yet many stories actually call for compassion towards mothers on welfare. A surprising number of stories profile mothers as recipients and attempt to humanize them as hardworking individuals. Although this may be seen as progressive and helpful in attempting to garner sympathy and public support for these mothers and their children, few articles substantively engage with identifying or calling out gendered inequalities that underlie many of the issues facing these women as mothers, workers, and recipients of social assistance. By failing to address these inequalities and removing gender-based inequalities from these analyses, many news stories fail to inform citizens about social policy reforms that may be more meaningful in addressing systemic social and economic barriers affecting women in Canada.

Overall, the results of this analysis speak to the growing need to interrogate depictions of welfare within and beyond the Canadian context. In general, news coverage of welfare mothers has decreased markedly in recent years, and as Maura Kelly notes, this lack of discussion on public assistance suggests that welfare is not an important issue and does not adequately educate the public about the problems with social assistance programs (92). The findings in this content analysis affirm that there is a continued need to illuminate the difficulties facing mothers on welfare and reconfigure conversations to more directly address the substantive gender inequalities underlying women's poverty in Canada and abroad.

Endnotes

1. This implicit and insidious signalling of race is consistent with recent racial mediation literature (Tolley).

2. Location parameters were set to Canada and regions within Canada to avoid discussions of welfare mothers outside the Canadian context.

3. These newspapers generally represent large regions within Canada, including Ontario, Quebec, British Columbia, and Alberta. However, it should be noted that this analysis excludes French-language publications and, thus, may not be entirely reflective of

news coverage, particularly in the Quebec region. Furthermore, unfortunately, there were no articles from major dailies with comparable readership rates in Atlantic Canada—such as the *Chronicle-Herald*—that specifically addressed mothers on welfare in the headlines. This analysis also excluded Indigenous-language publications. Future iterations of this research will aim to incorporate more diverse news sources to better reflect news coverage within the various regions and nations of Canada.

4. Although these time periods do not neatly portray distinct periods of governance at the federal or provincial level, they are reflective of specific economic or political conditions that facilitated the direction of policy change affecting mothers on welfare.

5. Effectively, a dendrogram builds a "word tree," so to speak, that shows how various terms and phrases branch off into coherent clusters or themes. For more information, please see Wallace (2018).

6. I measured the statistical significance of changes in the frequency of frames over the timeline using One-Way ANOVA and Tukey's Post-Hoc tests.

Works Cited

Bashevkin, Sylvia. *Welfare Hot Buttons: Women, Work, and Social Policy Reform*. University of Toronto Press, 2002.

Bezusko, Adriane. "Criminalizing Black Motherhood." *Souls*, vol. 15, no. 1-2, 2013, pp. 39-55.

Brodie, Janine. "Putting Gender Back In: Women and Social Policy Reform in Canada." *Gendering the Nation-State: Canadian and Comparative Perspectives*, edited by Yasmeen Abu-Laban, University of British Colombia Press, 2008, pp. 165-85.

Dobrowolsky, Alexandra, and Jane Jenson. "Shifting Representations of Citizenship: Canadian Politics of 'Women' and 'Children.'" *Social Politics*, vol. 11, no. 2, 2004, pp. 154-80.

Entman, Robert M. "Framing: Toward a Clarification of a Fractured Paradigm." *Journal of Communication*, vol. 43, no. 4, 1993, pp. 51-58.

Fraser, Nancy, and Linda Gordon. "Dependency Demystified: Inscriptions of Power in a Keyword of the Welfare State." *Social Politics*, vol. 1, no. 1, 1993, pp. 4–31.

Gilens, Martin. *Why Americans Hate Welfare: Race, Media, and the Politics of Anti-Poverty Policy.* University of Chicago Press, 1999.

Iyengar, Shanto. "Framing Responsibility for Political Issues: The Case of Poverty." *Political Behavior,* vol. 12, no. 1, 1990, pp. 19-40.

Jenson, Jane. "Writing Women Out, Folding Gender In: The European Union 'Modernizes' Social Policy." *Social Politics,* vol. 15, no. 2, 2008, pp. 131-53.

Kelly, Maura. "Regulating the Reproduction and Mothering of Poor Women: The Controlling Image of the Welfare Mother in Television News Coverage of Welfare Reform." *Journal of Poverty,* vol. 14, no. 1, 2010, pp. 76-96.

Lawlor, Andrea, Adam Mahon, and Stuart Soroka. "The Mass Media and Welfare Policy Framing: A Study in Policy Definition." *Political Communication in Canada,* edited by Alex Marland, Thierry Giasson, and Tamara A. Small. University of British Columbia Press, 2014, pp. 160-76.

Lawlor, Andrea, and Erin Tolley. "Deciding Who's Legitimate: News Media Framing of Immigrants and Refugees." *International Journal of Communication,* vol. 11, 2017, pp. 967-91.

Misra, Joya, Stephanie Moller, and Marina Karides. "Envisioning Dependency: Changing Media Depictions of Welfare in the 20th Century." *Social Problems,* vol. 50, no. 4, 2003, pp. 482-504.

Parker West, Laurel. "Soccer Moms, Welfare Queens, Waitress Moms, and Super Moms: Myths of Motherhood in State Media Coverage of Child Care during 'Welfare Reforms' of the 1990s." *Southern California Interdisciplinary Law Journal,* vol. 25, 2016, pp. 313-46.

Pennebaker, James W., Matthias R. Mehl, and Kate G. Niederhoffer. "Psychological Aspects of Natural Language Use: Our words, our selves." *Annual Review of Psychology,* vol. 54, 2003, pp. 547-77.

Tolley, Erin. *Framed: Media and the Coverage of Race in Canadian Politics.* University of British Columbia Press, 2016.

Wallace, Rebecca. "Contextualizing the Crisis: The Framing of Syrian Refugees in Canadian Print Media." *Canadian Journal of Political Science,* vol. 51, no. 2, 2018, pp. 207-31.

Winter, Nicholas J.G. *Dangerous Frames: How Ideas About Race and Gender Shape Public Opinion.* University of Chicago Press, 2008.

Chapter Eight

"Because We Are Mothers": The Invisibility of Migrant Mother Care Labour in the Canadian Context

Lindsay Larios

Women, especially mothers and those with primary caregiver responsibilities, face significant difficulties having the value of their care labour recognized, which represents for many an obstacle to full participation in the labour market and civil society (for example, Duffy et al.). For migrant mothers, these difficulties are multiplied and made more complex by such factors as structural racism, their migratory trajectories, pressures to integrate, and policy discourses that often explicitly label them as dependent on the state or their families (Arat-Koc; Boucher; Zhu). Bringing together four narratives of migrant mothers living in Montreal, this chapter examines the intersection of motherhood and immigration and suggests that although they do not directly engage in the formal labour market, migrant mothers' care labour allows for their partners, children, and other community members to integrate into a new community, become economically productive, and have sustained wellbeing, both locally and transnationally. These narratives show how care relationships and care labour can be a source of agency and resiliency (Tungohan), but when framed through the neoliberal lens, they can also become a challenge for migrant mothers' own integration and wellbeing. This role, as well as the intense emotional and physical labour that goes into it, is invisible in Canadian immigration and integration discourse and policy, despite the fundamental reliance on informal family and community work inherent within the neoliberal welfare state (Tronto; Zhu). Failure to recognize the important contributions that migrant mothers make in their families and communities through their care labour further marginalizes groups that already face significant challenges within Canadian society.

Migrant Mothers in the Canadian Refugee Policy Context

Canada's refugee immigration system consists of two main parts aiming to help people subject to involuntary migration or displacement due to war, persecution, and other threats to their livelihood (IRCC, *Refugees and Asylum*). The Refugee and Humanitarian Resettlement Program pertains to those applying from outside of Canada seeking protection, who, if selected, may enter as recognized refugees. The In-Canada Asylum Program pertains to people making a claim from inside Canada or upon arrival at the border, referred to as "refugee claimants" or "asylum seekers." To be accepted into Canada under either of these programs, an applicant must fit the definition of a United Nations Convention refugee, in accordance with the United Nations' Convention and Protocol Related to the Status of Refugees (1951), or a person in need of protection, as outlined in the *Immigration and Refugee Protection Act* (2002). Although the number of migrants accepted into Canada has increased overall, amid a highly scrutinized and securitized policy environment, the number of refugees accepted has steadily dropped over the last two decades, aside from a significant uptick in 2015 (IRCC, *Facts & Figures 2015*). Refugee, as well as family, migration is often characterized in discourses of dependency in public and policy spheres, in contrast to economic immigrants, who are represented as self-sufficient, contributing members of society, and generally more desirable to the state (Boucher).

Although almost as many females partake in refugee migration to Canada as males, the effects of this experience are felt in different ways. In particular, systemic barriers that make access to employment, education, and healthcare more difficult are felt more acutely by migrant women (CCR; Hill; Morris). This reality becomes especially apparent when examining income and economic security—for example, immigrant women with children under age fifteen are more than twice as likely as Canadian-born mothers to be living in low-income households (Statistics Canada). Refugee women have lower labour market participation rates than refugee men and compared to women immigrating under other programs. Furthermore, when immigrant women are employed, on average, they earn $2,000 less than Canadian-born women and $10,000 less than immigrant men (Statistics Canada). Integration in Canadian immigration policy and discourse has characteristically been constructed as a matter of economic productivity (McLaren and Dyck). Consequently, through this neoliberal lens, many migrant mothers—who are shown to have disproportionately lower labour market participation rates (Statistics Canada)—are often framed as noncontributing and dependent (Boucher; Zhu).

Although there are many factors that contribute to these outcomes, studies on migrant and transnational motherhood point to a number of ongoing issues, such as the lack of existing support networks, the lack of accessible and culturally appropriate care support services (Morantz et al.; Spitzer), difficulties arising from family separation and transnational care relationships with children and other family members (Bernhard et al.; Rousseau et al.), and problems navigating new and inconsistent discourses relating to being a good mother and a good immigrant (Spitzer et al.). Constructions of the "good mother" that are discursively endorsed both materially and symbolically by the state rely largely on assumptions of white, middle-class subjectivity and consumption, which are not equally attainable to marginalized mothers (Zhu; see also Cantillon and Hutton, this volume). A welfare state is largely defined by its broad range of public programs and services aimed at facilitating the health and wellbeing of citizens, yet the neoliberalization of the welfare state involves a divestment in public provisions as well as policies that restrict eligibility and increase surveillance. Public programs shift from being normalized and broadly used to marginalized and increasingly restrictive. The model for a "good mother," therefore, follows the model for the ideal citizen—someone who is able to navigate the demands of social reproduction through private means without reliance on public programs (Bezanson and Luxton).

Migrant mothers often lack access to services, programs, and opportunities that take into consideration "the reality of women's lives, especially the impact of their domestic and caretaking roles" (Hill 9).

These circumstances can present a challenge for migrant mothers' integration, as they are more likely to be isolated in their homes due to caring responsibilities and unable to fully participate in language-learning classes or in other education or employment opportunities (Hill; Morantz et al.; Stewart et al.). To this effect, their efforts to be good mothers and raise good citizens may inhibit their ability to embody the ideal citizen as constructed by the neoliberal welfare state. This research argues that the Canadian neoliberal welfare state positions migrant mothers in an impossible matrix of idealizations; it challenges this conception of the ideal citizen as failing to recognize contributions made through social reproduction. The narratives presented below highlight the lived experiences of migrant mothers in order to illuminate the role that mothering plays in the process of settlement and integration.

Methods

This research is part of a larger project exploring how various caregiving roles and responsibilities impact the lives of refugee women as well as how these caregiving experiences are shaped by Canadian immigration policies and the social value placed on care. This study uses in-depth qualitative interviews conducted over the summer of 2015 with six participants living in Montreal, who were recruited through advertisements at community organizations and through snowball methods. Interviews were conducted in the participants language of preference (three through the use of a translator). Guided by the ethics of care (Tronto), the interviews were analyzed thematically to get an understanding of the participants' lived exper-iences of the phenomena of caregiving, with particular consideration given to how society's treatment of caring relationships can facilitate or hinder a migrant mother's integration and wellbeing (Creswell et al. 57).

This chapter highlights four of those narratives, which emphasize the caregiving experiences of migrant mothers. The participants each migrated from countries within the Central Asia and Latin America due to experiences of violence. At the time of the interviews, they had been living in Canada between one and fifteen years and were in various stages of the Canadian refugee determination process. One participant entered Canada as a legally recognized refugee, whereas the other three engaged with the asylum-seeking process—waiting an initial refugee determination hearing, appealing a negative response from a hearing, and using an alternative migration pathway after a negative response. Although each migrated in response to violent situations, they have not all been recognized as fitting the formal definition of refugee by the Canadian state. For this reason, this chapter uses the broader term "migrant," as employed by the International Organization for Migration. Names and other identifying information have been changed to protect the anonymity of the participants.

Stories of Migrant Mothering

Maryam

Confronted with on-going war, Maryam fled her home country to take refuge in a neighbouring country with her husband and five children. Their temporary stay was soon extended, as violence grew worse in their home country. Maryam began organizing to help other refugees from her country who followed the same path. In the eight years she worked there, her organization was able to secure temporary residency permits and services for members of her community and connect with international and national refugee-helping organizations around the world for support. Maryam and her family were accepted to come as refugees to Canada fifteen years ago and now have Canadian citizenship. Settling in Canada had been dream of hers for her family, but she struggled to reconcile this with her caregiving role in her community.

> Canada accepted our [application]! And then, really, I [was] so surprised.... How is it possible to leave everything and go to Canada? Canada, my dream! What can I do? Believe me, many nights [I did] not well sleep.... I lost everything—position, people, activities, everything. I preferred to go with my children to Canada because they were going to study... [Where we were living], you have no right to study. Ah, [their government] closed the door for refugee people. Even [if] they have knowledge, even [if] they have talent, they stop them. That is the reason we came.

Her youngest child who was only one year old when they first fled was eight by the time they finally settled in Canada. She speaks with pride of the accomplishments of her children, who knew no English or French when they arrived and have now all gone on to pursue professional careers. She has again taken up an active leadership role in her community, helping refugee and newcomer women and organizing language-learning classes for the children in her community. Balancing family life with her community work, especially when Maryam first arrived and her children were still young, has been an ongoing negotiation: "It was a big family.... Fresh food ready. [I was] always responsible ... for the husband, and everything! ... Really. I woke up very early in the morning and cooked everything, then left."

Maryam's caregiving duties in her home occupy much less of her time now, since her children are adults and her husband has passed away. However, her passion for her work and the care and support she extends to other immigrant women in her community continues to keep her busy: "I wish for women to be educated. They need to learn. They need to learn for a new society, a new up and coming life.... I want to give them the opportunity." Maryam's story is one of constant rebuilding. She navigated a new career path and new service to her community in each new country she found herself in—a cycle largely shaped by her desire to protect her children from violence and put their access to healthcare and education above all else. She arrived in Canada as an educated and accomplished woman, but in Canada, these skills and her ongoing contributions are largely unrecognized.

Luisa

Luisa and her son left a life of poverty and violence in their home country and claimed asylum in Canada roughly ten years ago. At that time, their claim was rejected, and they returned to their home country. Concerned for her son's increased exposure to violence and determined to provide a better life for her family, she returned to Canada as a visitor. For the next two and a half years, her son lived with his grandparents in their home country. The separation weighed heavily on her and pushed her to work under the table and endure dangerous work conditions in order to be able to send money back home.

> [Migrant women], we live the situation in different ways than men. It's not more or less important, just different—because we are mothers. I mean, when you are in a precarious status,

sometimes you have to decide if you eat or if your son or family eats in [your home country]. It's like, how do I say, sabotage? Sabotage yourself, you know. Because you already earn less money than men, you know? And your money is not enough here. You have to eat. You have to put some money in your pocket. But at the same time, you normally send a lot of money, more than you have to. You just send. If you have $200, you will send $150. You will keep only $50, but it's nothing.

Luisa found the separation between her and her child difficult to endure:

That time was very hard—very, very hard—because he was an age that was very difficult. So, it was my parents [who were] in charge and the economic situation was not good. So, you always felt guilty, you know—"Why did I just leave my son? Why?" ... It's never enough. You work very hard, you send money, but it's always never enough because they tell you, sometimes, "Why are you there? Your son is here. He needs you." My son even told me, "I need you, no?" ... He was so angry, so angry—[it was a] very difficult moment.

While living in Canada, she met her husband, who later was able to sponsor her and her son to live permanently in Canada. She has since been reunited with her son and continues to send financial support to her family. However, after years of separation, rebuilding her relationship with her son took time: "[We are] very happy, but he is also going to therapy because we have a lot of trouble—not only [because of the separation] but because we have a background that is very difficult. So, when he came, he was so angry.... And now, finally after years, our relationship is perfect.... We support each other."

Throughout this time, Luisa has been an active volunteer in her community and now works in a community centre where based on her own immigration and employment experiences, she helps other women and newcomers. She is proud of her work and the life she is now able to share with her son:

Finally, we are building something. For example, one day I took him ... to the centre and I showed him my desk. And I said, "Do you remember when I was in the factory? When we were crying?

When we were separated? Now I have one place. I don't have to do the hard jobs. I fought for this, no? So, we are building this life ... and you are part of this we built, no?" And he said, "Wow." We made it together. He sacrificed also my presence. And this is what we wanted. [I told him], "I have a job now. You are here. You are building your dreams. You are building your life now."

Mothering for Luisa was a matter of sacrifice and compromise that led her to a place of material and emotional vulnerability. Despite this, she was able to leverage these experiences to create a safe and supportive home for her son, which empowered her to be an advocate for the wellbeing of other migrant mothers in her community.

Amal

Amal spent the first years of her marriage living with her husband's family, with whom she did not have a good relationship. When conditions in their home country became dangerous, she, along with her husband and young daughter, fled and applied for refugee status in Canada. She has been waiting over a year for a response to her claim while living in Canada. She described this as a difficult time filled with uncertainty and depression. Amal and her husband would argue frequently and intensely:

To get away from those arguments, 'cause my daughter used to feel upset in that environment ... I used to take her to the park and just sit.... At that time, I was very new to this society. I didn't have any circle of friends. I didn't know anything about this society, so I didn't know what to do. So, I used to just take my daughter out just to rest my mind and relax. (translation)

Her husband has since decided not to continue with the immigration process and disappeared. The trauma Amal endured prior and during migration and the ongoing stressed she has faced in her home environment triggered her epilepsy, which is now a constant concern. During this time she also gave birth to a second child, who arrived prematurely:

I am going through a very difficult period because when my husband left, I was really upset.... Without telling me, he left.... My health, my children, and doing everything on my own, was not easy for me.... The thing that satisfies me living here is that I am living a stress-free life [compared to] what stress I had in my life before. My daughter is going to school and settled, and I am happy that she is learning and she is growing.... And my son also has a doctor who is [caring for] him. We do regular checkups because he [was] born premature.... So, these things, really give me satisfaction.... The place where we are living, there are no threats to our lives, like where I was living back home. This is something. Although it is not easy, I am trying to make myself settled here. I am trying to make a good life for my children. (translation)

Amal spends her time caring for her children, handling the immigration process, managing her own health issues, and participating in community activities. She feels the pressure of being a single mother caring for two small children in a place that still feels new to her and a place where she is still uncertain that she will be accepted, yet she finds strength in being able to reclaim her decision-making power over her life and how to care for her children. She finds hope in the future she now sees open to them:

I want to go back to school to improve myself more because I want to help my daughter. So that is why I have started learning French, so I can help her with her homework. These are the steps I think of taking more so that I can be independent more. If you have a good standing in the society, you get respect. And this has positive effects on the children. If you are grounded, if you are settled, they also learn from you. This society gave me respect, and I like doing things that will help me to improve myself. And I am pretty sure that once my children are settled, I will do something. Right now, I have to take care of my son, but once he is going to school, I will have more time to think about that. (translation)

As Amal's story shows, mothering in this context means finding strategic ways to accomplish the physical tasks involved in providing care while learning how to live in a new and unfamiliar society. For Amal, despite the unexpected challenges, these care relationships represented empowerment and resiliency for her.

Yasmine

Yasmine and her husband left their home country and claimed asylum in Canada. They had been living in Montreal for approximately five years at the time of the interview. Their initial claim was rejected, and they were in the process of appealing the decision. Meanwhile, her husband works, and they have had a child, born in Canada. Her daughter was born with a medical condition that proved difficult to treat: "In the beginning, it was really difficult because it seemed like every day I [had] to take her to the hospital.... I was really sad, upset, depressed, [thinking] what is going to happen with my daughter? ... I never used to leave her alone because I never ... felt that she will be okay. Anytime anything can happen, so I used to be with her all the time, day and night" (translation).

Their two other children remain in their home country living with family members, waiting for their parents to receive the legal status necessary to reunite with them. Yasmine struggles with the emotional toll of the five-year separation: "[I] am calling and talking every day.... If I don't call them, then they start crying. They miss me and I miss them.... They need my love, my care. I was not able to give them. I am away from them" (translation). Yasmine and her husband send financial support overseas to support their children's education:

We send money back home so that they can go to school and whatever their needs are ... they should be met.... In the beginning, it was really difficult because at that time, my husband did not find a good job. He was doing work but not enough. But now he is making somewhat enough money that we are able to manage. We can send. It's not much, but at least we are able to send proper [amounts] back home for the children. (translation)

Now that her daughter's medical condition has stabilized and she feels more comfortable leaving her in the care of a childcare provider, Yasmine has begun taking French classes. She is also an active volunteer in her community. She works with other newcomers, introduces them to healthcare and public transportation services, accompanies them to immigration offices, and sometimes cares for their children while they attend appointments: "I like doing this work because [I have] gone through this process. When you know the things, why not help others? Whatever they need to know. Because I understand [their] situation. You are helpless. You don't know, and you need somebody to give you support. These things I have experienced, so I like giving that back to other people" (translation).

Yasmine's story shows mothering as a matter of balance. She had to make decisions that sometimes meant balancing material and emotional resources between her family in Canada, her responsibilities to her family abroad, and her community. She felt pain and a lack of control regarding her separation from her children but demonstrated her perseverance through her care labour for her child and community in Canada.

Migrant Mothering Interwoven with the Politics of the Welfare State

These narratives offer a glimpse into the lives of four migrant mothers, who due to conditions of violence and poverty have endeavoured to relocate their families to Canada. The examples shared in these stories include a wide range of experiences. Migrant mothers described forgoing language classes and experiencing isolation due to a lack of access to adequate childcare and protecting children from a violent partner when leaving the relationship may compromise her family's future in Canada. Others described rationing basic needs to send money to a child overseas and staying in exploitative employment to be able to do so. Each one of these mothers faced the challenges of balancing many different responsibilities: continuing their caregiving roles, supporting the wellbeing of their children and families, helping other women by volunteering in their communities, and maintaining their own personal wellbeing.

These narratives do not depict cases that neatly fit within conceptions of "ideal immigrant" or "good mother" as endorsed by the neoliberal welfare state (Zhu). As such, they challenge us to reimagine those conceptions. These idealizations use economic integration as the key measure, and they operate in a context in which service provision is not always attuned to the realities of family caregiving, and migrant mothers often struggle fit this criterion. This is so even with more highly skilled female migrants like Maryam, who never retained her professional employment status, those who work fulltime, like Luisa, who sent the majority of her earnings to family in her home country, and those with ambitions to learn the dominant language, like Amal and Yasmine, who had to postpose those classes to prioritize the immediate care needs of their children. These challenges were especially acute when mothers were separated from their children, as in the case of Luisa and Yasmine. Although they were able to financially support their children from abroad, they routinely sacrificed their own mental and physical wellbeing to do so. Despite this focus on caregiving, these cases of transnational motherhood, reliance on informal networks, and negotiating new parenting strategies also do not fit neatly within the neoliberal welfare state's conception of motherhood either.

Settlement services, language-learning classes, and employment transition services, alongside other health and social services are the primary ways that the Canadian welfare state supports newcomers. During the last decade, the funding model for immigrant-serving organizations overseeing settlement services for new immigrants has shifted from sustained core funding to limited project-based funding, and under the Harper government, the sector experienced massive cuts (Low et al.). Although it has since been reinstated, healthcare access for refugee claimants was also thrown into flux during the Harper-era with new restrictions to the Interim Federal Health Program (Villegas and Blower). Funding cuts and restricted access have also affected services at the subnational level, with Quebec restricting access to public childcare for refugee claimants in 2018 (Shingler) and Ontario implementing funding cuts to their Legal Aid program in 2019 (Law Society of Ontario). As these narratives show, accessing these services is not always straightforward or easy. Nonetheless, refugee families become part of communities whether formally supported by the state or not; however, without proper support, it happens slowly, unequally, and often with gendered implications.

It is important to recognize that this care work is not only a function of mothering but also a key part of how settlement actually happens (Ben Soltane). Upon arrival in a new country, migrant mothers take on a new care role and assume the weight of their partner's and their children's integration, even at the expense of their own integration and wellbeing. Migrant mothers who find themselves separated from their children may find more time for employment but still face limited opportunities, pushing them to accept harmful and exploitative work conditions to be able to send money to their children (Tungohan). Although many of these women may struggle to contribute directly to the Canadian economy—the neoliberal marker of immigrant success and integration—they contribute extensively through their mothering. Each woman's family, as well as other families in their communities, have thrived because of their mothering work. These stories demonstrate the value of care, as through care work, these four women have demonstrated that they have skills and have engaged in meaningful activities that contribute positively to the lives of those around them (see also Lovrod, Bustamante, and Domshy, this volume).

In a welfare context that would derisively cast each of them as dependent, their actions demonstrate their own resiliency and agency as well as the necessary role they play in the maintenance of the wellbeing of those around them, whether formally acknowledged by welfare state politics or not. Their narratives also demonstrate the negative impact of austerity policies and restricted access to services aimed at facilitating health, wellbeing, and integration. These families dealt with complex mental and physical health issues, and further restrictions to their access to health and social supports would have been devastating. As it is, they struggled to access language classes, childcare, and professional advice on their immigration files. The neoliberalization of the welfare state represents a real threat to the livelihood of refugee and asylum-seeker families within Canadian borders.

Such a situation has significant implications and should give us pause when considering current conceptualizations of idealized motherhood and immigration. The lived experiences of migrant motherhood presented in these narratives challenge these conceptions and require us as a society to examine our presumptions surrounding immigration and to call for more robust and caring state responses as well as support for all families within our borders.

Endnotes

1. This study was completed as a master of social work thesis at McGill University (2016) under the direction of Dr. Jill Hanley with ethics approval granted by the McGill University Research Ethics Board. I would like to extend my gratitude to Dr. Hanley for her knowledge and support during this process. I would also like to thank the women who contributed to this project by generously sharing their

time and their stories with me, and to the South Asian Women's Community Centre and the Afghan Women's Centre, among other community organizations in Montreal, for the essential work they do and their help in making this project happen.

Works Cited

Arat-Koc, Sedef. "Invisibilized, Individualized, and Culturalized: Paradoxical Invisibility and Hyper-Visibility of Gender in Policy Making and Policy Discourse in Neoliberal Canada." *Canadian Woman Studies*, vol. 29, no. 3, 2012, pp. 6-7.

Ben Soltane, Sonia. *Care and Immigration: Is It a Women's Job to Care?* A Question of Caring Workshop on Care and Migration, McGill School of Social Work, Montreal, QC.

Bernhard, Judith K., et al. "Transnationalizing Families: Canadian Immigration Policy and the Spatial Fragmentation of Care-Giving among Latin American Newcomers." *International Migration*, vol. 47, no. 2, June 2009, pp. 3-31.

Bezanson, Kate, and Meg Luxton, editors. *Social Reproduction: Feminist Political Economy Challenges Neo-Liberalism*. McGill-Queens University Press, 2006.

Boucher, Anna. "Skill, Migration and Gender in Australia and Canada: The Case of Gender-Based Analysis." *Australian Journal of Political Science*, vol. 42, no. 3, 2007, pp. 383-401.

Canadian Council for Refugees (CCR). *Gender-Based Analysis of Settlement, Research Report*. CCR, 2006.

Creswell, John W., et al. "Qualitative Research Designs: Selection and Implementation." *The Counseling Psychologist*, vol. 35, no. 2, 2007, pp. 236-64.

Duffy, Mignon, et al. "Counting Care Work: The Empirical and Policy Applications of Care Theory." *Social Problems*, vol. 60, no. 2, May 2013, pp. 145-67.

Hill, Diane Elizabeth. *Moving Forward: Advancing the Economic Security of Immigrant Women in Canada*. Women's Economic Council, 2011.

Immigration, Refugees, and Citizenship Canada (IRCC). *Facts & Figures 2015: Immigration Overview – Permanent Residents*. Annual IRCC Updates, Government of Canada, 2017.

Immigration, Refugees, and Citizenship Canada (IRCC). *Refugees and Asylum*. Government of Canada, 2017.

International Organization for Migration. "Key Migration Terms." *International Organization for Migration*, 2015.

Law Society of Ontario. "Law Society Expresses Grave Concern over Deep Cuts to Legal Aid Ontario." *Canada Newswire*, 11 Apr. 2019. www.newswire.ca/en/releases/archive/April2019/11/c4090.html. Accessed 20 July 2020.

McLaren, Arlene Tiger, and Isabel Dyck. "Mothering, Human Capital, and the 'Ideal Immigrant.'" *Women's Studies International Forum*, vol. 27, no. 1, 2004, pp. 41-53.

Morantz, Gillian, et al. "Resettlement Challenges Faced by Refugee Claimant Families in Montreal: Lack of Access to Child Care." *Child & Family Social Work*, vol. 18, no. 3, Aug. 2013, pp. 318–28.

Morris, Marika. *Gender-Sensitive Home and Community Care and Caregiving Research: A Synthesis Paper*. Women's Health Bureau, Health Canada, 2001.

Rousseau, Cécile, et al. "Trauma and Extended Separation from Family among American and African Refugees in Montreal." *Psychiatry*, vol. 64, no. 1, 2001.

Shingler, Benjamin. "Quebec Blocks Asylum Seekers from Public Daycare Network, Alarming Advocates." *Canadian Broadcasting Corporation*, 12 July 2018, www.cbc.ca/news/canada/montreal/quebec-daycare-asylum-seekers-1.4744103. Accessed 20 July 2020.

Statistics Canada. *Women in Canada: A Gender-Based Statistical Report*. 89-503–X, Government of Canada, 2015.

Stewart, M. J., et al. "Immigrant Women Family Caregivers in Canada: Implications for Policies and Programmes in Health and Social Sectors." *Health and Social Care in the Community*, vol. 14, no. 4, July 2006, pp. 329-40.

Tronto, Joan C. *Moral Boundaries: A Political Argument for an Ethic of Care*. Routledge, 1993.

Tungohan, Ethel. "Reconceptualizing Motherhood, Reconceptualizing Resistance: Migrant Domestic Workers, Transnational Hyper-Maternalism and Activism." *International Feminist Journal of Politics*, vol. 15, no. 1, Mar. 2013, pp. 39-57.

Villegas, Paloma, and Jenna Blower. "'Part of Being Canadian Is Having Access to Healthcare': Framing the Boundaries of Healthcare Deservingness for Non-Citizens through the Interim Federal Health Benefits Program." *Canadian Journal of Communication*, vol. 44, no. 1, 2019, pp. 69-88.

Zhu, Yidan. "Immigration Policy, Settlement Service, and Immigrant Mothers in Neoliberal Canada: A Feminist Analysis." *Canadian Ethnic Studies Journal*, vol. 48, no. 2, 2016, pp. 143-56.

Chapter Nine

Exploring Self-Sacrifice, Role Captivity, and Motherhood

Sara Cantillon and Martina Hutton

"I crook the bottle.
How you suckle!
This is the best I can be,
Housewife
To this nursery
Where you hold on,
Dear life..........."
—Eavan Boland (92)

T he few lines above from Boland's poem "Night Feed" about a night feed encapsulate some of the paradoxes of motherhood: the profound joy, the satisfaction of giving, the unique intimacy of breastfeeding as well as the challenges involved in raising a child, the loss of freedom, the guilt, and all of the other domestic care and housework involved. The line "this is the best that I can be" seems both to sanctify the value of motherhood while also exposing its vulnerability as well as the feelings of anxiety and inadequacy that accompany it. Much of the current literature on mothering is engaged in this discursive struggle, where cultural constructions of the ideal mother are important not only for how women define themselves as good mothers but also for they shape their identities as women (Arendell).

The ideology of intensive mothering is based on the notion that good mothers should first and foremost be caregivers, that they should invest their time, money, and emotional labour in their children, and that in order to maximize this provision they should reduce or eliminate their paid work (Hays). This idea of total self-sacrifice for your child (and its implicit message of emotional fulfilment) has been widely criticized as being too white and middle-class focused; too frivolous and excessive for its negative impact on maternal psychological wellbeing; and too physically and emotionally draining for mothers while not even necessarily being in the best interests of the child (Gunderson and Barrett). The ideal of intensive mothering requires women not only to put their child's needs before their own in every respect but to be able to display this to others through their everyday practices, such as consumption and food preparation (Cappellini et al.). The repercussions of intensive mothering include feeling under surveillance and being judged against a normalized mode of parenting, in which fathers can more easily opt out without being seen as a bad parent (Miller). For lower-income mothers in particular, J. A. Sutherland observes that "as long as mothers are exposed to this ideology, they risk being locked into a kind of prison, bound by the myths of motherhood" (313). However, while intensive mothering may well be represented as white and middle class, its discourse dominates many parenting cultures. The tenacity of institutional ideologies and social norms about motherhood and mothering persist regardless of race, ethnicity, social class, or the constraints faced by mothers in terms of structural inequality and poverty. For example, in a study of low-income Black single mothers, self-sacrifice and protection were repeatedly emphasized by the participants as what good mothers do for their children (Elliot, Powell, and Brenton). The issues of ideal motherhood and self-sacrifice are also explored in the chapters by Lynsey S. Race and Lorna Stefanick as well as by Roberta Garrett in this volume. Most mothers do, rightly, strive to protect their children and may often put their children's needs ahead of their own, but as Adrienne Rich argues, there are differences between motherhood as an institution and an experience—that is, the gap between cultural and patriarchal conceptions of motherhood and the physical, emotional, and gynaecological experiences of mothering itself.

This chapter explores the cultural demand of self-sacrifice in motherhood and focuses in particular on the concepts of choice and role captivity within households with children. Many feminist theorists have long argued that the family acts as a central mechanism in the reproduction of gender inequality, in which women are made vulnerable by the unequal division of labour in the family and by assumptions about childrearing and household responsibilities. An enormous literature exists on gender equality and the false dichotomy between public and private domains. For present purposes, our focus is on the material and psychological outcomes in relation to the assumption of mothers and self-sacrifice. The tendency for women, especially mothers, to channel their extra resources into household consumption has significant effects in terms of the differential levels of deprivation experienced by men, women, and children within the same family. In their review about the links between personal relationships and poverty, Judy Corlyon et al. argue that gender is an inescapable aspect of families, in view of the centrality of mothers in both experiencing poverty themselves and alleviating that of others. And as Benedetta Cappellini et al. show, such self-sacrifice involves contradictory emotional effects that generate not only pride and self-worth but also stress and anxiety.

This chapter draws primarily on two separate Irish studies undertaken by the authors. The first study, which draws on a large nationally representative sample of heterosexual married couples, examines gender differences in standards of living within households and at the woman's role in managing scarce resources, often at her own personal cost. It looks at why this extra work is often seen as a badge of honour or a sign of personal empowerment rather than as example of deprivation at the individual level or of gender inequality. The second study explores how mothers assume the role of consumer within and for their family and how the strain related to consumption is shouldered solely by mothers and legitimized as an extension of their caring responsibilities. We have combined insights from these two studies for several reasons. First, both studies focus on different aspects of the concept of self-sacrifice—one resource based and one consumption based. Second, both of these studies find that mothers are more likely to suffer deprivation and that this is implicitly sanctioned within a hegemonic family discourse, which sees the welfare of the children as the primary responsibility of the mother and which normalizes the idea that the mother should make sacrifices to this end.

Intrahousehold Differences in Standards of Living

Over the last twenty years, numerous studies on intrahousehold poverty and distribution have attempted to open the "black box" of sharing within the household (Bennett). These studies have mainly focused on gender inequality and have explored how differences in distributional outcomes and financial control are related to power imbalances between men and women. Such power differentials can also affect children's living standards within households, and various studies have found that when women have more control over household finances, a greater proportion is spent on children (Goode, Callender, and Lister; Middleton, Ashworth, and Braithwaite; Daly). A central insight concerning internal household processes is that this power differential in the household can be translated into gendered differences in standards of living. The tendency for women to channel their extra resources into household consumption—especially when compounded with the financial arrangement that gives the woman primary responsibility for household management but restricted access to household resources—has significant effects in terms of the differential levels of deprivation experienced by men and women within the same family (Rake and Jayatilaka).

Data from the most recent nationally representative poverty and social exclusion survey in the United Kingdom (UK) demonstrate that for a significant minority of children living in households where there is poverty, they themselves are not directly exposed. That is, either some (or all) of the adults in the household are poor, whereas the children are not poor. These children are living in households whose incomes and resources are insufficient to maintain the material living standards of all the family members, but the children's are maintained or ameliorated by the adults spending on their children's needs rather than their own (Main and Bradshaw). This finding reinforces earlier surveys in both the UK and Ireland suggesting that adults shelter children from the worst impacts of poverty by going without themselves (Goode, Callender, and Lister; Middleton, Ashworth, and Braithwaite; Ridge; Watson, Maitre, and Whelan). A key finding, however, in Gill Main and Jonathan Bradshaw's study is that "whilst a significant proportion of adults in households (where some adults are poor but children are not poor) are likely to be going without, not all adults in these situations are going without" (11). This finding echoed a foundational study from over a decade earlier, which found that were women more likely than men to "go without" (Goode, Callender, and Lister) and clearly implies that intrahousehold distributions are uneven. Although such distributions tend to work in favour of children versus adults, the burden of going without is not evenly distributed between adults. Gender, and particularly primary caring responsibilities, is a key variable, as mothers are more likely to go without and to favour spending on children over spending on themselves.

Our study of intrahousehold resource allocation in Ireland also explored the relative position of spouses and children in relation to living standards and material deprivation by analyzing the responses of 1,124 heterosexual married couples to questions specifically designed for inclusion in a separate ad hoc module in the annual Living in Ireland Survey, which was replaced by the annual EU Survey of Income and Living Conditions (Cantillon, Gannon, and Nolan.). While dated, having been undertaken in 1999, ours remains the only quantitative study carried out in Ireland on intrahousehold inequality. Later studies, under the EU Survey of Income and Living Conditions, focused on income pooling rather than material deprivation, the division of household decision making, or financial responsibilities. The questions related to levels of consumption and material deprivation and used standard deprivation measures, including heating use, food consumption, and access to social activities and to personal spending money. These items were specifically pursued, as a number of previous qualitative studies had shown their sensitivity to gender differentiation (Cantillon and Nolan). For example, Hilary Graham cites personal fuel consumption as an item in which women facing budget constraints felt there was scope for savings. The cutbacks in consumption were not, however, evenly spread among family members with excerpts from Graham's interviews poignantly illustrating this: "I put the central heating on for one hour before the kids go to bed and one hour before they get up. I sit in a sleeping bag once they have gone to bed.... I turn it off when I am on my own and put a blanket on myself. Sometimes we both do but my husband does not like being cold and turns the heating back on" (qtd. in Graham).

Likewise, the distribution of food often reflects the differences in status of family members. The issue of self-denial in relation to food consumption arises when a woman chooses a smaller portion, or none at all, in a situation where there is not enough for everyone. As Lynn McIntyre,

Suzanne Officer, and Lynne M. Robinson show, the majority of women in their study deprived themselves of food to feed their kids without thinking about it other than saying "that's what mothers do" (321). In this volume, Heather Bergen also writes about what mothers do to make their lives more liveable in her analysis of interdependence strategies between women living in Toronto. And Christine Delphy and Diana Leonard show that self-sacrifice is assumed to be second nature for women and, therefore, not something noticeable or worth reporting: "The mistress of the house takes the smallest chop without thinking, and if there are not enough for everyone, she will not have one at all. She will say she is not hungry, and no one is surprised, least of all herself, that it is always the same person who 'doesn't want any' and 'doesn't mind'" (150).

In the 1999 study, we also found that when there was a difference between spouses, there was a consistent, albeit not dramatic, imbalance in favour of husbands across all the selected nonmonetary deprivation indicators. In relation to food consumption, the results showed that the wife is consistently more deprived than her husband in relation to skimping on her own meal to try to ensure that the other family members have enough. In about 4.5 per cent of all couples in the nationally representative survey, the woman skimped and the man did not. The greatest differences between husbands and wives showed up in relation to social and leisure activities and in relation to spending money. Nearly 30 per cent of couples gave different responses in relation to having a leisure activity, and in about two-thirds of these, it was the husband but not the wife who had a regular leisure activity. A high proportion of wives who did not have an activity but their husband did cited lack of time (due to household or childcare responsibilities) rather than lack of money as the reason. Likewise, concerning the socializing question, childcare is given as the reason by 9.4 per cent of wives and 2.9 per cent of husbands for not having had an afternoon or evening out over the previous fortnight (Cantillon, Gannon, and Nolan).

Another difference in material living standards was the issue of control over resources. Several UK studies—both small scale and large nationally representative surveys—have explored different allocative systems for managing household resources and their implications for the living standards of individual members (Main and Bradshaw). A key characteristic of control over resources is the distinction between financial control and financial management, with the latter translating as women in poorer households having the added burden of responsibility for stretching scarce resources. Not surprisingly, the results showed that in relation to managing scarce resources, the burden falls disproportionately on women. In response to the question in our survey as to who takes the main responsibility for trying to make sure money, when it is tight, stretches from week to week, approximately 56 per cent of couples saw it as a joint responsibility. The remainder, about 34 per cent of the sample, saw it as the sole responsibility of the wife. In low-income households, those below the 40 per cent poverty line, joint responsibility was less common, and about 46 per cent of wives said they took sole responsibility for making scarce resources stretch. The results for this Irish study corroborate the consistency of this theme. Over and over, both qualitative and quantitative research reveals women as being more likely to manage the household budget in low-income families, which is more likely to be a burden than a source of power (Goode, Callender, and Lister; Daly and Leonard; Bradshaw et al.; Maplethorpe et al.). Very few studies have explored the intersecting relationship between intrahousehold inequality and the individual mothers' experiences of stress. Our second study addresses this link and reveals that consumption-related stress and differential wellbeing are rooted in the intersecting structural contexts of gendered and intrahousehold inequality.

Consumption and Role Captivity

Our second study examined the female experience of stress generated by consumption responsibilities and, in particular, how a group of low-income mothers coped with such pressure. Adopting an interpretivist approach, the study involved a series of focus group discussions and in-depth interviews with thirty women, who identified as living on a low income. The women ranged in age from twenty-six to fifty-eight; fifteen women were married, eight were single, four were separated, one was divorced, and two were widowed. Twenty-three of our participants were Irish white; two Nigerians, one German, and four women of Irish Traveller background (an Indigenous ethnic minority group in Ireland whose identity and culture are based on a nomadic tradition) also participated. This study demonstrated a tendency for women, especially mothers, to channel their extra resources into household consumption using material items as a conduit for social acceptance with respect to their dependent children (Hamilton, "Low-Income Families"). The psychological burden associated with trying to please all family members' consumption-related demands perpetuated power inequalities, as different individuals within the same household experienced different levels of wellbeing and deprivation. The cost to mothers' health was particularly evident, as they sacrificed their own wellbeing to buffer the effects of scarce resources. Feminist scholars are especially vocal about the stress experienced by individuals based on social categories, such as gender or socioeconomic status, which suggests they must cope not only with the chronic stress that arises from belonging to a relatively less powerful or stigmatized group but also with the daily experience of disproportionate role strain involving children, adults, and the juggling of economic resources (Belle; Hall, Williams, and Greenberg; Meyer, Schwartz, and Frost; Zwicker and DeLongis). Role strain is the difficulty associated with fulfilling role demands, and for women in particular, the gender-related power differentials and demands tied to mothering erode feelings of personal efficacy, as they endure the daily demands of role strain occupying too many roles for too long (Belle; Downey and Moen; Ennis, Hobfoll, and Schroder). The following exchange taken from an excerpt from the second study reveals how women articulate role captivity as it specifically relates to multiple household demands:

Joanne I have to not just make sure there is money in the house, but running the house and bringing up the children and even relationship wise. I'm like the foreign minister in the home.

All Yes. We're the mediators!

Kate We are the administrators!

Joanne We are the cook!

Joanne Different roles at different times...

Kate No not at different times. You are doing these roles at the same time.

Beth You have a variety of roles. You're like the teacher, the nurse, the jailer, the educator, the consumer, the whole lot! (Hutton).

These private, invisible realities of mothering draw attention to how the family system as a structural site reinforces emotional injustice for most mothers but especially those who are already economically and socially compromised.

The most dominant theoretical orientation regarding gender, strain, and inequality explains women's disadvantage in terms of the problems that arise within the boundaries of social roles, such as motherhood (Grove and Tudor; Meyer, Schwartz, and Frost; Pearlin). Indeed, both of our studies reveal how women recognize the gendered and captive nature of their role as mothers. One mother explained it in the following way: "I think there's a socialization a lot of us went through as well, where we were encouraged, even bullied, into not thinking about ourselves. You know women, we're taught to be nurturing. We're taught to be caring" (Hutton).

More specifically, our studies highlight how women reluctantly assume the role of consumer within and for the family; the strain related to consumption is shouldered solely by women and legitimized as an extension of their caring responsibilities. In particular, the anxieties and pressure arising from child-related spending and demands suggest that sacrifice is an expected consumption skill and responsibility of mothers. Commenting on how consumption is a taken-for-granted activity within the family, Delphy and Leonard propose that differential family status is part of the way in which actors perceive and realize their own and other people's relative statuses within this intimate sphere. We have found that for women in heterosexual relationships, the burden of responsibility for household consumption decisions is often reinforced by children and male partners, who tell women that they "like shopping" and are "good at it" (Hutton 15). Indeed, intrahousehold economic behaviour normalizes consumption, as it consists of commitments that cannot be quickly put aside once they have been accepted. The consumption domain is, therefore, a site of conflict and inequality resulting in intrahousehold stress derived from managing the expectations and demands of family members in low-income households. Scholars suggest that mothers' positive response to children's requests can be viewed as a rational choice, as it makes better financial sense to purchase food and clothing that children will eat and use to avoid wastage (Hamilton, "Those Left Behind"; John). In addition, feelings of guilt encourage parental cooperation, what Angela McRobbie refers to as "giving in," which is indicative of all the conflicts and anxieties around consumption.

The traditional view of conflictual family consumption suggests that disagreements only arise during the decision-making process—that is, during the purchasing stage, as family members strive to meet competing needs that are in line with the available financial resources (Hamilton, "Low-Income Families"). However, this view assumes that family decision-making roles are always in transition, depending on the nature of the product or service under consideration for purchase. Alternatively, our studies reveal that the role of consuming is fixed for women. Family discord does not centre on decision making per se, but on the outcome of women's decisions as appraised by other family members. In other words, women as mothers are implicitly sanctioned within a hegemonic family discourse to make the primary sacrifice of labour, finances, and consumption for their family (Larios, this volume). This conformity and sanctioning applied by other individuals in the household show how gender and role strains are acutely intertwined. We, therefore, suggest that stress experiences for mothers arise, at least partially, from patterned role circumstances that demand women's sacrifice and that directly reflect the effects of social inequality on allocations of resources, status, and power (Turner, Wheaton, and Lloyd.). The burden of self-sacrifice is, therefore, not randomly distributed in society but distributed based on power and related to structural, economic, and political processes (Brooker and Eakin). In the context of a consumption-led culture, the role of the mother as the consumer in the family is naturalized—a type of role captivity in which the stress related to consuming activities is shouldered solely by mothers. Indeed, "the various structural arrangements in which individuals are embedded," as Leonard Pearlin argues, "determine the stressors they encounter as well as their coping resources" (167). The invisibility of mothers' differential social status and associated role strains are bound up with their disadvantaged position of managing scarce resources within a household context. Sandra Harding suggests that although the private sphere is exploited by public sphere institutions, discussions regarding consumption are often ignored when focusing on how women's lives are organized in households.

Conclusion

The cultural construction of the ideal mother, rather conveniently for the state, is a version of privatized mothering; balancing work and care commitments become individual choices, and negotiations are almost always accompanied by feelings of guilt and stress. The greater the constraints created by structural inequalities, the greater the stress, burden, and hardship faced mothers; furthermore, more invidious and false dichotomies arise between stay-at-home and working mothers, married or single mothers, and so-called good and bad mothers. Both of our studies demonstrate that self-sacrifice is implicitly sanctioned within hegemonic family discourses, which understand the welfare of the children as the primary responsibility of the mother and which normalize the idea that mothers should make sacrifices to this end. Moreover, the impact of this responsibility increases as family income decreases; thus, mothers from low-income families are even more likely to experience personal deprivation in order to make ends meet.

Sylvia Chant argues that this feminization of responsibility can be detrimental if low-income mothers lack personal power because their identities are too closely tied to the interests of the household. If there is little opportunity for control over a situation, then changing the meaning of it may increase the individual's sense of control. That is, the ability to reframe obstacles is an important resource for resilience. We have seen the self-sacrifice of mothers in relation to compromising their food intake and other material indicators as well as others aspects of daily life, including social activities and personal spending money. However, rather than framing this going without as self-deprivation, we find it employed as a coping strategy and one that finds resonance in the socially acceptable role for mothers so that "it's not just poor moms who put themselves first" (McIntyre, Officer, and Robinson 320). Yet the possession of resources is instrumental in resilience, as the wellbeing of individuals is dependent upon their access to resources within their particular ecological niche in order for them to feel empowered (Hobfoll; Kelly). For the women in our studies, financial management was often the most common resource to draw on when dealing with constraint—one that was tied to feelings of competence and empowerment but was also involved in a great deal of self-sacrifice in terms of time and the juggling of the consumption effort and the expectations of family members.

A second source of mothers' resilience stemmed from actively managing the survival of social supports, such as family and friends, through relational coping or caring for others. In short, mothers actively rejected more individually beneficial coping strategies (Banyard), choosing instead to redistribute the experience of hardship particularly within the family setting (Heflin, London, and Scott). Our studies, therefore, highlight how self-sacrifice and empowerment coexist as narratives of motherhood in low-income families. But as the following chapter by Jacqueline Potvin shows, one can draw different conclusions from the idea of mothers engaging as rational actors. We argue mothers use sacrifice and empowerment as dynamic resources in the absence of economic means. Both serve as a functional and valuable means for surviving hardship, which, in turn, can have additional emotional benefits for women. Self-sacrifice and empowerment are creatively constituted resources, which foster agency, enabling women to (re)assert themselves in vulnerable contexts. As practices of sacrifice, thrift, and self-abnegation have become part of motherly subjectivities through their own self-discipline, women are able to feel optimistic for their families (Cappellini et al.). The seemingly conflicting narratives point to both the cultural construction of motherhood and to the structural inequalities that make adherence to that discourse so much more difficult for some mothers.

Works Cited

Arendell, Terry. "Conceiving and Investigating Motherhood: The Decade's Scholarship." *Journal of Marriage and Family,* vol. 62, no. 4, 2000, pp.1192–207.

Banyard, Victoria L. "Taking Another Route: Daily Survival Narratives from Mothers Who Are Homeless." *American Journal of Community Psychology*, vol. 23, no.6, 1995, pp. 871-91.

Belle, Deborah. "Poverty and Women's Mental Health". *American Psychologist*, vol. 45, no.3, 1990, pp. 385-89.

Bennett, Fran. "Researching within Household Distribution: Overview, Developments, Debates and Methodological Challenges." *Journal of Marriage and Family*, vol. 75, no. 3, 2013, pp. 58--97.

Boland, Eavan. "Night Feed." *New Collected Poems*, Carcanet Press, 2005, p. 92.

Bradshaw, Jonathan, editor. *The Wellbeing of Children in the UK*. Policy Press, 2011.

Brooker, Ann-Sylvia, and Joan M. Eakin. "Gender, Class, Work-Related Stress and Health: Toward a Power-Centred Approach." *Journal of Community and Applied Social Psychology*, vol. 11, no. 2, 2001, pp. 97-109.

Cantillon, Sara, Bertrand Maître, and Dorothy Watson. "Family Financial Management and Individual Deprivation" *Journal of Family and Economic Issues*, vol. 37, no. 3, 2016, pp. 461-73.

Cantillon, Sara., Brenda Gannon, and Brian Nolan. *Sharing Household Resources: Learning from Nonmonetary Indicators*. Combat Poverty Agency, 2004.

Cantillon, Sara, and Brian Nolan. "Poverty within Households: Measuring Gender Differences Using Non-Monetary Indicators." *Feminist Economics*, vol. 7, no. 1, 2001, pp. 5-23.

Cappellini, Benedetta, et al. "Intensive Mothering in Hard Times: Foucauldian Ethical Self-formation and Cruel Optimism." *Journal of Consumer Culture*, vol. 19, no. 4, 2019, pp. 469-92.

Chant, Sylvia. "New Contributions to the Analysis of Poverty: Methodological and Conceptual Challenges to Understanding Poverty from a Gender Perspective." *ECLAC Experts Meeting on Gender and Poverty*. United Nations, 2003.

Corlyon, Judy et al. *Personal Relationships and Poverty: An Evidence and Policy Review*. Joseph Rowntree Foundation, 2013.

Daly, Mary. *The Significance of Family in the Context of Poverty*. Conceptual Note No 6 Poverty and Social Exclusion in the UK: Economic Social Research Council, 2012.

Delphy, Christine, and Diana Leonard. *Familiar Exploitation: A New Analysis of Marriage and Family Life*. Cambridge: Polity Press, 1992.

Downey, Geraldine, and Phyllis Moen. "Personal Efficacy, Income and Family Transitions: A Longitudinal Study of Women Heading Households." *Journal of Health and Social Behaviour*, vol. 28, no. 3, 1987, pp. 320-33

Elliott, Sinikka, Rachel Powell, and Joslyn Brenton. "Being a Good Mom: Black Single Mothers Negotiate Intensive Mothering." *Journal of Family Issues*, vol. 36, no. 3, 2015, pp. 351-70.

Ennis, Nicole E., Stevan E. Hobfoll, and Kerstin E. Schroder. "Money Doesn't Talk, It Swears: How Economic Stress and Resistance Resources Impact Inner-City Women's Depressive Mood." *American Journal of Community Psychology*, vol. 28, no. 2, 2000, pp. 149-73.

Goode, J., C. Callender, and R. Lister. *Purse or Wallet? Gender Inequalities and Income Distribution within Families on Benefits.* Policy Studies Institute, 1998.

Graham, H. "Women's Poverty and Caring." *Women and Poverty in Britain in the 1990's,* edited by C. Glendinning and J. Miller, Harvester Wheatsheaf, 1987, pp. 221-40.

Grove, Walter R., and Jeanette F. Tudor. "Adult Sex Roles and Mental Illness". *American Journal of Sociology*, vol. 78, no.4, 1973, pp. 812-35.

Gunderston, Justine, and Anne E. Barrett. "Emotional Cost and of Emotional Support." *Journal of Family Issues*, vol. 38, no. 7, 2017, pp. 992-1009.

Hall, L., C. A. Williams, and R. S. Greenberg. "Supports, Stressors and Depressive Symptoms in Low-income Mothers of Young Children". *American Journal of Public Health*, vol. 75, no. 5, 1985, pp. 518-22.

Harding, Sandra. *Sciences from Below: Feminisms, Postcolonialities and Modernities.* Duke University Press, 2008.

Hays, Sharon. *The Cultural Contradictions of Motherhood New Haven*, Yale University Press, 1996.

Hamilton, Kathy. "Those Left Behind: Inequality in Consumer Culture." *Irish Marketing Review* vol. 20, no. 2, 2009, pp. 40-54.

Hamilton, Kathy. "Low-Income Families and Coping through Brands: Inclusion or Stigma?" *Sociology*, vol. 46, no. 1, 2012, pp. 74-90.

Heflin, Colleen, Andrew S. London, and Ellen K. Scott. "Mitigating Material Hardship: The Strategies Low-Income Families Employ to Reduce the Consequences of Poverty." *Sociological Inquiry*, vol. 81, no. 2, 2011, pp. 223-46.

Hobfoll, Stevan E. "Social and Psychological Resources and Adaptation." *Review of General Psychology*, vol. 6, no. 4, 2002, pp. 307-24.

Hutton, Martina. "Consuming Stress: Exploring Hidden Dimensions of Consumption-Related Strain at the Intersection of Gender and

Poverty." *Journal of Marketing Management,* vol. 31, no. 15-16, 2015, pp. 1695-1717.

John, Deborah R. "Consumer Socialisation of Children: A Retrospective Look at Twenty-Five Years of Research." *Journal of Consumer Research,* vol. 26, no. 3, 1999, pp. 183-213.

Kelly, J. G. "Ecological Constraints on Mental Health Services." *American Psychologist,* vol. 21, no. 6, 1966, pp. 535-39.

Main, Gill, and Jonathan Bradshaw. *Child Poverty and Social Exclusion: Final Report of the 2012 PSE Study.* Poverty and Social Exclusion in the UK: Economic Social Research Council, 2014.

Maplethorpe Natalie, et al. *Families with Children in Britain: Findings from the 2008 Families and Children Study (FACS).* Department for Work and Pensions Research Report, 2010.

McIntyre, Lynn, Suzanne Officer, and Lynne M. Robinson. "Feeling Poor: The Felt Experience of Low Income Lone Mothers." *Affilia,* vol. 18, no. 2003, pp. 316-331.

McRobbie, Angela. "Bridging the Gap: Feminism, Fashion and Consumption, *Feminist Review,* vol. 55, no. 1, 1997, pp. 73-89.

Meyer, Ilan H., Sharon Schwartz, and David M. Frost. "Social patterning of stress and coping; Does disadvantaged social statuses confer more stress and fewer coping resources?" *Social Science & Medicine,* vol. 67, no. 2008, pp. 368-79.

Middleton, S., Karl Ashworth, and Ian Braithwaite. *Small Fortunes: Spending on Children, Childhood Poverty and Parental Sacrifice.* Joseph Rowntree Foundation, 1997.

Miller, T. *Making Sense of Fatherhood: Gender, Caring and Work.* Cambridge University Press, 2011.

Pearlin, Leonard L. "The Sociological Study of Stress." *Journal of Health and Social Behavior,* vol. 30, no. 3, 1989, pp. 241-56.

Rake, Katherine, and Geethika Jayatilaka. *Home Truths: An Analysis of Financial Decision Making within the Home.* Fawcett Society, 2002.

Rich, Adrienne. *Of Woman Born: Motherhood as Experience.* Norton, 1987.

Ridge, Tess. *Childhood Poverty and Social Exclusion: From a Child's Perspective.* Polity Press, 2002.

Sutherland, J. A. "Mothering, Guilt, and Shame." *Sociology Compass*, vol. 4, no. 5, 2010, pp. 310-21.

Turner, R. Jay, Blair Wheaton, and Donald A. Lloyd. "The Epidemiology of Social Stress," *American Sociological Review*, vol. 60, no.1, 1995, pp. 104-25.

Watson, Dorothy, Bertrand Maitre, and Christopher T. Whelan. *Understanding Child Deprivation in Ireland*. Social Inclusion Report No 2, Department of Social Protection, 2012.

Zwicker, Amy, and Anita Coyne DeLongis. "Gender, Stress and Coping." *Handbook of Gender Research in Psychology*, edited by J. C. Chrisler and D. R. McCreary, Springer Science and Business Media, 2010, pp. 495-515.

Chapter Ten

Neoliberal Governance, Healthism, and Maternal Responsibility under Canada's Muskoka Initiative

Jacqueline Potvin

In June of 2010, former Canadian Prime Minister Stephen Harper led the G8 countries in developing and signing the Muskoka Initiative, an international agreement committing the signatories to addressing maternal, newborn, and child health (MNCH) at the global level. Lauded as putting MNCH at the centre of the global health agenda, the Muskoka Initiative also marked the beginning of a well-publicized campaign by the Harper government to establish Canada as a global leader in MNCH programming and to identify MNCH as Canada's top development priority. Between 2010 and 2015, Canada committed $2.8 billion to MNCH programming, followed by a commitment of $3.5 billion to be distributed between 2015 and 2020 (Keast 52). For many, Canada's commitment to maternal and child health was a significant victory, as it put women at the centre of development policy while addressing what has been identified as a key global health concern. However, the Muskoka Initiative also faced significant critique, particularly regarding its approach to family planning. Although the Muskoka Initiative engaged with family planning to a limited extent through contraception provision, it excluded any funds or support for access to safe abortion. This omission faced criticism in part because evidence has shown that unsafe abortion is a significant cause of maternal death (Webster).

Furthermore, analyses of the Muskoka Initiative have contended that the policy failed to engage with gender as a social relation, treating women as a homogenous category without addressing how gender roles and hierarchies affect the health of mothers and their children (Keast; Tiessen and Carrier). Rebecca Tiessen has also argued that the policy treated women as "walking wombs", as the policy narrowly addressed women's health concerns through the lens of childbearing and promoted a narrative of saving lives, which situated women as objects rather than agents of development. In this chapter, I extend these critiques and situate them within the Muskoka Initiative's broader reliance on neoliberal approaches to health and development, and specifically, on the responsibilization of women in the Global South through the mobilization of maternal healthism. Based on a critical discourse analysis of the programs funded through the Muskoka Initiative, I argue that although the Muskoka Initiative did succeed in mobilizing significant resources to improve the health and welfare of mothers and their children, these resources were aimed at creating conditions in which women in the Global South could be compelled to act as seemingly rational, risk-minimizing subjects. These women were therefore made responsible for maintaining not only their own health but the health of their children. Thus, while the Muskoka Initiative did situate maternal health as a problem that the global community, and in particular Canada, had a moral responsibility to address, the proposed solution to this problem was only to increase the ability of individuals to make seemingly better choices. This approach ultimately reinforced neoliberal frameworks of health as an individual responsibility. I argue that in treating maternal bodies as key sites of intervention, Canadian MNCH policy under the Muskoka Initiative relied on neoliberal frameworks of development that sought to govern, responsibilize, and, ultimately, instrumentalize women in the Global South. In doing so, it emphasized maternal responsibility while decentring and even excluding women's right to health for their own sake, including their right to access abortion services.

Methodology

This chapter is based on a critical discourse analysis of texts related to Canadian MNCH programming under the Muskoka Initiative from 2010 to 2015. The texts analyzed included thirty-nine webpages from the Government of Canada's website on MNCH health and eighty-eight project descriptions of programs funded through the Muskoka Initiative, as found on the webpage for what was then the Department of Foreign Affairs, Trade, and Development (now Global Affairs Canada).[1] The texts were analyzed using guided analysis sheets, with a focus on determining how maternal health was discursively constructed as a development problem and how Canadian interventions were constructed as appropriate solutions. Although several significant discursive constructions were identified through this analysis, in this chapter, I focus on the construction of maternal health as a problem of risk management and responses aimed at helping women to engage in risk management as a means of protecting their own health and the health of their children. My findings are interpreted through the lens of neoliberal governmentality and healthism, with a focus on the gendered constructions of maternal altruism and responsibility.

Risk, Responsibility, and Health

Over the past three decades, a significant body of research has been produced outlining how risk operates in neoliberal contexts, both as a framework for understanding social problems and as a means of governing health.[2] Although theoretical understandings of risk vary, scholars of governmentality have demonstrated how risk, while often a response to material threats, constitutes a particular way of understanding these threats and, perhaps more importantly, our ability to respond to and protect against them (Hannah-Moffat and O'Malley). Risk can operate differently as a tool of governance depending on the context. Neoliberal models of risk are associated with the individualization of responsibility, as they configure individual subjects as able to protect themselves against harm through rational and responsible risk management (Polzer and Power). The neoliberal model differs from the social insurance model of risk, as in the former "collective responsibility is replaced by [a model] in which individuals are ultimately apportioned responsibility, even for things (crime, health, job training) which are social in their scope" (Ruhl 102). The individualized model of risk draws on and reinforces the configuration of the contemporary neoliberal subject as a rational individual who pursues their own self-interest by making decisions that are understood as bringing the highest level of benefit at the lowest cost (Li). Thus, the role of the neoliberal state is understood as ensuring that individuals have the freedom to pursue their own self-interest rather than directing how they should live (Polzer and Power). Given this (presumed) freedom, individuals are, in turn, understood as responsible for their own wellbeing, with a lack of wellbeing situated as a failure to adequately protect oneself.

The emphasis on personal freedom and responsibility in neoliberal societies has meant that governance, while still, at times, deployed by direct means, more commonly operates at a distance through processes of self-regulation in accordance with dominant norms (Polzer and Power). As such, the individual's perceived ability to make personal choices remains intact, even as certain choices are constructed as abnormal, as irrational or irresponsible, and, hence, as untenable. Within neoliberal health regimes, risk has been theorized as an important tool of governance at a distance, compelling individuals to govern themselves in accordance with dominant understandings of risk minimization, which are often constructed through the dissemination of expert knowledge (Peterson and Lupton). Furthermore, although neoliberal health regimes situate health as an individualized project of risk management, individuals are compelled to maintain health through healthism, in which good health is considered both a moral imperative and an obligation of citizenship (Polzer and Power). In this model, individuals are considered free to make their own decisions but are held responsible for the costs to society should those decisions fail to result in good health. As such, neoliberal health regimes situate health as a moral and civic "duty to be well" (Greco). Poor health, furthermore, is seen as indicative of personal failure and an inability or unwillingness to make rational choices that would have preserved health (Crawford). Individuals are, thus, compelled to govern their behaviour; they must fulfill their duty to be well by reacting to risk responsibly, thereby protecting themselves from harm.

Risk and Maternal Healthism

Risk and healthism, despite a reliance on the seemingly neutral figure of the rational self-interested individual, operate differently based on gender (Hannah-Moffat and O'Malley; Polzer and Power). For women, who have historically been situated as responsible for the biological and social reproduction of the population, pregnancy and motherhood operate as key sites of governance (Lupton). During pregnancy in particular, women are expected to be exceptionally risk averse and to take significant measures to protect not only their own health but the health of the fetus (Lupton; Ruhl). The configuration of the pregnant woman as responsible for fetal health relies on an individualized risk model, and an understanding of risk as a set of dangers that can be guarded against through responsible decision making. In turn, undesirable fetal outcomes are configured, at least in part, as the result of poor maternal choices (Ruhl). This responsibilization of the pregnant woman is bound up in ideas and expectations of maternal sacrifice—a social norm that is explored in depth by Sara Cantillon and Martina Hutton in this volume. As Lealle Ruhl observes, a woman who fails to protect her fetus by defying expert medical advice "is made to feel both irresponsible (how could she be so cavalier about her future baby's health?) and guilty (she is placing her own desire ahead of her baby's wellbeing in clear contravention of our model of self-sacrifice)" (104). Thus, for pregnant women, maternal healthism encompasses not only a duty to protect the health of oneself and one's fetus but also a responsibility to protect the health of the fetus, even at the expense of one's own wellbeing. This expectation complicates the seemingly gender-neutral understanding of individuals as self-interested, risk-minimizing actors, as women are expected to act in contravention of their own interest in order to ensure the health of the other for whom she is responsible. This understanding of maternal healthism as a moral obligation to one's child and as a duty of reproductive citizenship can help us understand how women are uniquely governed through discourses of risk. Such understandings are, in turn, central to an analysis of how women have been included in Canadian MNCH policy under the Muskoka Initiative.

A Risk-Based Model of Maternal and Child Health

In the texts analyzed, Canadian MNCH policy is situated as an attempt to address preventable maternal and child deaths, primarily by increasing access to health services in countries where maternal and child mortality rates are highest. This focus on increasing access to health services is based on the Muskoka Initiative's construction of maternal and child mortality as the outcome of various medical risk factors that are situated as inherent to periods of pregnancy, childbirth and early childhood, and yet as able to be managed and protected against if the appropriate measures are taken. For example, one webpage states the following: "Common causes [of death] include severe bleeding after childbirth, infection, and high blood pressure during pregnancy. Most of these deaths, 99%, occur in developing countries, and most could be prevented" (Government of Canada, Maternal Health).

In this statement, specific medical risks are identified, whereas negative outcomes associated with these risks are established as preventable. In another text, preventability is also established while also being explicitly situated in access to healthcare during childbirth: "Mothers need skilled health workers like midwives during childbirth. This alone could prevent 42% of newborn deaths. Yet, more than 40 million women give birth without a skilled health worker every year" (Government of Canada "Improving Newborn Health to Reduce Child Mortality" 1:01-1:14).

In this statement, access to skilled health workers is situated not only as mitigating risk but also as directly preventing newborn death. In contrast, childbirth that occurs in the absence of skilled birth attendants is identified as high risk: "In Ethiopia, many women give birth in their homes, especially in rural areas. With some of the highest rates of maternal and child mortality in the world, these home births can put both the mother and the baby at risk." (Government of Canada "Canada Helps Deliver Childbirth Education in Ethiopia")

These statements clearly situate particular healthcare practices—in this case, childbirth attended by skilled medical professionals—as risk minimizing whereas others are situated as high risk. Furthermore, by constructing the problem of maternal and child mortality as a problem of managing preventable medical risks, the texts analyzed situate it as a problem that can be solved, specifically through increased use of healthcare services. This framing of MNCH as a problem that can be solved is epitomized in the name of the 2014 follow-up conference to the Muskoka Initiative, titled "Saving Every Woman, Every Child: Within Arm's Reach." The emphasis on preventability and saving lives signifies the use of a risk-based model in which risks are understood not in terms of probabilities but in terms of a direct cause and effect relationship, which can be disrupted through access to medical care. In turn, it also situates Canadian MNCH programming, which focuses on increasing healthcare access, as a necessary and effective solution. The Canadian programming described in the webpages and project descriptions shows a strong emphasis on increasing healthcare provision—both through programs that deliver services directly and through strengthening national healthcare systems by training medical staff, improving infrastructure, and enhancing the managerial capacity and data collection of local providers. Some project activities also sought to address barriers such as the economic cost of healthcare or the lack of transportation in rural communities.

In addition to addressing the provision of healthcare, programs funded through Muskoka also focused on encouraging women to seek healthcare services when available. This goal is detailed in one project description that outlines how their project "targets current challenges such as inconsistent quality of services and the fact that mothers, for a variety of reasons, hesitate to use such services when they do exist." (Department of Foreign Affairs, Trade and Development "Joint Government of Bangladesh-UN Maternal and Neonatal Health Project") Women's inability or unwillingness to make use of healthcare services is, hence, identified as a key component of high mortality rates, given the identification of healthcare access as central to mitigating risk to maternal and child health. In response, project descriptions detail activities, such as peer education programs, that teach women to access medical care during childbirth and to monitor their pregnancies so that they can recognize and act on signs of complications by seeking medical care. For instance, one webpage states that "thanks to awareness raising campaigns, 30 per cent more mothers are now aware of potential signs of complications during pregnancy and can seek care, if needed, in a timely manner" (Government of Canada "Maternal Health"). In addition to teaching women how to recognize and, hence, protect against risk factors during pregnancy, these programs continue to emphasize the benefits of formalized healthcare, as with one program that claims to "provide advice to mothers about their pre-natal care and speak of the benefits of delivering babies in an equipped government health centre or hospital where trained staff take care of the mothers and newborn babies" (Government of Canada "Canada Helps Deliver Childbirth Education in Ethiopia"). These program activities contribute to the construction of formalized, Western-style healthcare as the safe and, hence, rational choice for women who are pregnant and giving birth. In addition, the focus on awareness raising and education configures women in the Global South as capable of becoming rational, risk-minimizing subjects should they gain access to the necessary resources, including knowledge of maternal risk and of risk-minimizing strategies. This narrative of responsibilization aligns with contemporary discourses of empowerment as well as colonial narratives of a so-called civilizing mission, in which racialized women in the Global South, though initially positioned as victims in need of rescue, are configured as able to become agentic if they receive help from Western interventions (Batliwala; Wilson). Western intervention, in this case through the provision of formalized healthcare and health education, is seen as unlocking the capacity women in the Global South to become agentic, health-seeking subjects. Thus, the Muskoka Initiative perpetuated global hierarchies, casting Canada in the role of powerful saviour, while, nevertheless, situating responsibility for improved health within the individual actions of women within the Global South.

Responsibilizing Mothers

To a certain extent, the mobilization of risk discourse within the Muskoka Initiative seems to support a less individualized model of risk and responsibility than typical contemporary neoliberal risk frameworks. The emphasis on the need for Canada, as part of a global community, to participate in the project of saving mothers and children by improving access to healthcare can seem to indicate a model of shared social responsibility for risk management, which contrasts with individualized models of risk discussed above. Likewise, the texts' acknowledgment of the role economic and social barriers can play in limiting an individual's ability to access the services deemed necessary to address manage risk also challenges a purely individualized model, which situates risk management and outcomes as the responsibility solely of the individual themselves. Yet in another sense, the ultimate goals of the Muskoka Initiative exemplify neoliberal approaches to health, deploying a framework of risk as something that can be managed through individuals' participation in appropriate health-seeking behaviours. By focusing on increasing availability of health services while simultaneously raising awareness among women about when they should seek medical help, these programs seek to create a context in which particular choices, such as attended childbirth, are both available and will necessarily be chosen. Within these contexts, women are understood as having the capacity to manage their own health by mitigating the risks associated with reproduction, both to themselves and to their children. Awareness raising and education activities that seek not only to inform women of their choices but to promote particular choices as the right ones can, thus, be seen as endeavours to help women in the Global South develop a risk consciousness, which ostensibly shapes them into risk-minimizing actors who will use these services, once available, in ways deemed appropriate (Hannah-Moffat and O'Malley 3). Thus, despite a stated commitment to state- and community-supported health systems, programs funded through the Muskoka Initiative promote a healthcare model that relies on individualized notions of responsibility as well as neoliberal assumptions of rational subjects as risk-minimizing actors.

Maternal Health and Care Practices as a Site of Intervention

In constructing pregnancy and childbirth as periods of risk, the texts analyzed situate both pregnant women and children as vulnerable to the same risk factors. Thus, the same interventions are often positioned as helping to save the lives of both mothers and children, allowing the Muskoka Initiative to configure MNCH as one, cohesive project. Within this configuration, interventions promoting prenatal care and maternal nutrition are positioned as helping to ensure the health of the future child. For example, one project description states that it "aims to reduce infant mortality in three districts of the Kayes region [of Mali] by improving the nutritional status of children under the age of five and pregnant and nursing women" (Department of Foreign Affairs, Trade and Development, "Community-Based Nutritional Health in Southern Mali-I"). In this example, improving the nutritional status of pregnant and nursing women is explicitly identified as a strategy for reducing infant mortality. Such strategies rely on the understanding of maternal health as a potential site of risk to future children, illustrated by one webpage's statement that "when pregnant women suffer from under-nutrition, they and their babies are at higher risk of complications and death" (Government of Canada "Nutrition"). Along with maternal malnutrition, maternal infection and disease are also identified as sources of risk, with one webpage stating that "prematurity, complications, maternal infections, and hypertension are among the major causes of stillbirths" (Government of Canada "Newborns"). Other project descriptions outline the need to address "mother to child transmission of HIV," (Department of Foreign Affairs, Trade and Development "Supporting Systems to Achieve Improved Nutrition, Maternal, Newborn and Child Health"), situating the maternal body as a potential vector for disease and, hence again, as a site of risk to the fetus and/or child. These configurations of the maternal body as a source of risk contribute to the overall construction of maternal health as vulnerable to the same forms of risk as the fetus and as a means to ensure fetal, and ultimately child, health. By addressing maternal nutrition and infection, risks emanating from the maternal body can be mitigated and the health of the fetus and/or child is understood as being ensured.

In addition to program activities that target pregnant women's bodies, projects also situate care practices as a means by which to ensure child health. Breastfeeding in particular is encouraged as a means through which to improve child health, with one project identifying among its chief outcomes the "approximately 6500 infant's lives saved through breast-feeding practices" (Department of Foreign Affairs, Trade and Development "Improving Nutrition Through Homestead Food Production").

Several projects identify increasing the number of women who breastfeed as a positive outcome of their activities, positioning this increase as a means of saving lives. This positioning once again relies on a model of health in which positive outcomes are directly attributed to particular individual actions. Furthermore, the emphasis on outcomes demonstrates how practices such as breastfeeding are situated as right or desirable, and as easily adoptable. Yet this approach fails to engage with the potentially complex reasons why breastfeeding may be counter to a women's own interests (Van Hollen). As such, the programs strengthen the construction of particular actions as desirable, with benefits clearly seen as outweighing the costs.

Although maternal healthism is generally bound up in ideas of maternal altruism and sacrifice, within the Muskoka Initiative, the framework relies instead on the understanding that maternal and child health will benefit from the same interventions. By positioning MNCH interventions as mutually beneficial, the Muskoka Initiative is, in turn, able to obscure any possible tension between the health of mothers and their children. Whereas studies of maternal responsibility in the Global North have interrogated the way women's self-interest (or irresponsibility) can itself be understood as a potential site of risk to the fetus, in the case of Muskoka, the conflation of maternal and fetal interests means that this particular configuration of risk is absent. Even though, as outlined above, the maternal body is positioned as a potential site of fetal risk, such risks are configured as risks to both the maternal and the fetal body. The actions women are encouraged to take to minimize risk are, thus, not even recognized as sacrifices but merely changes in behaviour that will not have harmful effects on the women themselves. The analysis of the texts did not reveal any instances in which maternal health and child health may be at odds or in which there may be resistance from the women themselves to engage in celebrated practices once they were made aware of their benefits. Rather, resistance to practices deemed healthy was situated in a lack of awareness of **their** potential benefits **and was to be** addressed through education and awareness raising, such as those outlined above. This conflation of maternal and child health, thus, both simplifies and strengthens the positioning of particular choices as rational and as understood as being in the best interest of mothers and their children. Similarly, this conflation reinforces the way in which women are configured as responsible not only for their own health but also the health of the fetus and/or child.

Maternal Healthism Instrumentalization and the Exclusion of Abortion

In acknowledging the absence of any reference to resistance, I do not intend to deny or minimize the real feelings of altruism women may feel towards their children or to situate self-sacrifice as only ever the outcome of adherence to idealized maternal norms. Rather, I am interested in how the harmonious model of maternal healthism allows for the construction of a health framework that reentrenches the instrumentalization and responsibilization of women in development programming while allowing for the exclusion of abortion as a key component of maternal health. The inclusion of women in development programs is often based on discourses of instrumentalization, which emphasizes how women can benefit the project of development rather than what development can do to benefit women (Chant and Sweetman). Such language aligns with the social investment approach to state spending, in which funding for services that are seen as building human capital and, hence, as increasing employability are justified as investments that will bring worthwhile returns by allowing individuals to not only better their own lives but also enrich their communities (Jenson). This rationale is apparent in the model of gender equality as "smart economics" (Chant and Sweetman), which, as I have argued elsewhere, relies on discourses of maternal altruism, in which women are assumed to share any benefits they receive with their families and communities, thus constituting a good investment with high returns (Potvin).

Within the Muskoka Initiative, women are situated as risk-minimizing subjects, who when given access to the right resources will ensure their own health and the health of their children, and, in doing so, will ultimately help solve the problem of MNCH. Viewed through the lens of neoliberal healthism, this configuration justifies a focus on women's health both through the discourse of a moral imperative to save women and children as well as through the positioning of women's bodies as key sites of intervention through which to improve global health. This construction, in turn, relies on the configuration of women as risk-minimizing actors, who will fulfil their duty to protect their own health and, by extension, the health of their children. As such, the framework adopted by the Muskoka Initiative draws on and extends the emphasis on individual responsibility and empowerment that characterize neoliberal frameworks of both health and development (Li; Shani). As with the rise of the "mumpreneur," who can make do in hard times (See Roberta Garrett in this volume), the figure of the empowered woman in the Global South is constructed as able to become personally responsible for improving familial outcomes. Thus, the Muskoka Initiative, despite its focus on improving access to health services, contributes to the bootstrap rhetoric of empowerment that situates development success in improving the ability of individuals in the Global South to make rational, self-interested decisions in ways that are explicitly gendered.

Understanding the framework of maternal healthism within the Muskoka Initiative can help illuminate why maternal health was chosen as a key development priority by a Conservative government that had largely moved away from gender-sensitive approaches to global development (Tiessen and Carrier). By adopting an instrumentalizing approach to maternal health, the Canadian government was able to put women at the centre of the development agenda without prioritizing their needs or interests and while excluding any aspect of women's health that fell outside this instrumentalist framework. Although instrumentalist arguments in favour of increasing abortion access can, and have been made, by focusing on maternal health as a site through which to improve population and child health, the Muskoka Initiative was able to sidestep questions not only of women's right to health for their own sake but also their right to reproductive autonomy, including the right to abortion. The policy's silence around abortion was further facilitated by its presentation of maternal and child health as a cohesive project, in which women's health or interests are never in conflict with the health of the fetus. Because the circumstances under which abortion may be necessary or desired are never acknowledged, the policy was able to exclude reference to abortion either as a means of ensuring reproductive autonomy or as an important maternal health intervention.

Conclusion

By emphasizing the need for increased access to healthcare services for women in the Global South, the Muskoka Initiative appears, at first, to push back against a key tenet of neoliberalism, which, as Lynda Ross and Shauna Wilton outline in this volume, largely advocates for cuts to publicly funded services, such as healthcare, with dire consequences for the wellbeing of both women and children. Yet in seeking to increase the accessibility of healthcare services, the Muskoka Initiative situates these services as resources that will allow individuals to ensure health through the management of risk. In doing so, the Muskoka Initiative ultimately, reiterates rather than disrupts neoliberal config-urations of development as the outcome of responsible, individual choices. By positioning maternal health and care practices as sites through which to improve the health of children, the Muskoka Initiative also appears to acknowledge the interconnectedness of maternal and child health—in a sense demonstrating how maternal health, by its very nature, requires a rethinking of completely individualized models of health. Yet by deploying an individualized model of risk management, the Muskoka Initiative also denies this interconnectedness and any potential tension between maternal and child health. This denial allows women to be positioned as responsible for ensuring their own health, as well as the health of their children, by engaging in a particular set of healthy practices. Obscuring the ways in which women's and children's health may be at odds, these programs both hide and reinforce the assumption that a mother's own interests will not prevent her from prioritizing the health of her fetus and/or child. Not only does this model allow for the complete exclusion of abortion as an element of maternal health, it also supports a broader model of neoliberal responsibilization and instrumentalism, which has come to characterize women's inclusion in development. As such, this analysis can help elucidate how development interventions positioned as improving the welfare of mothers may, in fact, work to increase their burden of responsibility, govern their behaviour, and obscure and exclude their needs.

Acknowledgment

This chapter draws on research supported by the Social Sciences and Humanities Research Council through a Doctoral Fellowship Award.

Endnotes

1. For a full list of texts analyzed, see Potvin, *Biopolitics, Risk and Repro-ductive Justice.*

2. Edited collections by Polzer and Power and by Hannah-Moffat and O'Malley provide good examples of such research.

Works Cited

Batiwala, S. "Taking the Power Out of Empowerment—An Experiental Account." *Deconstructing Development Discourse: Buzzwords and Fuzzwords*, edited by A. Cornwall and D. Eade, Practical Action Publishing, 2010, pp. 111-22.

Chant, S., and C. Sweetman. "Fixing Women or Fixing the World? 'Smart Economics,' Efficiency Approaches, and Gender Equality in Development." *Gender & Development*, vol. 20, no 3, 2012, pp. 517-29.

Crawford, R. "Healthism and the Medicalization of Everyday Life." *International Journal of Health Services*, vol. 10, no. 3, 1980, pp. 365-88.

Department of Foreign Affairs, Trade and Development. "Community-Based Nutritional Health in Southern Mali-I". *International Development Project Browser*, w05.international.gc.ca/projectbrowser-banqueprojets/project-projet/details/A035102001. Accessed 7 Aug. 2020.

Department of Foreign Affairs, Trade and Development. "Improving Nutrition through Homestead Food Production." *Internatiaonl Development Project Browser*, w05.international.gc.ca/projectbrowser-banqueprojets/project-projet/details/M013707001. Accessed 7 Aug. 2020.

Department of Foreign Affairs, Trade and Development. "Joint Government of Bangladesh—UN Maternal and Neonatal Health Project." *International Development Project Browser*, w05.international.gc.ca/projectbrowser-banqueprojets/project-projet/details/A035190001. Accessed 7 Aug. 2020.

Department of Foreign Affairs, Trade and Development. "Supporting Systems to Achieve Improved Nutrition, Maternal, Newborn and Child Health." *International Development Project Browser*, w05.international.gc.ca/projectbrowser-banqueprojets/project-projet/details/S065377001. Accessed 7 Aug. 2020.

Government of Canada. "Canada Helps Deliver Childbirth Education in Ethiopia." *Government of Canada*, web.archive.org/web/20150918182312/http:/www.international.gc.ca/world-monde/development-developpement/mnch-smne/stories-histoires/ethiopia-ethiopie.aspx?lang=eng. Accessed 7 Aug. 2020.

Government of Canada. "Improving Newborn Health to Reduce Child Mortality" *YouTube*, 17 July, 2014, www.youtube.com/watch?v=v VI6iJ1R3sQ. Accessed 7 Aug. 2020.

Government of Canada. "Maternal Health." *Government of Canada*, web.archive.org/web/20160316171632/http:/www.international.gc.ca:80/world-monde/development-developpement/mnch-smne/facts-faits/maternal-meres.aspx?lang=eng. Accessed 7 Aug. 2020.

Government of Canada. "Newborns." *Government of Canada,* web. archive.org/web/20160325010935/http:/international.gc.ca/world-monde/development-developpement/mnch-smne/facts-faits/newborns-nouveau_nes.aspx?lang=eng. Accessed 7 Aug. 2020.

Government of Canada. "Nutrition." *Government of Canada,* web. archive.org/web/20160325014654/http:/www.international.gc.ca/world-monde/development-developpement/mnch-smne/facts-faits/nutrition.aspx?lang=eng. Accessed 7 Aug. 2020.

Greco, M. "Psychosomatic Subjects and the 'Duty to Be Well': Personal Agency within Medical Rationality." *Economy and Society,* vol. 22, no. 3, 1993, pp. 357-72.

Hannah-Moffat, K., and P. O'Malley. "Gendered Risks: An Intro-duction." *Gendered Risks,* edited by K. Hannah-Moffat and P. O'Malley, Routledge-Cavendish, 2007, pp. 1-29.

Jenson, J. "Inscribing Maternalism in the Social Investment Perspective." *Review of European and Russian Affairs,* vol. 9, no. 2, 2015, pp. 1-17.

Keast, J. "Missed Opportunity: a Discursive Analysis of Canada's Commitments to Maternal Health under the Muskoka Initiative." *Obligations and Omissions: Canada's Ambiguous Actions on Gender Equality,* edited by R. Tiessen and S. Baranyi, McGill-Queen's University Press, 2017, pp. 49-68.

Li, T. M. *The Will to Improve: Governmentality, Development, and the Practice of Politics.* Duke University Press, 2007.

Lupton, D. "'Precious Cargo': Foetal Subjects, Risk and Reproductive Citizenship." *Critical Public Health,* vol. 22, no, 3, 2012, pp. 329-40.

Peterson, A., and D. Lupton. *The New Public Health: Health and Self in the Age of Risk.* Sage, 1996.

Polzer, J., and E Power. "Introduction: The Governance of Health in Neoliberal Societies." *Neoliberal Governance and Health: Duties, Risks, and Vulnerabilities,* edited by J. Polzer and E. Power, McGill-Queen's University Press, 2016, pp. 3-42.

Potvin, J. "Mobilizing Motherhood : The Use of Maternal Myths in Popular Development Discourse." *Global Justice: Theory, Practice, Rhetoric,* vol. 8, no. 1, 2015, pp. 23-43

Potvin, Jacqueline, "Biopolitics, Risk, and Reproductive Justice: the Governing of Maternal Health in Canada's Muskoka Initiative" (2018). *Electronic Thesis and Dissertation Repository.* 5956.

Ruhl, Lealle. "Liberal Governance and Prenatal Care: Risk and Regulation in Pregnancy." *Economy and Society,* vol. 28, no. 1, 1999, pp. 95-117.

Tiessen, R. "'Walking Wombs': Making Sense of the Muskoka Initiative and the Emphasis on Motherhood in Canadian Foreign Policy." *Global Justice: Theory Practice Rhetoric,* vol. 8, no. 1, 2015, pp. 1-22 .

Tiessen, R., and K. Carrier. "The Erasure of 'Gender' in Canadian Foreign Policy under the Harper Conservatives: The Significance of the Discursive Shift from 'Gender Equality' to 'Equality between Women and Men." *Canadian Foreign Policy Journal,* vol. 21, no. 2, 2015, pp. 95–111.

Van Hollen, C. *Birth in the Age of AIDS: Women, reproduction and HIV/ AIDS in India.* Stanford University Press, 2013.

Webster, P. C. "Canada's G8 Health Plan Receives Praise and Criticism." *The Lancet,* vol. 375, no. 9726, 2010, pp.1595-96.

Wilson, K. "'Race,' Gender and Neoliberalism: Changing Visual Representations in Development." *Third World Quarterly,* vol. 32, no. 2, 2011, pp. 315-31.

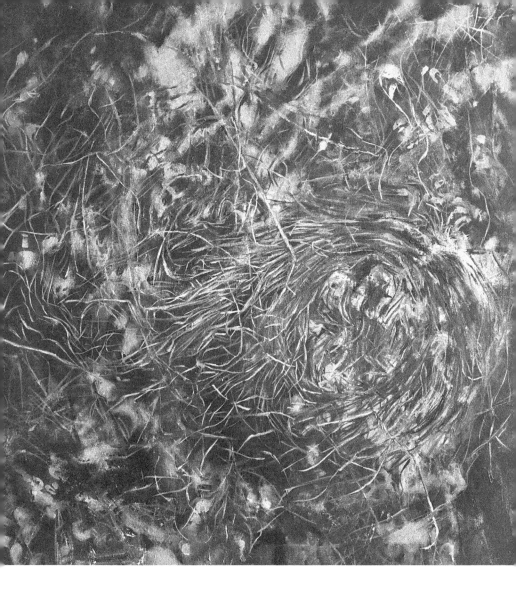

Part III

Reimagining Motherhood

"Money Isn't Everything, But It's Involved in Everything": Young Mothers' Experiences with Poverty, Their Survival Strategies, and Demands for Systemic Changes

Heather Bergen

This chapter focuses on the expertise of ten young parents in Toronto I had the privilege of interviewing. I spoke with these parents as part of research I conducted regarding what parents involved with the Child Protection System (CPS) identified as barriers to their parenting. One of the major obstacles all of the young mothers emphasized was a lack of financial resources. They saw this as constraining the choices they made as parents and perceived this as putting them at risk of CPS involvement. This chapter provides an overview of the struggles they pinpointed as coming from living in poverty as well as the strategies they developed to creatively negotiate their budget. While the young mothers I interviewed expressed pride in their strategies they also had clear ideas for systemic solutions. This chapter also highlights the contradictory role of the neoliberal state—shrinking its supportive functions while simultaneously expanding its policing functions in direct contradiction to the stated desire for small government. The impact of increased policing of mothers via CPS in tandem with fewer services—such as income support, subsidized housing, and affordable childcare—creates devastating repercussions that young mothers struggle to manage.

My interest in this research topic grew out of my decade of community work, particularly the last six years working with young mothers. I witnessed so many different parents struggling with the same barriers and undertook this research in an attempt to gain a better understanding and work towards systemic solutions. During 2015, I conducted two rounds of semistructured qualitative interviews with nine young mothers and one young father. Using an intersectional feminist theoretical framing, I examined how interlocking systems of power played out in the parents' interactions with CPS and how they resisted and strategized to keep their children safe (Crenshaw; Hulko; Bergen). I asked the mothers about what made their parenting more difficult, and they named lack of financial resources as the number one issue that hindered their parenting. Research relationships were an important part of the process when discussing such sensitive topics, and I interviewed eight parents with whom I had previous relationships. The two remaining mothers were referred to me by people I interviewed through snowball sampling (Csiernik et al.).

From an intersectional feminist framing, it is important to provide some background about the parents I spoke with and information about the larger social structures as a way of creating context. All of the parents had been involved with CPS—as children, as parents, or both. Everyone except Jessica had been a young parent; the mothers' age at birth of their first child ranged from fifteen to nineteen. Alicia identified as "Native and African, so mixed-race"; six others identified as Black, two as white. Chance identified as "Aboriginal: Cree and Ojibway." Seven of the mothers identified as single parents; Alicia and Matthew were a couple, and Jessica had a partner. Of the ten parents I interviewed, half of them were receiving social assistance' three others were pursuing postsecondary education and receiving student loans. One was receiving Employment Insurance (EI) for parental leave, and one parent was working.

Jessica, who was older and more established, was receiving EI while on parental leave from her permanent, fulltime, and unionized position. Alisha was working in social services, but was going from insecure contract to contract. Additionally, Alisha had lost her housing and was staying with her mother, so money remained a constant stressor.

Structural Context

To provide some background for how little money many of the families were living on, I estimated how much a mother with one child on social assistance (Ontario Works) would receive. The numbers are calculated for 2015—the year I conducted the interviews and are applicable to Toronto, Ontario, where the interviews took place. Since this time, there has been a slight increase in the child tax benefits and a more significant increase in the minimum wage, from $11.60 to $14 on January 1 2018 (Government of Ontario). Simultaneously, the average rent for a one bedroom has increased $158 between October 2015 and October 2018, from $1103 to $1261 (Canada Mortgage and Housing Corporation). As a result, the current financial situation is even more precarious for families receiving social assistance than it was when the research was conducted.

Based on the numbers from 2015, a family consisting of a mother and one child in Toronto receives $994 a month: $655 for rent and $339 for "basic needs." To this, I added all the government benefits they would be eligible for, which totalled $423 a month, leading to a monthly total of $1,417 per month or $18,924 per year. To give a point of comparison, the Canadian Centre for Policy Alternatives calculated a living wage for Toronto in 2015. The living wage is calculated for a family of four in Toronto to be $65,870.55 and includes what a family needs to survive:

> To meet its basic needs, participate in the economic and social fabric of their community, and purchase items that can help them escape marginal subsistence. The list of family expenses contains no extravagances. It doesn't allow families to save for their children's post-secondary education; it doesn't acknowledge that many working families also carry debt obligations. But it does recognize that things like rent, transportation, childcare, food, clothing, internet, and laundry costs are part of the basics that every family strives to meet. (Tiessen 5-6)

To create a ballpark figure for a family of two, I halved the living wage to $32,935.28. This highlights the stark reality that a single parent with one child receiving social assistance is living on $18,924, which is $14,011 less than the living wage. Understanding this helps make sense of some of the extremely difficult choices the parents reported having to make, for example between rent and groceries or between new clothes for growing kids and school supplies for parents.

Canada does not calculate a poverty line; however, the low-income cut off (LICO), low-income measure (LIM), and the market basket measure (MBM) are used as approximations of a poverty line (Aldridge). The LIM is used across Organization of Economic Cooperation and Development (OECD) countries and measures families that live 50 per cent below the average income, although it does not account for community size (Aldridge). For a lone parent with one child in 2015, the LIM was calculated at $25,498 after taxes were paid (Khanna). Even by this conservative measure, the people I spoke to were living on $6,574 less than that—on a budget in which every dollar makes a significant difference.

The reality of how little money single mothers receiving social assistance are living on is integral to orienting policy and advocacy efforts. The public conversation around social assistance and how people receiving it should spend their money quickly becomes judgmental. From individual welfare caseworkers to broad public narratives, mothers are continuously shamed while receiving insufficient resources (Hunter, this volume). Even making the most perfect, rational choices, the budget is so small that mothers are forced to skip meals or be late paying bills. Many of the choices made by more privileged mothers that are lauded as self-care—such as getting your nails done or hiring a babysitter for a date night—are demonized as wasteful or frivolous when marginalized mothers on social assistance make the same choices. Parents reported that this stigma and judgment make an already difficult situation more stressful.

Mothering When Money's Tight: Striving to Make It Work

Although the numbers and stories from the parents paint a grim picture, they also reported feeling pride in the varieties of strategies they used to make it work. This complexity is important to create a meaningful picture of their mothering; they did not see themselves as helpless victims but rather as active agents striving to overcome structural barriers. It is also important not to romanticize the struggle of marginalized mothers. In a country as rich as Canada, there is no reason that parents should have to make the types of choices they are routinely forced to make (Khanna). It is in this tension between their pride in balancing budgets and the hardship endured from trying to care for their families in such straitened circumstances that some part of their experience can be understood. As the quote in the chapter title describes, the mothers knew that "money isn't everything" and that love and care are integral parts of raising children, but they were also aware that money shapes and constrains so many parenting choices. These tensions were at the heart of many of our conversations.

The mothers reported that not having enough money to make it through a month led to a variety of struggles. Being tight for money led to increased isolation, not having enough food, second-rate childcare options, unsafe and isolated housing options, and difficulties leaving abusive relationships. They made hard choices and moved farther out of the city, away from support networks to more affordable apartments, which subsequently led to more money being spent on transportation. Through trial and error, parents figured out ways to make their budgets work; for example, several parents mentioned attending up to four parenting groups a week so that they could receive $10 food vouchers. This added up to $160 a month to their budget but also took a lot of time and energy travelling all over the city with their children to attend these groups. The mothers benefited from online mommy groups to trade or buy used baby equipment. Several of them also used social media quite extensively to connect with other mothers and create meaningful support networks that decreased their sense of isolation. The mothers were also generous and helped one another out. Paige explained this in terms of struggling for money herself but still pitching in to help others: "We need to help each other; it's not just help yourself, you know? Some people are like that but not me. I'm a low-income family, so I like to help out other moms and help other people that are struggling." These values were grounded in an ethic of care and interdependence that helped make their struggles more liveable.

When asked about how having more money would impact their lives, all of the parents said that it would give them a better range of options for food, housing, and childcare; it would meaningfully decrease stress, as the pain that came from being unable to meet their children's needs was palpable. They wanted their children to not just have winter coats when they needed them; they wanted them to have birthday parties, to play with their friends, and to enjoy after school activities. The parents often made large sacrifices to ensure their children could get experience these events. As discussed by Sara Cantillon and Martina Hutton (this volume), mothers have internalized societal beliefs about the importance of sacrificing for one's children, and they have done everything in their power to shield their children from poverty.

Parents were experts in figuring out how to make things work, but living on a budget with no margin of error is hard. Many of the mothers reported pride in their advocacy skills and adeptness in navigating bureaucracies. For example, Shadae shared her pleasure in getting her five-year-old daughter enrolled in free municipal swimming lessons despite all of the paperwork. However, this was tempered by her subsequent chagrin when a snowstorm after swimming class led to her bus being delayed. Since her daughter was cold and wet and there was no bus in sight, she decided to take a taxi home. Unfortunately, that single taxi ride destabilized her carefully calibrated budget for the whole month. These little expenses that middle-class parents would never notice can cause serious hardship for low-income parents, and since there was no flexibility month-to-month for unexpected expenses, such a month can be very to recover from. Parents are left with limited options, as they try to rebalance a bare-bones budget by not eating for several days, paying rent late, staying with family or friends, or going deeper into debt. Several of the parents talked about how relatively minor unplanned expenses had led to them using their credit cards; they explained how quickly debt spiralled out of control and their hopelessness about being able to repay it, unless their financial situation dramatically improved. Chance reported that she was so happy when she was offered subsidized housing, despite it being in an isolated suburb with little public transportation access. At the time, she had been working a summer job that paid well and was an extension of her college placement, so she had purchased a cheap car and paid the minimum insurance. However, she had a car accident and lost her job just as school was finishing up, and she described the consequences:

> I went from school and working and like everything was so good, and steady income coming in, and then January hit me, and once the car hit me, like, no steady income, no resolutions, like my mind went blank and I was like, "What am I going to do?" and I'm like, "I can't get a part time job because I have no childcare." ... I applied at like six different places. I got like four interviews,

and all of them said to me, "How are you going to get here?" And I'm like, "I don't know," and they're like, "You understand you're applying for an evening shift that goes from eight o'clock to like three a.m., right?"

The precarious nature of the balancing act becomes devastatingly apparent in her narrative, as she reported struggling to even pay the minimum interest on her credit card every month. Her choice to take subsidized housing meant that she needed a car, and while she was working, this was manageable. However, as soon as she lost her temporary daytime job and her car, she could no longer get evening retail jobs, as she had no childcare, and even if she could have arranged it, she no longer had a car, which she needed for late night shifts. All of the single parents highlighted the intersection between lack of resources and lack of safe, affordable childcare. They also cited the lack of flexible childcare hours, or the lack of money to pay for a caregiver, as something that impeded their ability to get jobs. As Shadae explained, "Many of the jobs I'm qualified for aren't traditional nine-to-five jobs, so I can't even apply because I have no one to watch my daughter." Struggles with childcare also affected what courses they could take, as several mothers needed to take two-hour transit rides to reach their postsecondary institutions, which meant they could only able take courses offered in the middle of the day. Despite their ingenuity and resourcefulness, these parents' lack of resources led to serious struggles, and all of them were aware that they were being closely monitored and any mistake could trigger further CPS intervention.

Increased Risk of CPS Involvement

Although the mothers' concerns that poverty would put them at increased risk of CPS involvement may, at first, seem exaggerated, the statistics and experiences of marginalized mothers are quite clear. Using myself as an example, as a white, middle-class girl, I was ignorant of how CPS operated, and I never knew of any CPS involvement within my community. This is not to say that I didn't have friends who experienced abuse or who had parents that struggled with substance use or mental health, but rather that CPS was not present in my community due to our intersecting privilege. Violence in the lives of children is common; one in three Canadian adults reports having experienced or witnessed abuse in their childhood, which would be grounds for CPS involvement with a family, yet only 7.6 per cent report any involvement with CPS (Afifi et al.). Alarmingly, of that small percentage, the families with CPS involvement are disproportionately poor, Indigenous, Black, racialized, and/or led by single mothers (King et al.; Roberts; Fallon et al.; Fong). A lack of financial resources puts parents at risk for CPS involvement in a variety of ways, including accusations of neglect and increased surveillance. For example, a parent who leaves an abusive partner and can afford an independent rental unit will never become involved with CPS. However, a parent who needs to move to a domestic violence shelter will find that CPS is automatically called and that staff at the shelter observe their parenting around the clock. Similarly, the more parents interact with helping professionals that have a legal obligation to contact CPS if there is even a suspicion of neglect or abuse, the more likely it is that CPS will become involved (Fong). These are just a couple examples of how living in poverty can lead to CPS involvement. This connection between poverty and CPS points to a frustrating contradiction that even as the neoliberal state pulls back from providing basic income support, it simultaneously invests in punitive functions, creating situations in which the apparatus to investigate marginalized families grows while the infrastructure to support them shrinks.

The Paradoxical Role of the Neoliberal State

The women I spoke to knew that as young mothers, they were constantly scrutinized and held to impossible standards, especially since they fell outside of racist, colonial, classist and ageist ideals of motherhood (Turnbull; O'Reilly; Lovrod, Bustamante, and Domshy, this volume). Furthermore, they were hyperaware that failure to maintain those standards could lead to the loss of their children. Alisha spoke about trying to keep her toddler's clothes clean at all times, an almost impossible task, and Shadae talked about parenting differently in public in order to avoid tantrums. Dirty clothes and embarrassing toddler meltdowns are part of most parents' experiences, yet for parents who are disproportionately targeted by CPS, this could bring allegations of neglect, attachment issues, and abuse (Miller et al.). Being poor also means parenting in public more than more privileged parents. Whether in public transit, cramped apartment buildings, laundromats, or different social service agencies, there are simply more eyes on poor mothers, whereas those mothers who have a car, live in a detached house, and have no need to access social services do not face such scrutiny. This heightened visibility—combined with increased stigma for mothers who are not married, straight, white, middle class, or of the appropriate age—leads to constantly having to perform as the perfect mother (Rebecca Wallace, this volume). The stress of constantly having to make difficult parenting choices based on the lack of money, while constantly being judged and found wanting based on stereotypes rather than actual parenting, had a profound impact on the mothers. A study in Oregon found that "This issue [stress] was particularly pronounced in communities of color and suggested that the need for public assistance and child maltreatment become blurred in the minds of mandated reporters"(Miller et al. 1637). Many, if not all, mothers feel the pressure to be perfect, but for marginalized mothers, the judgment is external as well as internal and can lead to devastating outcomes if they perform less than perfectly in front of the wrong person.

This stress occurs without CPS involvement; the constant vigilance of trying to avoid having them called becomes even more stressful when a mother is already involved with CPS. Matthew explained that despite being confident in his own parenting, "It's a heavy load on your shoulders, just feeling there's a government worker looking at you and your child. For what? Trust me; it brings stress." Matthew knew that despite his son being happy and healthy, the fact that he was a young, poor, and racialized father, who had grown up in CPS care himself, meant that he was automatically positioned as a risk to his child.

The heightened policing of marginalized families is where some of the hypocrisy of neoliberal discourse about shrinking the state becomes apparent. In actuality, neoliberalism entails a decrease in supportive functions—such as income support, housing, and childcare—but an increase in punishing functions, such as the police, immigration enforcement, and CPS (Bergen and Abji). In the American context, Dorothy Roberts discusses the impact on Black families: "Focusing on the regulation of black mothers brings to the fore the child welfare system as a critical institution of social supervision, on a par with workfare and prisonfare ... [the child welfare system] reflects a political choice to investigate and blame mothers for the cause of startling rates of child poverty and other forms of disadvantage rather than to tackle their societal roots. " (1778). The Canadian context is similar; Nico Trocmé and colleagues reviewed the changes in CPS investigations in Ontario between 1993 and 1998, during which time there was a doubling of neglect cases. This dramatic increase was attributed to cuts to social assistance rates by 21 per cent in Ontario in 1995 (Trocmé et al.). In 2013, the second largest reason for CPS to become involved with a family was neglect, at 24 per cent of cases (Fallon et al.). Although neglect can be a serious form of child abuse in which parents actively withhold necessities from their children, the vast majority of cases involved with CPS are neglect due to poverty. Parents are blamed for issues like inadequate housing, insufficient food, or other concerns stemming from a lack of income due to systemic failings rather than abusive intent. This means that almost a quarter of CPS cases could be resolved by supporting parents in accessing sufficient resources to provide for their children.

In the United States, a study found that "child protection intervention is most frequent in states with punitive social policy regimes and suppressed in states with social policy regimes that favour redistributive interventions" (Edwards 590). This relationship over time can be found in Canada as well; social supports continue to be cut, and the total number of CPS investigations went from 44,900 in 1993 to 64,800 in 1998, and all the way up to 125,281 in 2013, the most recent year for which statistics are available (Trocmé et al.; Fallon et al.). There are a variety of reasons for this dramatic increase—most notably, changes to legislation regarding witnessing intimate partner violence and a decrease in the level of risk that is needed to make a report (Fallon et al.). These changes point to a willingness by the state to increase its jurisdiction in a punitive area while pulling back from responsibility for the social safety net. The mothers were acutely aware that they were being held to high standards for their parenting with insufficient resources. When asked about what sort of systemic supports would be useful, the mothers had a variety of suggestions.

Structural Changes

The young mothers I interviewed came up with a variety of concrete suggestions for structural and policy changes, which would support their parenting and reverse some of the negative impacts stemming from cuts to services. In general, the mothers would have preferred to have good work and be able to provide for their families without recourse to any type of social assistance. They knew, and had internalized to varying degrees, the public narratives about social assistance and would have preferred to work good jobs and make sufficient money to make ends meet. However, they also clearly identified the unjust nature of social assistance—since it falls so far below minimums, such as the living wage or the LIM—as well as the large gap between the wealthiest Canadians and the poorest ones. Paige argued the following:

I think they need to have more resources for young parents especially, because we're the ones that are suffering the most. Like there's people living in mansions and here we are basically eating off the floor.... Welfare doesn't really give you anything; they need to bring up everything for low-income families basically because right now it's not fair for our children, and for us too.

Other mothers I interviewed echoed this sentiment and believed that people with power clearly did not understand how hard it is for one person to survive, let alone raise children, on so little money. Chance maintained that politicians could not possibly understand how little money they were asking families to live on, and Shadae said that she would like to see politicians try to support their families for a week on her budget.

The mothers also had a wide range of proposals for how people in power could contribute to improving their financial situation and the overall context of their mothering. The unanimous suggestion was increasing the amount of money they received, through a variety of strategies. Some of the policies the mothers suggested included implementing a basic income as described by Jenni Mays (this volume); others suggested increasing social assistance rates and raising the minimum wage. The next most popular suggestion was the need for free, flexible childcare. Especially for single mothers, it was impossible to pursue education or get a job without free, or affordable, high-quality childcare. Many of the mothers also mentioned the shift in the economy from traditional nine-to-five jobs to service industry jobs, which necessitate early morning or evening work and provide no childcare. Mothers were creative and found ways to navigate the lack of supports; they practiced childcare swapping with other parents and got support from grandparents, their ex-partners, and godparents, but they felt that these were not permanent, reliable solutions.

Many of the parents also advocated for an increase in high-quality and well-located subsidized housing. By the end of 2015, cutbacks had led to a situation in which there were 95,280 households, or 173,816 people, on the wait list for subsidized housing in Toronto, and this number has only grown (Housing Connections). As well, the mothers wanted the units located in a variety of neighbourhoods, preferably close to public transportation so that they could remain connected to family and other social supports as well as to schooling and employment opportunities. They also strongly advocated for the existing housing stock to be renovated and maintained. Matthew and Alicia were lucky to live in subsidized housing but had struggled with neglected and poorly maintained housing. Matthew discussed his experience:

The wall fell off over there on [son's] room, on the outside, like the bricks, like boom, thousands of bricks came falling down.... It really shook up the building, and news reporters, police, everybody came and they interviewed me and stuff. I told them how I felt about it and what could be done and stuff. But after that, after the police and the news reporters and everybody left, all the constructions workers left! ... So my number one thing would be housing.

Matthew and Alicia were both actively involved in advocating for their building to be maintained; they talked and organized with their neighbours and spoke with reporters, but they felt trapped and forced to choose, for economic reasons, to continue living in subsidized housing that they feared was fundamentally unsafe for themselves and their child. Tragedies like the Grenfell Towers fire in London illustrate how dangerous it can be when corners are cut, and they serve an important role in the public conversation around subsidized housing and the importance of maintaining the existing housing stock (Shildrick). However, Matthew and Alicia's experience shows how stressful it is to live with more mundane but still dangerous issues, such as mould and crumbling infrastructure. Their experience points to the importance of not cutting costs when building units and committing to maintaining housing after it has been built.

The parents also strongly advocated for affordable, efficient, stroller, and wheelchair accessible transportation. Most imagined this as improved public transportation, but Chance also advocated for access to a car for those living in isolated suburbs. They also wanted support in accessing good, permanent, and fulltime employment and wanted universal healthcare expanded to include free dental care, mental health support, and prescription drug coverage. Chantall also understood the concept of health to include access to healthy, affordable food. Another proposal from Jessica, which was inspired from her own childhood before the austerity cuts of the 1990s, was to increase access to free after-school programs, such as dance, homework and science clubs. Jessica strongly advocated for their return and talked about how they had increased her confidence, provided stability, and offered her enrichment opportunities that she would not have otherwise had. Moreover, several of the parents suggested free postsecondary education as a way for mothers to have access to education and better jobs without being burdened by massive debt.

For the most part, structural solutions for mothers and families living below the poverty line are not complicated; they need more money. As income inequality rises, it becomes increasingly important to commit, as a society, to ensuring a minimum standard below which it is unacceptable for people to live. The mothers have valuable insights into the sorts of changes that need to be made at the policy level to support their families. Their visions provide inspiration for what it could look like for the state to reengage with social supports in a meaningful way and how beneficial that would be for mothers and their families.

Endnotes

1. In accordance with my intersectional feminist framing, participants chose whether to use a pseudonym. Jessica and Chantall are pseudonyms; all other names are their own.

Works Cited

Afifi, T. O., et al. "Relationship between Child Abuse Exposure and Reported Contact with Child Protection Organizations: Results from the Canadian Community Health Survey." *Child Abuse and Neglect*, vol. 46, 2015, pp. 198-206. *Scopus*, doi:10.1016/j.chiabu.2015.05.001.

Aldridge, Hannah. *How Do We Measure Poverty?* Maytree Foundation, May 2017, maytree.com/wp-content/uploads/How_do_we_ measure_poverty_May2017.pdf. Accessed 22 July 2020.

Bergen, Heather, and Salina Abji. "Facilitating the Carceral Pipeline: Social Work's Role in Funneling Newcomer Children from the Child Protection System to Jail and Deportation." *Affilia,* vol. 35, no. 1, 2019, pp. 34-48.

Bergen, Heather. *Teen Moms Talk Back: Young Mothers Strategizing Supportive Communities.* 2016, York University, dissertation.

Canada Mortgage and Housing Corporation. "Toronto—Historical Average Rents by Bedroom Type." CMHC www03.cmhc-schl.gc. ca/hmip-pimh/en/TableMapChart/Table?TableId=2.2.11& GeographyId=2270&GeographyTypeId=3&DisplayAs=Table& Geograghy Name=Toronto. Accessed 6 Aug. 2020.

Crenshaw, Kimberlé. "Demarginalizing the Intersection of Race and Sex: A Black Feminist Critique of Anti-discrimination Doctrine, Feminist Theory and Anti-Racist Politics." *University of Chicago Legal Forum,* no. 1, 1989, pp. 139-67.

Csiernik, Rick, et al. *Practising Social Work Research: Case Studies for Learning.* University of Toronto Press, 2013.

Edwards, Frank. "Saving Children, Controlling Families: Punishment, Redistribution, and Child Protection." *American Sociological Review,* vol. 81, no. 3, June 2016, pp. 575-95.

Fallon, Barbara et al. "Exploring Alternate Specifications to Explain Agency-Level Effects in Placement Decisions Regarding Aboriginal Children: Further Analysis of the Canadian Incidence Study of Reported Child Abuse and Neglect Part C." *Child Abuse & Neglect,* vol. 49, 2015.

Fallon, Barbara et al. *Ontario Incidence Study of Reported Child Abuse and Neglect- 2013 (OIS-2013).* Child Welfare Research Portal, 2015.

Fong, Kelley. "Child Welfare Involvement and Contexts of Poverty: The Role of Parental Adversities, Social Networks, and Social Services." *Children and Youth Services Review,* vol. 72, Jan. 2017, pp. 5-13.

Government of Ontario. *Minimum Wage Increase, Ontario,* 26 Jan. 2018, www.ontario.ca/page/minimum-wage-increase. Accessed 22 July 2020.

Housing Connections. *Housing Connections—Annual Statistical Report 2015. Housing Connections,* 2016, www.housingconnections.ca/pdf/ annualReports/2015/2015%20Annual%20Report.pdf. Accessed 22 July 2020.

Hulko, Wendy. "Operationalizing Intersectionality in Feminist Social Work Research: Reflections and Techniques from Research with Equity-Seeking Groups." *Feminisms in Social Work Research: Promise and Possibilities for Justice-Based Knowledge,* edited by Stephanie Wahab, Ben Anderson-Nathe, Christina Gringeri, Routledge, 2015, pp. 69-89.

Khanna, Anita. *2017 Report Card on Child and Family Poverty in Canada: A Poverty-Free Canada Requires Federal Leadership.* Family Service Toronto, Nov. 2017, campaign2000.ca/wp-content/uploads/ 2017/11/EnglishNationalC2000ReportNov212017.pdf. Accessed 22 July 2020.

King, Bryn, et al. "Factors Associated with Racial Differences in Child Welfare Investigative Decision-Making in Ontario, Canada." *Child Abuse & Neglect,* vol. 73, 2017, pp. 89-105. *Scholars Portal Journals,* doi:10.1016/j.chiabu.2017.09.027.

Miller, K. M., et al. "Individual and Systemic/Structural Bias in Child Welfare Decision Making: Implications for Children and Families of Color." *Children and Youth Services Review,* vol. 35, no. 9, 2013, pp. 1634-42.

O'Reilly, Andrea. *Matricentric Feminism: Theory, Activism, and Practice.* Demeter Press, 2016.

Roberts, Dorothy. "Complicating the Triangle of Race, Class and State: The Insights of Black Feminists." *Ethnic and Racial Studies,* vol. 37, no. 10, 2014, pp. 1776-82.

Shildrick, Tracy. "Lessons from Grenfell: Poverty Propaganda, Stigma and Class Power." *Sociological Review,* vol. 66, no. 4, July 2018, pp. 783-98.

Tiessen, Kaylie. *Making Ends Meet: Toronto's 2015 Living Wage. Canadian Centre for Policy Alternatives,* 2015, www.policyalternatives.ca/sites/ default/files/uploads/publications/Ontario%20Office/2015/04/ CCPA-ON_Making_Ends_Meet.pdf. Accessed 22 July 2020.

Trocmé, Nico, et al. *The Changing Face of Child Welfare Investigations in Ontario: Ontario Incidence Studies of Reported Child Abuse and Neglect (OIS 1993/1998)*. OIS 1993/1998, *Centre of Excellence for Child Welfare*, 2002, cwrp.ca/sites/default/files/publications/en/OIS93-98.pdf. Accessed 22 July 2020.

Turnbull, Lorna A. *Double Jeopardy: Motherwork and the Law*. Sumach Press, 2001.

Chapter Twelve

The Missed Bus: Intersecting Law, Motherhood, Advocacy, and Privilege[1]

Shauna Labman

*T*he *final days of August, and school begins next week. I am looking at my schedule and wondering if I can perch in front of my son's elementary school and count how many kids get off the bus.*

I write here of my own experience with the law as both a lawyer and a mother. The law entangles these dual identities and the relationship between my employment and my family in terms of societal expectations and understandings that move beyond my individual experience. My regular research looks at movement and migration, international law, and the journeys of asylum seekers from points of persecution to safety found across continents. This essay is also about movement but only the travels of my five-year-old son to and from school. It explores our schoolboard's transportation policies and the provincial law that influences those policies and leaves families, most notably mothers, vulnerable.

The law at issue is the Manitoba Public Schools Act. The precise section is 43(1): "In all cases where transportation of pupils is required, it shall be provided for those pupils who would have more than 1.6 kilometers to walk in order to reach school." This is a simple rule to facilitate the safe transport of children to school.

I learned of this law as I prepared for my son to start kindergarten. Kindergarten where I live is half-day, which is a mere 2.5 hours. A common assumption is that parents value kindergarten as free childcare.

Indeed, my daycare offers a half-day, half-price option if a child is in attendance for fewer than four hours a day. The reality of schedules, work distance, and traffic concerns made this option unviable for my family. We enrolled my son in afternoon kindergarten but continued to pay for full-day daycare as well. This is when the 1.6 kilometres distance requirement in Manitoba's Public Schools Act entered my life. My son does not trigger this law. We live 1.2 kilometres from the local school. We picked our neighbourhood partially for this proximity.

We have only 1.2 kilometres from home to school. But no one is home. I am not home. My partner is not home. My children are not home. While my partner and I work, our children, aged two and five, are at a daycare. Daycare is close. Close enough that I breathed a sigh of relief when we finally got into the daycare when my son was four and my daughter was approaching one. Prior to that, I had been driving six kilometres from home to my son's daycare, the only daycare we could get into despite being on waitlists since I was pregnant, and another thirteen kilometres from daycare to work. Driving directly from home to work was also thirteen kilometres, so daycare was an absolute, but necessary, six kilometre detour each way. That I could choose to drive and to detour are privileges and are not an option for many mothers whose experiences are represented in this volume.

The waitlists I had been on since 2011 finally paid off in 2015, when I got the call to place my son, and soon after my daughter, in a neighbourhood daycare a mere three kilometres from our house and almost en route to work. As an aside, Manitoba's daycare waiting lists were approaching fifteen thousand in July 2016, an all-time high (Klowak). Back in 1970, the Royal Commission on the Status of Women Report called for the creation of a national daycare program as women, including mothers, entered the workforce. Four national childcare conferences took place in 1971, 1982, 2004, and 2014; the 1971 event was in Ottawa, and the following three conferences took place in Winnipeg. As I write, childcare waits remain, costs soar and political promises continue.[2]

Having successfully secured childcare, my challenge was now getting my son from care to school. This is where I hit the law and the gendered geographic obstacle course we needed to travel. Rebecca Johnson's "Leaky Woman" guides me in her exploration of the gendered space created by legal regulation (181). Johnson's piece focused on her connection and necessary physical attachment to her children while breastfeeding. She examines the exclusionary consequences that result from liquor licensing regulations that prevent her from nursing her newborn in a pub. Her identity as a mother is quite literally dripping into the analysis. For me, the moment of law's intersection with my motherhood is in the absence of my child and the spatial distance between us. It is my absence, my inability to be present, and the disconnection from my son that bring me up close to the law. But Johnson's work is important because it helps me to situate a personalized local event, and a provincially particular law into a broader analysis of gender, jurisdiction, and injury (184).

Within the Public Schools Act, the reliance on residence reflects a societal understanding that a parent is home to deliver and receive the child. Historically, this was the mother. Joan Williams argues that "Domesticity is a gender system comprising most centrally of both the particular organization of market work and family work that arose around 1780, and the gender norms that justify, sustain, and reproduce that organization.... The ideology of domesticity held that men 'naturally' belong in the market because they are competitive and aggressive; women belong in the home because of their 'natural' focus on relationships, children, and an ethic of care" (1). A mother not only would be home but also needs to be home to facilitate educational transport. Yet the number of Canadian families with a single income earner and a stay-at-home parent decreased from 1,487,000 in 1976 to 493,000 in 2015 (Statistics Canada). I was born in 1977, and in the span of my life, that is almost one million fewer Canadian parents at home. In 1976, fathers accounted for approximately one in seventy of stay-at-home parents in Canada; by 2015, it was one in ten (Statistics Canada). Although the number of stay-at-home mothers has been decreasing yearly since I was born, the number of stay-at-home fathers has increased, even if one in ten is still a significant gap. Nevertheless, the gendered division of labour, with men in the market and women at home, has changed, resulting in fewer parents at home, more women at work, and more, but still few, fathers at home.

As a child of privilege in the 1980s, I grew up with both a stay-at-home mother and the notion that I could do anything. Education and a professional career were assumed, and work-life balance was an aspiration. Formal barriers to my participation were long passed;

assumptions and stereotypes were tackled, and strong feminist scholars were challenging the foundations of the public-private divide before I started law school (Boyd 5-8). My assumption when I encountered the 1.6 kilometre requirement was, thus, that the provincial law and school board policy that ignored the realities of childcare and the residence of school-aged children outside the home during the day was a simple oversight. Indeed, the provincial law that was confronting me had not changed since it was introduced in 1959 (Statutes Manitoba section 35(3)).[3]

On March 14, 2016, I presented as part of a delegation to the Winnipeg School Division Board of Trustees to discuss whether the distance requirement could encompass either the residence or daycare location for transportation criteria (WSD, "Building/Transportation" 25). The policy at the time, "EEA Transportation of Pupils," had been in operation since the last revision on May 7, 2007:

2. DISTANCE REQUIREMENTS 2.1 Daily transportation to and from school as provided for in the Board Policy statement, sub-sections 1.3, 1.4, 1.5, and 1.6 is subject to the following requirements: (a) that in all cases the resident address of the pupil shall be used to determine the eligibility of a student to be transported; (b) that all measurements shall be from the nearest point of the residence property to nearest point of public access to the school grounds; (c) that the minimum distance for elementary pupils to qualify shall be as follows: Kindergarten— Grade 6–1.6 kilometers (1 mile). (WSD, "Building/Trans-portation" 30)

Nothing in the 2007 policy referenced the reality that often kindergarten children do not require transportation to and from their residence but from their daycare where they spend the remainder of the work day. My presentation offered the simple proposal to recognize the exceptional circumstances of half-day kindergarten and to assess transportation eligibility from daycare locations (still within catchment but beyond 1.6 kilometres). Other school divisions in Winnipeg had already adopted similar policies (St. James-Assiniboia School Division).

The relationship between law and the resulting public policy is interesting here. The school division is bound by the provincial law and creates policy accordingly. When I first contacted my local school trustee in March 2016 with my concerns, she replied, "It is important to understand that the requirements and provisions for bussing are provincially legislated.... I agree that the provincial mandates have not moved with the times" (Naylor). I, therefore, contacted the provincial minister of education. I received a response from a staff member stating the following:

The Winnipeg School Division is the local authority for decision making and for policy development when considering the extension of school bus transportation service levels beyond the minimum legislated requirements of *The Public Schools Act* and regulations. Therefore, your request for an alternate transportation arrangement is appropriately left with the division for a response. (Hagen)

Although both responses are technically accurate, they combine into a game of issue avoidance, which left me feeling like the monkey in the middle, unable to catch the ball. The province could amend the law and the school division could change the policy beyond provincial requirements. Neither was willing.

The question of childcare only further muddies the regulation. As the board members of the Winnipeg School Division repeatedly reminded me, they have neither the jurisdiction nor the budget line to address daycare (Rollins). Although daycare, schooling, and before and after care blur into a juggling act for working parents to ensure learning, supervision and safety; from a legal perspective, these responsibilities are divided. Both childcare and education fall within provincial jurisdiction, but the specific ministries and laws addressing them differ. The distance between my son and his school is nothing compared to the distance between the discussion of education and childcare.

The Winnipeg School Division did, ultimately, change their policy in April 2017 (WSD, "Building and Transportation"). The new policy recognizes that kindergarten-aged children may be in daycare. But before the success of my advocacy is celebrated, the new policy makes the following clear:

3. DISTANCE REQUIREMENTS 3.1 Daily transportation to and from school as provided for in the Board Policy statement, sub-sections 1.3, 1.4, and 1.5 is subject to the following requirements: (a) that in all cases <u>both the resident address/</u>

daycare of the pupil shall be used to determine the eligibility of a student to be transported. (WSD, "EEA Transportation of Pupils")

Eradicating any uncertainty and silencing pushy parents, the new policy made clear that both residence and daycare must be beyond the 1.6 kilometre distance—either/or would simply not do. The new policy also ended the "fee-for-service" option, which enabled children within the 1.6km kilometers to access transportation for a fee. When the revised 2017 policy notice was announced, parents of school-aged, and soon to be school aged, children were enraged.[4] A Facebook group commenced with the name "Access to Transportation in the WSD is a Feminist Issue." Within a month, the group's name was changed to "Access to Transportation within the WSD," so as not to limit the impact or scope of the group. The group administrator explained: "I recognize the word 'feminism' is often maligned, and I did not want to limit the impact the group might have if people interested in the bussing issue and its complexity were affronted by the word 'feminist' in the group's title. I still see this as a largely feminist issue" (Vickers). The policy is an affront to women because of the gendered assumptions on the division of labour, but the "killjoy" (Ahmed) feminist assertion suggested an agenda or implied an exclusion of fathers who had taken on increased parenting responsibilities. The first delegation of parents who presented to the board of trustees following the policy change included four mothers and three fathers (WSD, "Special Board Meeting").

For me, both the name and the name change make sense. I understand. But I don't. This is a feminist issue, and the removal of the word is both disappointing and infuriating. Erin Wunker recognizes this frustration:

The difficulty of trying to articulate the banal frustration upon realizing (again, and again, like a dull hammer on the heart) that mothering and child care are feminized labour. That they are feminized labour is not new. That there are still uphill battles that are being waged in my mind, on my body, and on the sidewalks of cities and the hallways of workplaces is not new. (172)

Sidewalks and workplace hallways are the very locations that pull at me. The letter sent home to parents announcing the policy change recognized that "this will require some families to make adjustments"

(WSD, "Transportation Policy Changes"). The "adjustments" required to get a child from daycare to school or back mid-day require parents to either quit, change, or reduce employment or, alternatively, not to put their children in kindergarten. Neither the parent nor the child is at the forefront of the school division's gaze. If all advocacy efforts fail, the latter option—nonenrolment in kindergarten—will be the reality for my daughter. Children and parents are positioned in a tug of war between the parents' work and their children's schooling. Which is valued? Which is necessary? There is no winner in this.

Quitting or reducing work is the reestablishment of a parent in the home, which is only an option of the privileged. Doreen Massey outlines how "The construction of 'home' as a woman's place has, moreover, carried through into those views of place itself as a source of stability, reliability and authenticity" (180). The Winnipeg School Division Board of Trustees is asking for parents to restabilize the home as a location of reliability and authenticity while refusing to acknowledge the resituating of this source of stability, reliability, and authenticity to the daycare.

With the revised policy, my anger and advocacy moved beyond the circular dance between the school division and the provincial ministry to the media. As a professional advocate, I was both comfortable being interviewed and had the sufficient flexibility in my schedule to be interviewed. I reluctantly became the voice of this personal advocacy within my community of parents. I was interviewed on the radio and by the local television from my office at the university. While my children's photos and artwork were visible during the television interview, I remained apart from them, and my voice as mother and professional blur in the locational representation of privilege. A corresponding online CBC article (Annable) allowed me to see reactions to my arguments. My work was attacked by the commentators, some of whom googled me. They said that I feel "entitled to [my] entitlements," that I was "paid to go to school," and that I "support illegal immigrants." What has this to do with access to transportation? My own roles as mother, refugee advocate, and professor were challenged by my pursuit of this issue in a public forum. My ability to voice particular concerns was twisted into accusations of entitlement and critiques of my unrelated research. In this way, my voice and my arguments were dismissed.

My own identity furthers the assertion that this issue is a private affair beyond the welfare obligations of the state. Katherine Teghtsoonian has suggested that "In Canada, caring for children is an activity that appears to be firmly anchored on the 'private' side of the ideological division between 'public' and 'private'" (177). In the absence of any evolution of the Manitoban law or the school board policies, this judgment will continue. A CBC commentator suggested "Remember babysitters. Retired folks looking for a bit of extra cash. Why should I have to pay for services for you, that my parents paid out of pocket. To [sic] many whiners in today's population" (Annable). Another asked "Why can't they take their own kids?" The simple answer is that, of course, like 75 per cent of other mothers, I work (The Canadian Press). My work positions me to speak and establishes financial stability. Yet because I have the ability to speak, I should be silent. Because I can afford to pay for alternatives, I should not ask for services. But what about those parents and their children who lack a voice and stability (Bergen, this volume)?

I have developed thick skin working in an area of divisive public opinion. The challenges to my parenting pierce deeper. This hurts in ways that rattle me. I long for that idyllic vision of slow walks with my children to school as we discuss the world around us or, more realistically, their obsession with potty humor. Instead, I make rushed exits dodging sticky-handed hugs in the kitchen, and drive across town. But my ideal comes from a position of privilege that is another mother's necessity. Is it a "motherhood sacrifice" to stay home with my children or to leave them to work (Horne and Brietkreuz 4)? Lisa Pasolli and Susan Prentice note that childcare programs prior to 1970 "were designed around the belief that working mothers signaled some kind of family 'failure'" (27). These authors discuss a climate in the 1970s "that remained deeply suspicious of working mothers (or at least, believed that childcare was a private family responsibility)" (28). Although the suspicion has faded, the personal guilt remains. My fierce actions as a mother play out in the law library stacks digging for the origins of the distance provision, and now writing these words, rather than beside my children.

Across this gendered space, my distance from my children disrupts my own sense of self. Why am I spending my time fighting for others to transport my son? Should I either be working or spending time with my children and not stuck in this muddled middle ground? I research refugees and the reach of protection. In the vastness of refugee journeys, filled with inherent risks and numerous tragedies, the distance of

1.6 kilometres in a residential neighbourhood is laughable. It is both absurd and insignificant. Recently, a Ghanaian woman, who was both a mother and a grandmother, died near our border from exposure (in May after so many risked the bitter crossing in winter months) and I end a media email on point to dig into the Public Schools Act. Can I possibly rank importance between my children and desperate strangers? What is the value of my advocacy and agency alongside mothers like those interviewed by Heather Bergen and Lindsay Larios in this volume? How do I navigate and reconcile my roles? My time? My voice?

Erin Wunker's *Notes from a Feminist Killjoy* explores the "chafing positions" of feminist and mother (172) and helps me to locate in the identity blurring space of this narrative. I have workshopped this piece with feminist scholars, and they joked that I should have titled it "The Law Professor Encounters the School Bus." It is oh so true, but where is my motherhood in that title? Where is my child? The distance is too far, and this is not just about me. Wunker closes her work with the recognition of a "false dichotomy" between the personal and the professional and the "crucial places where mothering and feminism bruise against each other until I let them coexist" (187). Here then is my reconciling. My co-existence.

The reverberation against the transportation policy is the expectation that a mother will be home. Johnson asserts that "It is crucial to attend to the stories we tell about those spaces" (187). Her work warns of law's power "to persuade us that the world described in its image is the only world in which we would want to live" (195). Presented with an old law and stubborn policies that fail to recognize my reality or the modern realities of parents, my actual and metaphorical distance from their assumptions is challenged both internally and externally. I am pulled to the sidewalk space to walk my son and back to the page to challenge the law.

Addendum

On October 3 2017, after parents changed schedules, plans, and daycares to either facilitate or opt out of the September start of the school year, the Winnipeg School Division announced a new "courtesy seat policy" to students who do not qualify for transportation. The policy does not apply to noon-hour kindergarten and nursery runs, and it can be cancelled with seven-day notice any time in the school year, if a qualifying student requires the seat.

Endnotes

1. Many thanks go to those who provided feedback during the feminist legal scholars workshop held in Toronto in September 2017 hosted by the *Canadian Journal of Women and the Law* and The Institute for Feminist Legal Studies at Osgoode. Thanks also to the Legal Research Institute at the University of Manitoba, which supported the invaluable research assistance of Segen Andemariam and Anna Tourtchaninova on this piece.

2. A 2017 nationwide study found that childcare fees had risen faster than inflation in 71 per cent of Canadian cities since 2016 and in 82 per cent of them since 2014. Although Manitoba has the second-lowest childcare costs for spots in non-profit subsidized childcare in the country, 75 per cent of respondents in a Manitoba survey still indicated that childcare was too expensive in the province (David Macdonald and Martha Friendly).

3. Though in 1987, the law did take the progressive step of moving to metric measurements, striking out the words "one mile" and replacing this with "1.6 kilometers." (Revised Statutes Manitoba section 43(1)).

4. Parents were advised on March 14, 2017, the day after the board of trustees passed a budget for the 2017-2018 year, which removed the fee for service option. The new policy was not passed until April 10, 2017.

Works Cited

Ahmed, Sara. "Hello Feminist Killjoys!" *Feministkilljoys,* 26 Aug. 2013, feministkilljoys.com /2013/08/26/hello-feminist-killjoys/ Accessed 23 July 2020.

Annable, Kristin. "Winnipeg Parents Irate after New School Bus Policy Leaves Them Stranded." *CBC News,* 29 Mar. 2017, www.cbc.ca/news/canada/manitoba/daycare-winnipeg-school-buses-1.4045050. Accessed 23 July 2020.

Boyd, Susan B. "Introduction." *Challenging the Public/Private Divide,* edited by Susan B. Boyd, University of Toronto Press, 1997, pp. 3-34.

The Canadian Press. "Fewer Canadian Mothers Work Outside Home Than Those in Many Rich Countries." *CBC News,* 4 Aug. 2016, www.cbc.ca/news/business/mothers-work-outside-home-1 .3707227. Accessed 23 July 2020.

Hagen, Chris (Senior Field Officer, Public Transportation Unit, Manitoba Education and Advance Learning). "Kindergarten Transportation Issue." Received by Shauna Labman, 12 Apr. 2016.

Horne, Rebecca M., and Rhonda S. Brietkreuz. "The Motherhood Sacrifice: Maternal Experiences of Child care in the Canadian context." *Journal of Family Studies*, vol. 24, no. 2, 2016, pp. 126-45.

Johnson, Rebecca. "Law and the Leaky Women: the Saloon, the Liquor Licence, and Narratives of Containment." *Continuum: Journal of Media & Cultural Studies*, vol. 19, no. 2, 2010, pp. 181-99.

Klowak, Marianne. "Waiting List for Child Care in Manitoba at All-Time High." *CBC News*, 24 Aug. 2016, www.cbc.ca/news/canada/ manitoba/child-care-wait-list-pat-wege-manitoba-1.3733870. Accessed 23 July 2020.

Macdonald, David, and Martha Friendly. *Time Out Child Care Fees in Canada in 2017*. Canadian Centre for Policy Alternatives, December 2017.

Massey, Doreen. *Space, Place and Gender*. Polity Press, 1994.

Naylor, Lisa (Ward 4 School Trustee). "Re: Kindergarten-Bussing-Daycare." Received by Shauna Labman, 3 Mar. 2016.

Pasolli, Lisa, and Susan Prentice. "Reflect, Regroup, Renew." *Our Schools/Our Selves*, vol. 24, no.4, 2015, pp. 25-33.

Public Schools Act. Continuing Consolidation of the Statutes of Manitoba, c.P250.

Revised Statutes Manitoba, 1987 Supplement, c.26.

Rollins, Sherri (Ward 1 School Trustee). "Re: Kindergarten Bussing." Received by Shauna Labman, 15 Mar. 2016.

St. James-Assiniboia School Division, "EEAA Policy #88356: Student Eligibility for Transportation Services" 25 October 2011.

Statistics Canada. "Changing Profile of Stay-at-Home Parents." *The Daily*. 28 Sept., 2016, www.statcan.gc.ca/pub/11-630-x/11-630-x2016007-eng.htm. Accessed 23 July 2020.

Statutes of Manitoba, 1959. 2nd Session. c.47.

Teghtsoonian, Katherine. "Who Pays for Caring for Children? Public

Policy and the Devaluation of Women's Work." *Challenging the Public/Private Divide,* edited by Susan Boyd, University of Toronto Press, 1997, pp. 113-43.

Vickers, Shannon. "Re: Question/Quote." Received by Shauna Labman, 30 Aug. 2017.

Williams, Joan. *Unbending Gender: Why Family and Work Conflict and What to Do About It.* Oxford University Press, 2001.

Winnipeg School Division. "Building and Transportation Committee Report 2-2017." *Winnipeg,* 10 Apr. 2017, www.winnipegsd.ca/Governance/minutes-and-summaries/Documents/April%2010%202017.pdf. Accessed 23 July 2020.

Winnipeg School Division. "Building/Transportation Committee Meeting." *Winnipeg,* 4 Apr. 2016, winnipegsdca.civicweb.net/document/12882. Accessed 23 July 2020.

Winnipeg School Division. "EEA Transportation of Pupils." *Winnipeg,* 10 Apr. 2017, www.winnipegsd.ca/Governance/policy/Documents/EEA%20-%20Transportation%20of%20Pupils.pdf. Accessed 23 July 2020.

Winnipeg School Division. "Special Board Meeting." *Winnipeg,* 17 Apr. 2017, winnipegsdca.civicweb.net/Portal/MeetingInformation.aspx?Id=220. Accessed 23 July 2020.

Winnipeg School Division. "Policy EEA Transportation of Students-Courtesy Transportation Seats." *Winnipeg,* 3 Oct. 2017, www.winnipegsd.ca/About%20WSD/deptservices/buses-and-transportation / Pages/Courtesy-Transportation-Seats.aspx. Accessed 23 July 2020.

Winnipeg School Division. "Transportation Policy Changes." 14 March 2017, *Document Cloud,* www.documentcloud.org/documents/3526686-Transportation-Policy-Changes.html#document/p1. Accessed 23 July 2020.

Wunker, Erin. *Notes from a Feminist Killjoy: Essays on Everyday Life.* BookThug, 2016.

Chapter Thirteen

Single and Desperate?
Lone Mothers and Welfare

Rachel Lamdin Hunter

The purpose of this chapter is to show how storytelling research approaches can be used to transform ways of working with mothers who are reliant upon welfare. "Welfare," as termed in those Western democracies driven by capitalist directives, is often framed as the provision of services for those in material need. Another use of the word can be applied to the idea of doing well. This application invites consideration of the physical and mental health, as well as the happiness, of human beings. In countries where neoliberal ideas have shaped the form of economic and social directives, formal systems of welfare provision have changed from the recognition of state responsibility for the welfare of its citizens—which is typically associated with Keynesian economics after the Second World War—to a market-driven and businesslike approach to the organization of humanity. Neoliberal advocates for radical global economic and sociopolitical transformations found traction for their ideas in Reaganomics in the United States, Thatcherism in the United Kingdom, and Rogernomics in Aotearoa New Zealand. Such ideas also took root in European and Canadian jurisdictions from the 1980s onwards. Neoliberal directives included the reduction of the direct state provision of services to those in need. User pay systems were used to encourage entrepreneurial, market-driven remedies to meet diverse human needs. Philanthropy would fill the gap between residual state provision and market opportunities (Grant and Humphries). Gender disparities remain in all jurisdictions where neoliberal directives prevail. Mothers' lives have been particularly negatively affected by the changes of welfare provisions and the pressure to find employment under this regime (VandenBeld Giles).

Lone mothers and their children are among those historically deemed to need support under both the postwar welfare system and the later neoliberal regime. The narratives of cause and remedy differ between these two orientations to welfare. The two narratives share concerns about life in single-parent families as beset by vulnerabilities and risks. For children, these supposed risks include behavioural problems, addictions, and crime. The lives of their mothers are characterized by stress, struggle, and deficiency (Amato, "Consequences"). Lone-parent families are typically reported to experience greater material poverty, housing insecurity, and poorer health compared with their two-parent counterparts (Amato, "Consequences"). UNICEF cites poorer health, economic, and social outcomes of families with single parents at the helm, including "a greater risk of dropping out of school, of leaving home early, of poorer health, of low skills, and of low pay" (23). Paul Amato connects "inept parenting by resident single parents" to "negative outcomes among children, including poor academic achievement, emotional problems, conduct problems, low self-esteem, and problems forming and maintaining relationships" ("Impact" 83); he further states that "many single parents find it difficult to function effectively as parents" and are "less emotionally supportive of their children" ("Impact" 83). American policy advisor Ron Haskins reports on "the collapse of the two-parent family" and blames rising poverty rates on the "malign impact" of lone-parent families (134), in numbers described by some scholars as "precipitous" and continuing "unabated" (Ryan et al. 112).

This chapter argues that such depictions are not only inaccurate but also damaging representations of life for many such mothers. Patriarchal arrangements fuse with the radical individualism of neoliberal orientations to make mothers more dependent, as they are unable to operate as independent, self-contained beings, making it difficult for them to care for others and themselves. The feminization of poverty and dependence are evidence of patriarchy in action, culminating in the proportion of women and children living on welfare.

This chapter demonstrates the transformative potential of the application of antenarrative methodologies. These are intended to disrupt the harmful, limited, and limiting narratives of lone mothers as an 'expense' for the social welfare system. Antenarrative also offers yet-to-be told possibilities for mothers and their children. The chapter begins with an explanation of the transformational potential of the antenarrative as described by Margaret Vickers and David Boje. The explanation is followed by two versions of the same short story—one told by the mother, named Susan, and one by the case worker, Alex (names included here are pseudonyms). Subtle shifts between them enable different conversations and outcomes, with new stories made possible. The stories taken together demonstrate how a narratively imagined conduit to potentially life-changing interactions could change policy. The chapter concludes with a challenge to researchers and policymakers to renew the possibilities for improvement of social policies and practice in the interests of maternal and family wellbeing.

The Transformational Potential of Amplifying Antenarratives

The emergence of narrative theory is documented by the need of a form of research inquiry that tells the stories of people in their own words and from their own lived perspectives (Clandinin and Connelly). This form of social analysis considers the many realities people experience daily. A critical reading of those dominant narratives that have served to fabricate, embed, and justify various forms of injustice has transformational possibilities. For Vickers and Boje, dominant narratives that embed prejudices and limitations get in the way of a more just narrative to guide the future. They offer the concept of an "antenarrative," which refers to a "bet [that] a proper narrative can be constituted", in the words of Boje—a prestory or prequel that could take thought and practice into a different direction.

For Vickers, an antenarrative is stimulated by a semifictional con-structed vignette, which stories an alternatively imagined future for the actors in a specific scenario ("Taking a Compassionate Turn" 174). The generation of such antenarratives are widely demonstrated in the work of Boje. The concept of antenarratives and their transformational intent was applied in my PhD research that began with an intention to challenge the dominant narratives about sole parenting I had come to experience personally as destructive, disheartening, and maddeningly untrue.

Narrative methodologies offer the potential to tell people's stories and hear a variety of voices in the sharing of research findings—voices that create possibilities for unpredicted and untold perspectives to be shared (Clandinin and Connelly; Denzin and Lincoln). Both Boje and Vickers recommend antenarratives to use smaller snapshots of a story from individual perspectives, eschewing the coherent, beginning-middle-end narrative in order to air fragments and ideas told "from the middle of things" (Vickers, "Taking a Compassionate Turn" 42). The word "antenarrative" carries a double meaning. First, it is a bet or gamble on where a particular story will be channelled to go and how it may develop and eventually be resolved (Boje 10). Second, an antenarrative is a process that takes place before a grand narrative can be formed; thus, it is a progression directed to bringing about a particular, new ending for the actors. A story told as an antenarrative constitutes a type of prequel, which propagates "transformational potential in the form of writing or talking a new future into being, including many possibilities, some new and untested" (Rosile et al. 558). It is an in-between process, which attends to stories that may otherwise be marginalized or silenced As such, this method of storytelling can be used to funnel the stories of frontline workers including social workers, healthcare practitioners, or teachers into imagined possibilities for new ways of acting and responding. Examples provided by Vickers include the use of constructed vignettes. Stories with aspects of true life-events and/or fiction are woven, told, and retold from different perspectives, with changes made to expression, events, or utterance as the author deems necessary to evoke a response in the reader.

I gathered detailed stories from a small group of research participants with whom I met individually during my PhD fieldwork. The stories these mothers shared with me generated my own reflection concerning the conversations we had. The narrative I demonstrate here as an example of the formulation of an antenarrative is created from a story told to me by one such research participant. The first story is how it was told. The second version reimagines the tale differently. This retelling with its creative amendments opens the way for innovative possibilities to emerge for mothers in which they can thrive.

Story One: Susan

Susan is a single mother. She is out of work and is becoming desperate. Along with Rose, her child, she is hungry. Her isolation and struggle is evident.

Susan

I grit my teeth and square my shoulders as the double doors hum open in front of me. I feel the gaze of the security guard. It's my third time at this office asking for help. I hate asking! Anyone who calls beneficiaries "bludgers" or parasites has clearly never been into one of these offices. It is so horrible and public and exposed, and you feel so small and stupid and gross, even when they are nice to you, which isn't often.

Someone calls my name. He's so young—honestly. He takes my paperwork; studies it for so long that I begin to wonder if I've done it wrong. My stomach churns. He says, "So, what can I do for you this time?" I hesitate, but then I remember the frightened look on Rose's face and the empty fridge. I lift my chin, look him in the eye, and say, "I need an emergency food grant. I got cut from my casual job, and my benefit got stopped. I'm really behind in all my bills. We've got no food. It's just me and my daughter, and I want to apply for a food package or something just to tide us over 'til the next benefit payment." I breathe out and wait.

His name is Alex, according to his name tag. His last name is covered up with a sticker—to prevent harassment I guess. He stares past me and says, "You know you'll have to pay it back, whatever you get today. How will you do that?"

My stomach drops, and I stare. Hot tears prickle behind my eyes. "I can't pay it back. Well, I mean, it'd take a long time. You'd have to take it out of my benefit. But it is not even enough to cover the basics! When would I have to start repaying?" I'm babbling. I take a deep breath and hold it.

Alex focuses on me again. This time he grins. "Just kidding. It's okay. We won't make you pay it back. I was just having a joke with you."

The prickling tears tumble down my cheeks. Relief? Anger? My face flushes and I sigh. What kind of dumb pathetic joke is that? Not even funny. Just cruel. A lame attempt at humour in a grim dark place of desperation and dependence. I sigh again and look around me at the stack of forms beside Alex. Does he do this with every "customer"? What if they (like me) believed him, and he got them to pay the money back into his own account?

Alex is tapping into his computer; he turns away slightly as the printer beside him buzzes while I wait for an answer. He hands me a piece of paper as it emerges, warm from the machine. "Here. The money will be in your account tonight. Okay?" He turns away. Okay? I think. Is that it? All that drama and adrenaline, and it's done? Is any of this okay?

Story Two: Alex

Alex is a 'customer services officer. To Susan he looks like a very young man. Indeed, he is not long out of his training.

Alex

I greet the woman and say, "Hi. I'm Alex. You're... Susan?" I grin. "Take a seat. What brings you here today?" She hesitates. "I need an emergency food grant. I got cut from my casual job, and my benefit got stopped. I'm really behind with my bills. We've got no food. It's just me and my daughter, and I want to apply for a food package or something just to tide us over 'til the next benefit payment."

She breathes out like she's been holding in air for a long time. That's not uncommon around here. People hold in everything for as long as possible. By the time they pluck up the courage—or desperation—to come here and face us, they have probably needed help much earlier but would have been too uncomfortable to ask. I don't blame them. Needing others is so uncool these days. I remember the lecture we had about the history of the old welfare state. Needing help was a fact of life and nothing to be ashamed of. People weren't blamed for their plight. Was it because poverty was so prevalent after the Great Depression? Back then, everybody knew they were only a pay check away from desperation.

Oops! My mind has wandered. She's now looking at me, waiting, wondering what the problem is. I've been told not to think too deeply in this job. But the whole media conversation about beneficiaries and welfare spins my thoughts when I see people who are forced to come here and beg—and these are tax-paying citizens!

I return my focus to Susan. "What happened with your job?" She explains, and again it's very familiar. With a pool of flexible (read: desperate) workers, those companies are pretty cutthroat in their approach to workers—short notice, low pay, take it or leave it. She couldn't do it, so she resigned and lost all her benefit entitlements. Every time she comes here for another meeting, it's more appointments, waiting, and form filling. Not very efficient for a government department trying to save money!

I scroll down my computer screen to see that Susan is not getting some entitlements that she should. Her review date is two weeks from now, but... "If you like, we can do your benefit review now," I suggest. "Maybe your money can increase from today seeing as you're already here."

Susan's eyes cloud with uncertainty. Beneficiaries have been told there is no flexibility in the system. But our new branch manager has told us to be creative and to use terms such as "quality" and "customer service" for our "customers" like Susan.

The relief and gratitude on Susan's face are disarming. I'm only doing my job, and people have a right to decent service, don't they?

Lone Mothers: Surviving or Thriving

In retelling Susan's story through the view of a reconfigured Alex, a new perspective comes into view. This Alex bases his response on relational, thoughtful, and humane service, informed by the basic values of respect and decency. Small aspects of the story are intentionally reworked to demonstrate different interactions. Alex's demeanour shifts from disinterest and vague disapproval to engagement. Some aspects remain the same; for example, looking over Susan's shoulder can be read in different ways—either boredom and inattention or contemplation and deep thought. For Susan, a different Alex is likely to generate a differently shaped view of herself and her situation, a capacity to conduct herself with purpose and positivity and enhanced wellbeing. In the second story Alex's willingness to help reflects such capacity and hope. A new, overhauled welfare system or government initiative is not the focus here. Small interactions conducted with respect, reflexivity, and understanding can produce different outcomes. These differences can be achieved on a daily basis. For institutional purposes that can be construed as moves towards efficiency, effectiveness in the lives of clients results in better organizational outcomes.

Transforming Stories as Activist Research Reporting

The disapproval and indifference of welfare workers noted by recipients are reported by Louise Humpage and is given graphic illustration in the first story. Susan's experience reflects the experiences of mothers in many countries where policies are aimed at encouraging people into paid work despite hardship, lack of suitable employment, and little acceptable or affordable childcare. Such reforms represent a neoliberal reasoning that situates such problems within private (privatized) families (VandenBeld Giles 10).

Most lone-parent families are headed by mothers (OECD 28). Lone mothers, researchers tell us, "have fewer rules, dispense harsher discipline, are more inconsistent in dispensing discipline, provide less supervision, and engage in more conflict with their children" (Amato "Impact" 83). Haskins associates rising costs of social programs used by families with a "depressing effect on child development associated with single parenting and father absence" (147). Dominant narratives of disaster and collapse reinforce his statement that "We must face the fact that we are likely to always have millions of female-headed families" (134). In this grand narrative of risk and disadvantage revealed here, the increased likelihood of lone mothers as recipients of welfare contributes to the exacerbation of their disadvantage and demonization.

Aotearoa New Zealand: A Case in Point

In the late 1980s, Aotearoa New Zealand embraced neoliberal ideologies. Jane Kelsey predicted that these reforms would result in degrading social consequences, and her predictions largely came true, as evidenced by the work of New Zealand's Child Poverty Action Group between 2000 and 2010. In 2013, austerity measures further reduced available social support, rendering those in need less likely to receive necessary assistance. Within such frameworks, customers of the beneficiary industry, (i.e., mothers like Susan) are portrayed as overly dependent users of welfare support and unworthy of basic respect. Alex finds it acceptable to make troubling jokes at a difficult time, give inaccurate information, and ignore Susan's evident distress. Researchers, policymakers, and case workers are charged with "moving people off benefits and into paid work" and are pressured to find solutions to "benefit dependence" (Ministry of Social Development). Sole mothers and their children are understood as problems to be solved rather than as examples of the systemic obstacles to equality of opportunity that neoliberalism creates.

Frontline case workers and welfare officers regularly interact with struggling citizens. Service users report that the treatment they receive from those officials is, at times, rude, punitive, unprofessional, and legally questionable (Morton et al. 43; Lamdin Hunter, "She Watches" 245). Case workers anecdotally disclose the pressure they face to understand and apply complex and changing policies and to discourage or even limit benefit use (Morton et al. 43). Mothers have been ordered to undertake unreasonable or unsafe employment in order to remain eligible for benefit assistance (Sudden 61), which has resulted in news stories and social media commentary about the power-laden relationships between welfare systems, workers, and mothers. The belief that paid work is the only way out of hardship or dependence has been critiqued in New Zealand by Alicia Sudden, echoing work in the United States by Barbarra Ehrenreich. Both authors note the punitive coercion of people into low-wage employment, despite the legitimate barriers posed by family and other commitments. Appropriate paid work is elusive for lone mothers with children, partly due to scarce support and precarious work conditions, including zero-hour contracts and only casual employment opportunities (Lamdin Hunter, "Single-Parent Families 230). And like Susan's experience, such casual employment can come to a sudden end with dramatic consequences for the breadwinner.

Conclusions and Implications: Surviving or Thriving. It is our story to tell into being

Human dependence upon others for welfare and wellbeing is natural. All people move through dependent stages, as infants, as the elderly, or as anyone requiring help to function because of changed circumstances. Among mothers who require assistance, lone mothers and their families are the most visible (Lamdin Hunter, "Single-Parent Families" 228). In most places where the neoliberal market-driven narrative has gained traction, the typical subject of policy and law is assumed to be the rational, competitive individual—self-sufficient, independent, and unencumbered by others (VandenBeld Giles). This construct, informed by Enlightenment philosophies, was intended to free some men from limited and shackling ideas about themselves and life. The continued application of this construct to women and children is problematic; they are deeply and necessarily entwined with each other (Lamdin Hunter, *"She Watches"* 134).

The antenarrative story I present refers to the welfare meeting between a mother and a worker, taking place as a prequel to events in the mother's life, which contribute to the grand narrative of vulnerability and risk. The retelling of the story shows previously unseen ways in which the meeting could unfold differently for the mother, her child, and the worker. For organizations that act punitively, creative texts producing antenarrative threads of possibility offer possible ways to respond differently to service users—in this case, mothers.

Between each of the narratives, Susan's words and the outcome of the predicament remain constant, insofar as the approval of the emergency grant is concerned. Yet the unfolding of the story, the antenarrative, demonstrates shifts that signify different possibilities for Susan and Alex. The stories constitute antenarratives, as they recount episodes from "before the narrative" of one's life (Vickers, "Antenarratives" 175). The "alternative responses, understandings, and meanings" (Vickers, "Taking a Compassionate Turn" 53) used in telling a semifictional story signal potentially transformative situations for actors. In an organizational context, the raising of silenced voices potentially leads to "compassionate and workable situations" (Vickers, "Taking a Compassionate Turn" 51) for those in the story by providing a 'catalyst for inspiration" as well as "a trigger for new ways of looking at things" (Vickers, "Taking a Compassionate Turn" 42). The shifts open new possibilities for the system and all those within it.

Antenarrative storytelling has the potential to disrupt structural power inequalities by highlighting powerful effects of language in the evocation of life stories. Small shifts in expression have reworked the plotline to emerge in a more just way. The boundaries of storytelling have been extended to transform as well as recount people's experiences. Experimenting with these new possibilities in stories is one of many ways to address the survival of mother-led households and promote thriving.

The space between surviving and thriving takes many forms. An instantaneous change in circumstances or a gradual shift of social and economic situation is possible. Equally possible are intricate shifts in perception and the revised telling of old stories, with new plot lines and twists as well as different meanings and new interpretations. These reimaginings make space for improving the wellbeing of mothers. Storytelling is not merely a method of reporting a value-free event. Storytelling has constitutive power to construct reality and create versions of truth that are credible, promising, and hopeful. For families to thrive, new tales of thinking and practices in line with humane relational tactics can engender wellbeing and thriving for lone mothers.

Works Cited

Amato, Paul. "The Consequences of Divorce for Adults and Children." *Journal of Marriage and Family*, vol. 62, no. 4, 2000, pp. 1269-87.

Amato, Paul. "The Impact of Family Formation Change on the Cognitive, Social, and Emotional Wellbeing of the Next Generation." *The Future of Children,* vol. 15, no. 2, 2005, pp. 75-96.

Boje, David. *Storytelling Organizational Practices: Managing in the Quantum Age.* Taylor & Francis, 2014.

Clandinin, D., and F. Connelly. *Narrative Inquiry: Experience and Story in Qualitative Research.* Jossey-Bass, 2000.

Denzin, Norman, and Yvonna Lincoln. *The Landscape of Qualitative Research.* Thousand Oaks: Sage, 2013.

Ehrenreich, Barbara. *Nickle and Dimed.* Henry Holt Publishers, 2001.

Grant, Suzanne, and Maria Humphries. "Critical Evaluation of Appreciative Inquiry: Bridging an Apparent Paradox." *Action Research,* vol. 4, no. 4, 2006, pp. 401-18.

Haskins, Ron. "The Family Is Here to Stay—Or Not." *The Future of Children,* vol. 25, no. 2, 2015, pp. 129-53.

Humpage, Louise. "'A Common Sense of the Times?' Neo-Liberalism and Changing Public Opinion in New Zealand and the UK." *Social Policy and Administration,* vol. 50, no. 1, 2015, pp. 79-98.

Kelsey, Jane. *The New Zealand Experiment: A World Model for Structural Adjustment?* Auckland University Press with Bridget Williams Books, 1995.

Lamdin Hunter, Rachel. *"She Watches Over Her Household": Wellbeing of Mothers and Children in Motherled Households.* 2017. University of Waikato, PhD dissertation.

Lamdin Hunter, Rachel. "Single-Parent Families, Mother-Led Households, and Wellbeing." *Motherhood and Single-Lone Parenting:*

A Twenty-First Century Perspective, edited by Maki Motapanyane, Demeter Press, 2016, pp. 225-42.

Larner, Wendy. "Guest Editorial: Neoliberalism?" *Environment and Planning D: Society and Space*, vol. 21, 2003, pp. 509-12.

Ministry of Social Development New Zealand (MSD). "More People into Work and Out of Dependency." *Ministry of Social Development*, www.msd.govt.nz/about-msd-and-our-work/publications-resources/corporate/annual-report/2013-2014/ministry-outcomes/more-people-into-work.html. Accessed 23 July 2020.

Morton, Kim, et al. *Access to Justice for Beneficiaries: A Community Law Response*. Community Law Canterbury. 2014.

Organization for Economic Co-operation and Development (OECD). *Doing Better for Families*. OECD Publishing, 2011.

Rosile, Grace, et al. "Storytelling Diamond: An Antenarrative Integration of the Six Facets of Storytelling in Organization Research Design." *Organizational Research Methods*, vol. 16, no. 4, 2013, pp. 557-80.

Ryan, Rebecca et al. "Associations between Family Structure Change and Child Behavior Problems: The Moderating Effect of Family Income." *Child Development*, vol. 86, no. 1, 2015, pp. 112-27.

Sudden, Alicia. *Putting Wellbeing Back into Welfare: Exploring Social Development in Aotearoa New Zealand from Beneficiaries' Perspectives*. 2016. Victoria University of Wellington, PhD dissertation.

United Nations Children's Fund (UNICEF). *An Overview of Child Wellbeing in Rich Countries: A Comprehensive Assessment of the Lives and Wellbeing of Children and Adolescents in the Economically Advanced Nations*. Report Card No. 7. UNICEF, 2007.

VandenBeld Giles, Melinda, editor. *Mothering in the Age of Neoliberalism*. Demeter Press, 2014.

Vickers, Margaret. "Taking a Compassionate Turn for Workers with Multiple Sclerosis (MS): Towards the Facilitation of Management Learning." *Management Learning*, vol. 42, no. 1, 2011, pp. 49-65.

Vickers, Margaret. "Antenarratives to Inform Health Care Research: Exploring Workplace Illness Disclosure for People with Multiple Sclerosis (MS)." *Journal of Health and Human Services Administration*, vol. 35, no. 2, 2012, pp. 170-206.

Chapter Fourteen

Mothering, Welfare and Political Economy of Basic Income in Australia: Potentials for Mothers with Disabilities

Jenni Mays

> "I thought he wouldn't follow me [interstate].... He found me in a shelter on the weekend.... He was doing things about threatening to turn up at my son's school. I was very angry that the shelter workers wouldn't let me keep my son at home.... I was ineligible for government assistance. Very over stretched services. You've really got to be in crisis. So I moved back into his house. He started being violent within the first week."
> —Sarah[1]

D omestic violence continues to be a pressing social problem in modern society. As the above excerpt suggests, for mothers with disability, domestic violence represents a complex inter-action between personal and political dimensions, in which meeting basic need (material, social, and political) is challenging. For these mothers, domestic violence is compounded by structural dimensions of gender, disability, and the broader political economy of neoliberalism. Neoliberalism upholds the preeminence of economic over social objectives and subscribes to a market-oriented economy (deregulation of markets, privatization of public services, and labour market adjustments) and society. The dominance of neoliberalism in Australia has eroded the social protection mechanisms and welfare safety nets required by the most socially and economically vulnerable groups (Mays, *Disability, Citizenship*). Over time, these policies have had a profound impact on mothers with disability, demonstrated by the tightening of eligibility to social protection (Watts 69) as well as a decreasing ethos of social justice underpinning social policies.

Inequalities and poverty gaps are widening rather than closing, particularly in advanced Western capitalist economies (as in Australia and Canada) (Piketty 232). This widening gap continues, despite neoliberal claims (and promises) of strong economic growth, strong economies, and wealth generation (Mays, *Disability, Citizenship*; Piketty). Australia's poverty rate has risen markedly above the Organization for Economic Co-operation and Development (OECD) average (11.3 per cent), with 14.4 per cent of Australians living in (relative) poverty (Alvaredo et al. 5; Whiteford 92). Yet Australia's overall welfare expenditure remains persistently below the OECD average, which has generated higher levels of economic insecurity, precarity, and increased income inequality over time. These increasing levels are associated with labour market restructuring, a rise of automation in conjunction with decline in fulltime jobs as a proportion of the labour market, an increase in casual employment, and a rise in long-term unemployment (Whiteford; Hague et al.). Precarious employment is reflected in the changing nature of the labour market from permanent, secure, and well-remunerated jobs to highly precarious, insecure, and often underremunerated and low-status jobs (Whiteford 92). Structural and social inequalities have grown substantially under neoliberalism, and in turn reduced egalitarian collective responses. The neoliberal pursuit of activation policies (welfare-to-work requirements) have constructed attachment to the labour market and work as the only policy response to inequality and poverty, thereby silencing socially just and collectivist alternatives (Alvaredo et al.; Hague et al.).

The growing concern for increasing structural inequities and deteriorating social conditions (seen in poor working conditions) have prompted calls by academics and activists for alternative policy measures based on egalitarianism that offer greater social protection to all people in society. The insights drawn from policy discussions on alternative universal models of basic income (BI) support reveal possibilities for securing freedom, autonomy, and dignity through poverty reduction, fairer wealth distribution, and gender equality (Klein et al.; Mays, "Feminist Disability Theory"; *Disability, Citizenship*). For mothers with disability experiencing domestic violence, exploring the potential of universal BI to redress poverty and structural inequalities is crucial for determining whether such a scheme can indeed provide greater economic and social security and enhanced freedom. There is a limited literature exploring the connection between mothers with disability, domestic violence, BI, and social protection. Such a critical exploration allows us to understand the feasibility of a universal and socially just alternative, which contrasts with the current targeted social protection system.

Using a feminist disability social theory lens, this chapter critically analyses two BI ethical principles—distributive justice (meeting basic need) and freedom from the stigmatizing effects of categorization—to determine its potential for securing the socioeconomic freedom of mothers with disability experiencing domestic violence (Mays et al., *Neoliberal Frontiers* 4). In employing qualitative data from my previous study[2] on mothers with physical disability (some of whom identify as having mental health issues) experiencing domestic violence in Australia, this chapter explores whether there is a case for BI in securing just outcomes for mothers with disability.

Backdrop of Structural Violence in the Australian Political Economy

The lived experience of mothers with disability experiencing domestic violence involves extreme poverty, economic hardship, injustice, and unequal gendered power relations. For many mothers with disability, the gendered nature of the violence is demonstrated in the interaction between gender, disability, and mothering dimensions (Garland-Thomson; Hague et al.; Harpur and Douglas; Mays "Feminist Disability Theory"). As one participant from my early study noted, "I was from a lower socioeconomic group ... working in a factory at the time.... [After I left my husband and work because of my disability] ... I didn't have enough money for food ... after paying all my bills ... I was depending on people". Acknowledging the interrelating identities for women—including gender, disability, sexual orientation, ethnicity, and age, together with their identity as mothers—provides insight into the experience of structural violence and oppression in the domestic sphere.

Compared with women without disability, women with disability, particularly mothers, have a greater likelihood of encountering violence (approximately 37.3 per cent) (Harpur and Douglas 408). Domestic violence centres on the exercise of power and control by one person over another in a domestic setting through the use of coercion, force, or threat and, consequently, results in harm, oppression, and disadvantage to the other person (Lockton and Ward 7). Domestic violence can incorporate physical, sexual, psychological, spiritual, and verbal abuse (Lockton and Ward 7). Dominant features consistently identified in the literature include social isolation, economic deprivation, and enforced dependency by a perpetrator, as a means of maintaining power and control (Lockton and Ward; Morley and Dunstan). Material dependence and control, together with gendered and/or disablist social relations and social forces (such as constructs of the traditional family), prevents mothers with disability from leaving a violent situation (Hague et al.; Lockton and Ward; Morley and Dunstan).

Disability and gender inequalities construct and legitimize notions of male privilege, dominance, and entitlement, which are reflected at the political and societal levels through restrictive policies, such as welfare-to-work policies (Morley and Dunstan 45). Inequality is exacerbated for mothers with disability who also experience higher levels of violence than mothers without disability, who also have low levels of reporting an abusive incident or having perpetrators prosecuted (Frohmader and Ricci 27). The prevalence of structural gender-based violence leads to a heightened exposure to abuse and exploitation, a subordinate social position, and exclusion from the labour market (Frohmader and Ricci; Morley and Dunstan). For mothers with disability in a violent relationship, there is a greater likelihood of being reported to child protection services and having their child removed from their care and put into the foster care system, as compared to other parents. The disability-gender interaction is predominant in instances in which the removal centres on concerns based on the mother's disability experience, not substantiated child neglect (Frohmader and Ricci 27). Despite some recent advancements in gender wage parity, mothers with disability continue to encounter wage gaps and experience interrupted career trajectories (created by her disability and/or having children); they can typically only access insecure, highly causal, or part-time work (Apps; Commonwealth of Australia).

The Australian Welfare State and Mothers with Disability

The Australian system of social protection provides social security through income support (pensions and allowances) and social services. It originally functioned as a safety net to prevent poverty and inequality. The Australian Commonwealth government is charged with the statutory responsibility for implementing income-support policies through the social security system. The provisions relevant to mothers with disability include the disability pension, single parents' pension, carers' pension, and the unemployment benefit (Whiteford 91). Notably, the targeted nature of income support means different rates of payment exist between pensions (which tend to be higher) and allowances/benefits (which are at lower rates) (Whiteford 91; see also Itaborai, this volume). Mothers with disability continue to live below the poverty line (on average AUD$135 per week below the poverty line) and often remain outside of the labour market (Australian Council for Social Services [ACOSS], "Poverty in Australia" 12).[3] In Australia, there are around three million people (13.3 per cent of the Australian population, including approximately 739,000 children) experiencing significant poverty and extreme financial hardship (ACOSS, "Poverty in Australia" 6). Approximately 60 percent of those whose income falls in the lowest 20 per cent of households rely on a pension or allowance as the predominant source of income (ACOSS and University of New South Wales, "Inequality in Australia" 17). The groups overrepresented in the lowest 20 per cent of households by income include sole parents (36 per cent), people with disabilities who received the disability pension, parent payment, or carer payment (36.2 per cent), and unemployed people (77%) (ACOSS and University of New South Wales, "Inequality in Australia" 17). These vulnerable groups experienced increased exclusion from the labour market (Khoury).

The dominance of neoliberal policies leads to an erosion of social protection measures. Neoliberal policies emphasize the preeminence of earned rights through productive citizenship (not social citizenship) and stronger connections to the labour market (Khoury 29; Garrett, this volume), which translates into conditionality—fulfilling specific activity requirements to be eligible for the disability pension, single parents' pension, or unemployment benefits (Mays, *Disability, Citizenship*; Tomlinson; Watts). The challenges for mothers with disability experiencing domestic violence suggest the need for gender and disability justice through redefining and reconstituting the nature of social protection from targeted models to more universal, unconditional ones.

A universal and unconditional approach to social protection has potential to promote fair income and wealth distribution based on needs, justice, and dignity (Cox 73). The renewed interest in universal provisions not attached to labour market requirements, workforce participation, or other social controls offers the opportunity to critically examine gender and disability justice under capitalism for mothers with disability in a violent situation and to determine the feasibility of an alternative grounded in social justice and egalitarianism. Issues of gender and disability justice centre on the extent to which motherhood, family responsibilities, and interacting disability dimensions are considered in conceptions of domestic violence and social protection (Cox 73). To understand the potential of BI, there are specific structural injustices in terms of gender and disability relevant to to mothering dependent children (e.g., unequal divisions of household labour, a punitive welfare state, and unequal access to jobs) (Cox 74) that need deeper consideration.

BI: A Transformative Alternative?

Universal BI represents the foundation of an egalitarian provision available for all permanent citizens. Egalitarianism is the notion that all people should enjoy equal rights and opportunities to participate in society and share in the equal distribution of goods and services for collective benefit (Tomlinson 56); it centres on participatory democracy, rights, and collective solidarity. This focus on equality of opportunity, social inclusion and the right of citizenship status provides a moral and ethical shift away from traditional targeted and conditional measures to more egalitarian forms of income-support provision (Tomlinson; Torry). BI is an unconditional grant (tax-free payment) paid by government to all citizens who are permanent residents at regular intervals and set at a modest rate to offer a decent standard of living (Cox; Mays et al., *Neoliberal Frontiers*). Partial BI grants or other payments, such as participation income or negative income tax, while useful for transitioning to BI, can retain existing regulations, conditionality, and categorization. The BI literature suggests that a nation-state determines the unit of payment (Torry 8). For Australia, there is consensus that a full BI payment would go directly to individuals rather than households or family units (Bowman et al.; Mays et al., *Neoliberal Frontiers*). A child BI (smaller amount) can also be introduced for children to eliminate poverty and reduce economic precarity when there is a single parent in receipt of a pension or a single earner (Levy, et al. 63). To date, a full BI has not been implemented. Yet there are examples of partial BI models (such as in Norway, and the Alaska Permanent Fund, which are social dividends paid annually to all nation-state deemed "permanent citizens" and derived from natural resources [oil] revenue) (Widerquist and Howard 4). These examples suggest there is potential to design and implement a feasible and sustainable model of BI.

BI has been subject to much debate and criticism. Objections to BI tend to be concerned with issues of idleness and deservingness in income-support provision. Embedded in the concern with idleness is the lack of incentives or conditions attached to BI, in which there is no in-built mechanism to compel people to work (Birnbaum 8). For critics of universal BI, socioeconomic freedom must have a corresponding participation obligation. Malcolm Torry counters that BI has an incorporated incentive, given the amount is modest, which allows people to supplement their income through work or other meaningful activities chosen by the individual (8). As a policy instrument, BI provides an equalization of opportunities for income and wealth through a distributive mechanism attached to citizenship and rights, as opposed to attachment to the labour market or a specified need (Torry 8). BI contributes to redefining and revaluing feminized jobs that are traditionally underremunerated and undervalued by allowing new conceptions of social contribution in terms of collective representation, citizens' rights, and responsibilities rather than via paid work or pursuit of profit (Cox 73). In this way, BI reflects an equitable nongender or nondisability form of distribution, which promotes the value of mothering, care work, and unpaid labour. If the grant is set at an appropriate yet modest level, it has the potential to ameliorate poverty and material hardship (Torry 8), and existing income-support payments could be consolidated into one provision to redress poverty. The mothers in Heather Bergen's chapter in this volume speak eloquently about their need for dignity and power.

Cost factors and feasibility are cited as additional barriers against BI (Birnbaum; Torry). Yet social and economic modelling of BI revealed several options that point to its feasibility (Spies-Butcher and Henderson 165). As Jurgen De Wispelaere states, "while much resistance persists among both policy-makers and the general public ... basic income has nevertheless become a credible alternative to orthodox thinking on combating poverty, economic inequality and crisis austerity" (617). He adds that the current policy interest in BI provides a "policy window" to advance the BI agenda (De Wispelaere 618).

BI represents one way to consolidate many existing income-support transfer schemes, but it does not replace other social programs. It is not a complete solution for poverty and inequality reduction. Instead, BI represents one component of an inclusive strategy designed to strengthen the state overall and embed universal provisions in other programs—such as health, childcare, job training, social services, and other welfare provisions—for the benefit of all in society (Forget 13).

BI, Distributive Justice and Meeting Basic Need

The distributive justice principle provides the philosophical and theoretical basis for equalizing income and wealth distribution in society to protect the most vulnerable people in society (Birnbaum 28). Social justice is concerned with the way the social (welfare) state and other institutional and social arrangements distribute (equally and equitably) basic values, fundamental rights and duties, as well as income and/or wealth to produce shared solidarity and social co-operation in society (Birnbaum 22). BI is genuinely emancipatory for mothers with disability in an abusive situation, as it invokes the fairness principles of freedom, autonomy, and decency (Torry 88) rather than conservative paternalism and "deserving poor" ideals (Zelleke 37).

The preconditions of universality, justice, and fairness have significant implications for mothers with disability experiencing domestic violence. These mothers experience a loss of freedom, security, and control.

My earlier study on mothers with disability in domestic violence situations demonstrated their limited economic and social freedom, which made it difficult for them to leave a violent relationship:

It was very hard. I couldn't get a house to rent because I didn't have the references ... no prior rental history. It was very hard to go anywhere else. So I moved back into his house ... after six months of being out. He started being violent within the first week. ... If I had any power before I certainly didn't have any now. I used to take the kids to kindy [kindergarten] and come home and sit on the bed and just cry.[4]

This excerpt illustrates the gendered and disability inequality in the relationship and beyond. The heightened economic and social vulnerability was intensified by a lack of power and control over financial matters and a devalued social and economic status (Evans 56). Without economic means, the mothers with disability were forced to remain in an abusive situation for longer periods of time and, in turn, were subjected to further abuse (Thiara et al. 761). The complex interaction of these structural barriers increased the vulnerability of these women and prevented them from leaving (Thiara et al. 761).

The lack of material resources, emotional degradation, and control was exacerbated by a sense of powerlessness. The outcomes of violence tended to result in internalized feelings of powerlessness and subordination, a diminished sense of worth, as well as experiences of marginalization, disempowerment, and alienation. The use of economic violence, the mothers' impairments, and previous experiences of abuse made it harder for them to seek assistance. One mother's story exemplifies this pattern:

He used the fact that I had the physical problems. Things like if [child] was naughty, it would be "Your mum will let you get away with that, but I won't ... Your mum's not strong enough to stop you from doing this, but I am." So he would play on the fact that physically as my [child] got bigger, I was less able to restrain [the child] from doing things [like] trying to run on the road.... It was his [perpetrator] power issue of I'm the big powerful person and the mother is the weak disabled person.

The accounts powerfully depict the unequal gendered-disablist relations and oppressive conditions that occur in highly controlling environments (Morley and Dunstan; Frohmader and Ricci). Contemporary public narratives (Domestic Violence Resource Centre Victoria [DVRCV]) reveal similar experiences of power and control underpinning violence and poverty. Perpetrators control the finances through means, such as withholding Keycards[5] or compelling mothers with disability to pay bills (DVRCV). These experiences of power and control mirror early narratives of regulation and control through economic and social means (Thiara et al. 761). The erosion of freedom and social protections leaves mothers with disability vulnerable to poverty, dependence, and further violence, exacerbating existing inequalities and hardship.

The need for strengthening the material and social existence of mothers with disability is evident in these accounts. Gaining financial and social independence from partners, caregivers, or the state for subsistence is crucial for redressing power imbalances within the household and beyond (workplace or community). BI potentially reconstitutes power imbalances and agency in instances of unequal social relations (such as with partners or the state) (Raventós; Torry; Zelleke (see also Itaborai, this volume) and safeguards power and justice to the most vulnerable in society (Zelleke 38).

BI removes the need to rely on others (Zelleke 38) and offsets the insecurity brought about by income variations and precarity, fears about becoming a sole parent or having their child removed, as well as interrupted income flows. BI is transformative for mothers with disability because it is freedom enhancing rather than freedom restricting (Zelleke 38); it allows emancipation from spouses, the state, and the broader labour market. A BI supplemented by other support services (e.g., housing and subsidized childcare) and benefits (e.g., family payment) significantly improves the economic and social wellbeing of mothers with disability and contributes to greater socioeconomic independence, which, in turn, has beneficial outcomes for children (Atkinson and Marlier; Cox; Mays, *Disability Citizenship*).

BI and Freedom from the Stigmatizing Effects of Categorization

A universal BI promotes dignity and autonomy through another ethical principle: freedom from stigma and categorization. An unconditional grant is free from stringent controls, work requirements, as well as classifications of motherhood and disability. This is in direct contrast to the current Australian targeted approach to income support, which generates categories of both motherhood and disability based on gendered notions of mothering, parental status, as well as disabling criteria of capacity and deficit (Evans; Zelleke). Targeted and conditional measures stigmatize mothers with disability. The categories in the disability pension and parent pension suggest the applicant is undeserving and defective. Disability is medicalized for the purpose of bureaucratic categories of entitlement.

BI redresses the tendency for stigma on the basis of categories of gender and disability by removing gender and disability as the central defining features of receiving income support or social services (Raventós 126). The social construction of gender and disability is found in accounts from my early study and in contemporary narratives of the DVRCV. In all narratives, stigma interacts with familial abuse, institutional practices, as well as power and control, which place mothers with disability in a subordinate position through an inferred secondary citizenship status and classification (Frohmader and Ricci 27). Such stigma through the classification of mothering and disability experiences reinforces gendered and disability injustice when in a violent situation.

> [My partner] was hiding what he was doing [domestic violence] ... but he had the whole town up against me and really believing that it was really in my mind. They [the community] sort of threw it on you and shunned you ... the tendency is ... if they can't find a cause for why things are happening ... they blame the mother [with the disability] ... and that was the way the town thought ... it does leave a stigma.

Rather than see mothers with disability as citizens in their own right, gendered mothering and disability categories have been used to reinforce and perpetuate categories of difference and differential treatment. Under a BI, mothers with disability in a violent relationship would no longer be targeted as a separate category or subject to stereotypes according to classifications of disability or motherhood. BI transforms targeted and unequal pension and benefits regimes into an egalitarian system that promotes social citizenship and rights (Torry 18). This nonstigmatizing effect of BI is most freeing for mothers with disability experiencing domestic violence.

Conclusion: BI, a Way Forward

BI can respond to the structural gender and disability dimensions inherent in a violent relationship. It responds to both distributive justice in meeting basic needs and providing freedom from the stigmatizing effects of categorization. BI as a valid alternative to targeted measures is gaining momentum nationally and globally, which is encouraging for mothers with disability experiencing domestic violence.

It is BI's inherent moral, ethical, and economic principles grounded in social justice and social citizenship that provide legitimacy for the proposal. It is essentially one step towards egalitarian pension regimes and an equitable society (Piketty 399), as it can relieve mothers with disability from precarity and disadvantage due to their reliance on perpetrators, carers, and the state. BI represents one way to secure economic freedom and dignity. As the accounts suggest, the long-term consequences of domestic violence—including extreme material dependency, financial hardship, and work precarity—often prevent mothers with disability from leaving a violent relationship. When they do leave, they find themselves in poverty, as the levels of pensions and benefits in Australia are well below the poverty line.

BI offers an optimal approach to ameliorating poverty (Torry 3), but this does not preclude the need for other social support services based on need if extra assistance is required (e.g., health) (Piketty; Torry). Thus, BI needs to be a part of an overall strategy that leads to the reconfiguration of other unequal structures, such as the taxation system, the labour market and employment conditions, and public provisions (e.g., adequate childcare and social housing). BI can have an overall positive social and economic effect for mothers' with disability and can potentially disrupt the ideology of neoliberalism and oppressive gender-disabling inequalities through its transformative strategy and notions of social justice and social citizenship.

Endnotes

1. Pseudonyms were used to protect privacy, uphold confidentiality and anonymity, and safeguard participants. Ethical clearance was obtained from the University Human Research Ethics Committee (Reference number: QUT1264H).

2. See my master's thesis on the perception of women with physical disability (who identified as mothers) and their lived experience of domestic violence for a comprehensive overview of the research design and methodology.

3. ACOSS "Poverty in Australia" explains that estimating levels of poverty after considering housing costs reflects "the median value of income after subtracting the cost of housing and set[ting] the 'after-housing' poverty line at 50% of that median. This results in new poverty lines equal to $353 for singles and $742 for couples with two children. We then estimate after-housing poverty by subtracting housing costs from the incomes of each household in the ABS income survey sample and comparing the resulting incomes with the after-housing poverty lines" (12).

4. The women with disability in the study had experienced violent relationships and received disability pensions and additional supports through women-led services, such as refuges and community groups.

5. Keycards in Australia are like debit or credit cards and are used to access money from an automatic teller machine or at a point of service. Money is generally held in a current savings or other account in a bank and accessed through these Keycards.

Works Cited

Atkinson, Anthony B., and Eric Marlier. *Income and Living Conditions in Europe.* Eurostat, 2010.

Australian Council of Social Services [ACOSS]. "Poverty in Australia 2018." *ACOSS and University of New South Wales*, 2018, www.acoss. org.au. Accessed 24 July 2020.

Australian Council of Social Services. [ACOSS] and University of New South Wales. "Inequality in Australia 2018." *ACOSS and University of New South Wales*, 2018, www.acoss.org.au. Accessed 24 July 2020.

Alvaredo, Facundo, et al. "World Inequality Report: Executive Summary. *World Inequality Lab*, 2018, wir2018.wid.world/. Accessed 24 July 2020.

Apps, Patricia. "Gender Equity in the Tax-Transfer System for Fiscal Sustainability." *Tax, Social Policy and Gender: Rethinking Equality and Efficiency*, edited by Miranda Steward, ANU Press, 2017, pp. 69-98.

Birnbaum, Simon. *Basic Income Reconsidered. Social Justice, Liberalism, and the Demands of Equality.* Palgrave Macmillan, 2012.

Bowman, Dina, et al. "Basic Income: Trade-offs and Bottom Lines." *Brotherhood of St Laurence*, 2017, www.bsl.org.au. Accessed 24 July 2020.

Commonwealth of Australia. "Re: Think Tax Discussion Paper." *Australian Government*, 2015, bettertax.gov.au/files/2015/03/TWP_combined-online.pdf. Accessed 24 July 2020.

Cox, Eva. "Feminist Perspectives on Basic Income." *Implementing a Basic Income in Australia: Pathways Forward*, edited by Elise Klein, Jennifer Mays, and Tim Dunlop, Palgrave Macmillan, 2019, pp. 69-85.

De Wispelaere, Jurgen. "Basic Income in our Time: Improving Political Prospects through Policy Learning?" *Journal of Social Policy*, vol. 45, no. 4, 2016, pp. 617-34.

Domestic Violence Resource Centre Victoria [DVRCV]. "True Stories from Women with Disabilities." *DVRCV*, 10 Dec. 2017, www.dvrcv.org.au/stories. Accessed 24 July 2020.

Evans, Patricia. "Lone Mothers, Workfare and Precarious Employment: Time for a Canadian Basic Income." *International Social Security Review*, vol. 62, no. 1, 2009, pp. 45-63.

Forget, Evelyn. "Do We Still Need a Basic Income in Canada? *Basic Income Guarantee Series, Northern Policy Institute*, May 2017, www.northernpolicy.ca/upload/documents/publications/reports-new/forget_do-we-need-a-big-en.pdf. Accessed 24 July 2020.

Frohmader, Caroline, and Cristina Ricci. "Improving Service Responses for Women with Disability Experiencing Violence: 1800RESPECT." *Women with Disabilities Australia*, 2016, wwda.org.au/wp-content/uploads/2016/09/1800RESPECT_Report_FINAL.pdf. Accessed 24 July 2020.

Garland-Thomson, Rosemarie. "Integrating Disability, Transforming Feminist Theory." *The Disability Studies Reader*, edited by Lennard J. Davis. 2nd ed., Routledge, 2006, pp. 257-273.

Hague, Gill, et al. "Disabled Women and Domestic Violence: Making the Links, a National UK Study." *Psychiatry, Psychology and Law*, vol. 18, no. 1, 2011, pp. 117-36.

Harpur, Paul, and Heather Douglas. "Disability and Domestic Violence: Protecting Survivors' Human Rights." *Griffith Law Review*, vol. 23, no. 3, 2014, 405-33.

Khoury, Peter. "Neoliberalism, Auditing, Austerity and the Demise of Social Justice." *Social Alternatives*, vol. 34, no. 3, 2015, pp. 25-33.

Klein, Elise et al. "Introduction: Implementing a Basic Income in Australia." *Implementing a Basic Income in Australia: Pathways Forward*, edited by Elise Klein, Jennifer Mays and Tim Dunlop, Palgrave Macmillan, 2019, pp. 1-20.

Levy, Horatio et al. "Toward a European Union Child Basic Income? Within and Between Countries." International Journal of Microsimulation, vol. 6, no. 1, 2013, pp. 63-85.

Lockton, Deborah, and Richard Ward. *Domestic Violence*. Routledge, 2016.

McDonald, Catherine, and Greg Marston. "Workfare as Welfare: Governing Unemployment in the Advanced Liberal State." *Critical Social Policy*, vol. 25, no. 3, 2005, pp. 374-401.

Mays, Jennifer. "Perception of the experience of domestic violence by women with a physical disability", unpublished master's thesis, Queensland University of Technology, Brisbane, Queensland, Australia, 2003.

Mays, Jennifer. "Feminist Disability Theory: Domestic Violence against Women with a Disability." *Disability & Society*, vol. 21, no. 2, 2006, pp. 147-58.

Mays, Jennifer. "Disability, Citizenship, and Basic Income: Forging a New Alliance for a Non-Disabling Society." *Basic Income in Australia and New Zealand: Perspectives from the Neoliberal Frontier*, edited by Jennifer Mays, Greg Marston, and John Tomlinson, Palgrave Macmillan, 2016, pp. 207-51.

Mays, Jennifer, et al. "Neoliberal Frontiers and Economic insecurity: Is Basic Income a Solution?" *Basic Income in Australia and New Zealand: Perspectives from the Neoliberal Frontier*, edited by Jennifer Mays, Greg Marston, and John Tomlinson, Palgrave Macmillan, 2016, pp. 1-25.

Morley, Christine, and Joanne Dunstan. "Putting Gender Back on the Agenda in Domestic and Family Violence Policy and Service Responses: Using Critical Reflection to Create Cultural Change." *Social Alternatives*, vol. 35, no 4, 2016, pp. 43-48.

Piketty, Thomas. *Capital in the Twenty-First Century.* Translated by Arthur Goldhammer, The Belknap Press of Harvard University Press, 2014.

Raventós, Daniel. *Basic Income: The Material Conditions of Freedom.* Translated by Julie Wark, Pluto Press, 2007.

Soldatic, Karen and Barbara Pini. "Continuity or Change? Disability Policy and the Rudd Government." *Social Policy and Society,* vol. 11, no. 2, 2012, pp. 183-96.

Spies-Butcher, Ben, and Troy Henderson. "Stepping Stones to an Australian Basic Income." *Implementing a Basic Income in Australia: Pathways Forward,* edited by Elise Klein, Jennifer Mays, and Tim Dunlop, Palgrave Macmillan, 2019, pp. 163-78.

Thiara, Ravi K., et al. "Losing Out on Both Counts: Disabled Women and Domestic Violence." *Disability and Society,* vol. 26, no.6, 2011, pp. 757-71.

Tomlinson, John. "Australian Basic Income: Efficiency and Equity." *Basic Income in Australia and New Zealand: Perspectives from the Neoliberal Frontier,* edited by Jennifer Mays, Greg Marston, and John Tomlinson, Palgrave Macmillan, 2016, pp. 54-68.

Torry, Malcolm. *The Feasibility of Citizen's Income.* Palgrave Macmillan, 2016.

Watts, Rob. ""Running on Empty": Australia's Neoliberal Social Security System, 1988-2015." *Basic Income in Australia and New Zealand: Perspectives from the Neoliberal Frontier,* edited by Jennifer Mays, Greg Marston, and John Tomlinson, Palgrave Macmillan, 2016, pp. 69-91.

Whiteford, Peter. "Social Security since Henderson." *Revisiting Henderson: Poverty, Social Security and Basic Income,* edited by Peter Saunders, Melbourne University Press, 2019, pp. 89-119.

Widerquist, Karl, and Michael Howard. "Introduction: Success in Alaska." *Alaska's Permanent Dividend Fund: Examining its Suitability as a Model,* edited by Karl Widerquist and Michael Howard, Palgrave Macmillan, 2012, pp. 3-11.

Zelleke, Almaz. "Feminist Political Theory and the Argument for an Unconditional Basic Income." Policy & Politics, vol. 39, no. 1, 2011, pp. 27-42.

Chapter Fifteen

Lesbian-Parented Families: Negotiating the Cultural Narrative of Hetero- normativity through Leisure and Sport Experiences[1]

Dawn E. Trussell

Although leisure is acknowledged by the United Nations as a human right and is considered a key pillar in at least two major social justice frameworks (see Fraser; Nussbaum, for example), scant attention has been paid to leisure in relation to public policy. Leisure has been widely shown to have a positive impact on wellbeing in multiple spheres, including physical, cognitive, emotional, social, and spiritual domains. Long considered to encapsulate a state of freedom, autonomy, individual choice, self-expression, and satisfaction (Shaw, "Conceptualizing Resistance"), leisure affects individuals, families, and communities, and can result in increased wellbeing, family cohesiveness, social support, and community engagement (Hebblethwaite; Iwasaki et al.; Trussell).

Federal, provincial, and municipal governments acknowledge the role of leisure in individual and community development, improving quality of life, and enhancing social functioning (e.g., Canadian Parks and Recreation Association; Canadian Sport Policy). Leisure policy, however, has not escaped recent shifts in the Canadian social policy landscape, and the politics of leisure has become an increasing concern.

During the last two decades, the Canadian welfare state has been increasingly identified as a social investment state (SIS), thereby eclipsing the social security state that had emerged during the postwar period (e.g., Saint Martin). Moreover, guided by the National Recreation Statement (Interprovincial Sport & Recreation Council), municipalities carry the primary responsibility for implementing provincial policies and services, which often results in unequal access for marginalized groups, including women, the unemployed, and persons with disabilities (Frisby et al.; Havitz et al.).

Yet it is clear too that leisure is recognized as a site of resistance, wherein power relations that oppress individuals or groups based on categorical definitions, such as gender, race, class, and sexual identity, are challenged (Shaw, "Conceptualizing Resistance"; Shaw "Resistance"). Although people learn through leisure about social roles influenced by the dominant culture (Johnson), leisure can also facilitate the transition of social systems and policies to enhance equity and inclusion of marginalized and vulnerable citizens (Mair et al.). For example, research on LGBTQ-parented families and youth sport organizations reveals that parents challenge incidents of enacted stigma and sexual prejudice by addressing inclusive language and policies with league organizers (Trussell et al., "LGBTQ Parents' Experiences").

This chapter illustrates the ways in which leisure and public policy shape the lived experiences of lesbian-parented families[2] through a story that is presented in three parts (i.e., Child, Mom, and Mama) and was developed from interview transcripts. Aligned with other chapters in this volume (Cantillon and Hutton; Labman; Larios), this chapter also understands individual narratives and stories to be particularly informative in examining the lived effects of policy because they question mainstream and deficit notions of particular human experiences, such as motherhood (Butler-Kisber). Before presenting the story, I provide a brief background of the importance of family-centred leisure meanings and experiences and consider how lesbian-parented families confront the cultural narrative of heteronormativity.

Performing Family within a Culture of Heterosexism

Though dominated by a heteronormative conceptualization of the family unit (i.e. two heterosexual parents and school-aged children), research has explored the role of leisure for families with young children (Trussell et al., "Revisiting Family Leisure"). Parents organize leisure activities to build and strengthen family relationships through a sense of togetherness and child socialization (Harrington). Parents also believe that shared leisure activities provide other benefits, including inculcating life lessons and moral values as well as promoting children's physical development (Shaw, "Family Leisure"). Family leisure is deliberately used to provide opportunities for positive interactions that establish a sense of family. In turn, family-centred activities are romanticized, and there is often a "gap between parental ideals and reality" (Shaw and Dawson, "Contradictory Aspects" 179). In part, the idealization, motivation, and expectations for family-centred leisure activities are connected to broader parenting ideologies, such as the ideology of intensive motherhood (Hays; Cantillon and Hutton, this volume).

Susan Shaw and Don Dawson suggest that family leisure is "a form of purposive leisure, which is planned, facilitated, and executed by parents in order to achieve particular short and long-term goals" ("Purposive Leisure" 228). Maureen Harrington draws attention to the performative character of purposive leisure "as a way of being, doing, or 'practicing' family both at home and in the public space ... which aligns with the concept of family leisure as a performative space" (329). Through gendered identities, family identity is "forged and experienced through class, religion, or other cultural processes" (Harrington 331). The performing of family then becomes a public act in the community, whereby families seek to attain cultural idealizations of a so-called "good family" and instill life lessons through their leisure practices (Harrington; Trussell and Shaw).

Organized youth sport, in particular, is perceived as an important component of family leisure activities and a way to achieve the ideal of being a good parent (Trussell and Shaw). As Jay Coakley has theorized, there are important cultural connections between organized youth sport and ideologies of parenting and gender. Susan Shaw and I have examined the connection of organized youth sport to cultural values and the practise of contemporary heteronormative parenting ideologies (i.e., involved fathering and intensive mothering). We posit that "Parenting goes beyond the home environment and becomes a public act that is observed by other parents, with these observations creating the basis of what is deemed to be a good parent" (377). That is, children's extra-curricular participation and their family leisure engagements may reflect and contribute to broader and complex sociocultural changes in contemporary parenting ideologies and provide not only an idealization of childrearing practices but also a set of criteria by which parents are judged.

Yet organized youth sport may also become a contentious space for lesbian-parented families, as sport has a long history of homophobia that prevents "gay men, lesbians, and transgendered people from fully participating" (Davison and Frank 178). Research undertaken to understand diverse family structures within sport organizations has documented tensions and difficulties that families experience. The power of heterosexism, homophobia, and stigma is reflected in the ways that all family members' leisure experiences with sport clubs, churches, work colleagues, and close friends may be adversely altered, including both LGBTQ+ and heterosexual family members (Trussell; Trussell et al. "LGBTQ Parent's Experiences"). As Corey Johnson indicates, the interpersonal aspects of leisure can be used "to promote and enforce mainstream discourses and ideals ... and to keep individuals and/or groups of individuals in a state of inequality" (247).

Previous research on lesbian- and gay-headed families also points to parents' conscious awareness of their own role accountability related to the intentional socialization of their children's gender within the prescribed norms (Berkowitz and Ryan; Kane). Dana Berkowitz and Maura Ryan argue that "By virtue of their sexual minority status, lesbian and gay parents are subject to increased moral judgment than that of their heterosexual counterparts" (333). Research examining the attitudes and beliefs of heterosexual adults towards lesbian and gay parents indicates an enduring concern for the potential impact on the child's wellbeing and how the children will be socialized to behave in gender appropriate ways (Pennington and Knight).

Although interpersonal relationships may reproduce heterosexist parenting practices, feminist scholars have also challenged the ways in which gendered discourses shape the interactions, practices, and structures of leisure and sport organizations that maintain patriarchal, heterosexist norms (Fink; Shaw and Frisby; Trussell et al., "LGBTQ Parent's Experiences"). With this backdrop, the story presented below illuminates the lived experiences of lesbian-parented families within the context of community-based youth sport and leisure organizations and how they negotiate the cultural narrative of heteronormativity.

Methods

This research is part of a larger project investigating the lived experiences of LGBTQ-parented family structures within community-based youth sport and leisure organizations (i.e., municipal government as well as nonprofit). In phase one of the study, seventy-three parents from Australia, Canada, and the United States participated in online asynchronous focus groups. In phase two, parents were contacted one year after completing the online focus group to determine their interest in participating in semistructured interviews to advance the insights from phase one. Nine lesbian-parents responded to the call; six of the parents were in a committed relationship with one another. At the end of each interview, parents were asked to consider having their children participate in the study, but only one couple from Canada agreed to this. As the child's story presented in this chapter illustrates, children have an important perspective to share. When the data were collected, same-sex marriages were legal in Canada and the United States and became legal shortly thereafter in Australia.

This chapter highlights one family's experiences (i.e., Child, Mom, and Mama) that are presented in the form of a story (Sparkes and Smith). Data analysis in both phases of the project was guided by an inductive approach to help understand the participants' experiences. In crafting the story, my primary aim was to stay as true to the voices of the individual family members as possible through the use of direct quotations. Words were edited slightly, and sentence order was sometimes modified to present a coherent story of the child's and lesbian parents' experiences. I also chose to focus on the lesbian parents' experiences that traversed the majority of the participants shared stories throughout both phases of the larger study. At the same time, the complexities and nuances of each family member's experiences within this particular family unit are also demonstrated. What follows is one family's story that emerged from this process.

Negotiating the Cultural Narrative of Heteronormativity: A Story in Three Parts

Child (Nine Years Old)

I can't really imagine what it would be like to have a mom and a dad or two dads. I find it a lot different. Sometimes, people make assumptions that my parents are straight—that I have a mom and a dad—and then it's kind of confusing. It's kind of hard when I have to correct them because I don't always know how to say it. It's just like, "Actually I have two moms," and then they are like, "Oh, that's interesting."

Sometimes when people don't understand having differences, they make fun of differences to make themselves feel better. If people don't understand, they think, "Oh, it must be a bad thing." And it makes the people with those differences feel really bad. It's happened to me. Once, someone said something to me about having a mom and a dad. And I said, "Oh, actually, I have two moms." And they said, "That doesn't make sense" or "That's weird!" But really, it doesn't make sense that they think it's bad. Another time, I was cutting out paper people, and I said, "These two characters could just be lesbians," and my friend said, "I find that kind of wrong." And then she remembered that I had two moms, and she apologized.

Sometimes, it is hard to have two moms. Sometimes, when they sign me up for stuff, the forms say, "parent/guardian," but sometimes, they say "mother/father." It's annoying. I know there are lots of people in the world that are straight. But there are also lots of people in the world who are gay or lesbian. So why not just put "parent/parent?" But my parents come and support me when I play sports, like when I did hockey, dance, or soccer. They came to watch every practice. But, sometimes, they just watched the big recital or the big show. I like that they are there. In that big ocean of people, somebody there will know who I am!

I have a picture of my family with Kate Reid at the Toronto gay pride parade a couple of years ago. She's a lesbian singer. It was a special day for me. It was the first time I ever remember going to Pride. And I just find that cool. I like the idea that we can all be proud of our differences. And I love rainbows. They make me proud and happy about my family. Life is not black and white, so rainbows make sense.

Mom

I didn't identify as a lesbian until I was an adult. When I was twenty-seven years old, I came out. My wife and I were in angst; for two years we were in the closet before we told our families. But with a child, we had no choice but to be outed in the community. I was my daughter's soccer coach, and my wife was there on the sidelines. On the first day, she helped me set up and get all of the pylons out. So, people saw that … I think I might have introduced her as my wife. We have never lied about our relationship in front of our daughter because we don't want her to ever feel shame.

Our daughter really wanted me to coach her again in soccer after that first year. But I also thought it would be good for her if I didn't do it. She had a male coach, which I also thought was good because, other than her granddad and uncles, all her caregivers, like in any context—education and daycare—have been women. So, it was like "Yay! A dad is doing this!" It's important that our daughter is exposed to different leadership styles and opportunities. If she was to only have positive interactions with adult women in her life, then how does she navigate the world? The world doesn't just exist with adult women. But we also feel that it's important that she is exposed to powerful female role models, and that's why we loved the all-female hockey program that she was in—the players as well as coaches were all female. It is important that she is exposed to empowering female environments because she is a female child. We want our daughter to have that. So, I really appreciated that there were all women coaches on the ice. If we had a male child, would we want to see him in empowering female-led environments? Yes. But would we also want a son to have more empowering male figures? Most likely.

We have asked our daughter, "Hey, what's your gender?" She knows about gender fluidity and that if she ever wants to be called something else or by a different gender, she understands that we would support her. So, my daughter and I both have Pride tape on our hockey sticks. When my wife and I took her to hockey for the first night, I said, "Do you want Pride tape on your stick?" She's like, "Yeah!" She loves it. She's got a rainbow stick. And, then, on her hockey helmet, we put on a rainbow mohawk. It's interesting because the ball hockey league that I've played in, we are not supposed to have tape on our stick. But I broke the rules because I really like the tape. I figured if someone tells me to take it off,

I will take it off. So not a lot of people have tape, but I get a lot of compliments on my tape from the referees and other players. It's neat because with my daughter, she wanted to use it, too. She likes the Pride tape. She knows why we bought it. I love that it's on both of our sticks. I'm hoping that she learns we are political advocates to inclusivity, and this is why we wear tape on our sticks. I mean we are not "rah-rah proud," but it's important for her to see us advocating for inclusivity.

I think kids' extracurricular activities are somewhat inclusive of diverse families. But my first impression is that they are heteronormative. Sport organizations have to be inclusive now. If you run the city soccer league and somebody phones the mayor or talks to the media and says, "This organization has not been inclusive to me," it will have a negative impact on the organization. In my experience, the people in the decision-making positions have a huge influence, especially if they are open minded. For example, if you run the city soccer league and you have lesbian moms who are on the board, then you're probably going to get that part right. In the same way that if you have racial minorities on the board, you're probably going to get that part right. If you have a single-parent family, you're probably going to get that part right. But if you don't have that diversity on the board and the organization is isolated in their social circle, its members might not mean to do harm to families, but they do it without knowing.

Inclusive language is the place to start because that's the first entry point that someone has with an organization. Change your forms. A transitioning parent can also have difficulties with community spaces that don't have their own bathrooms or inclusive signage. There is a lot of subtle ways that you can show support, like by putting a rainbow flag on everything. Even if I walk by a store and I notice a little rainbow flag, I smile to myself. It's basically saying, "Hey, you and your family are okay here." A sport organization can make it not just a tolerant space but an accepting place for all families. "So even something like an organizational statement: 'We accept all families' does make a difference."

Mama

I feel like there is silent judgement, which means that I have never actually seen or heard any judgement. But in my head, there's just a sort of silent judgment. I feel like there are eyes on what we do sign her up for. And I think it's more in terms of what's gendered and what's not gendered. When she was four and into pink and skirts, she wanted to do ballet. But she's not into that kind of thing anymore. She's into geekier, nerdy stuff. She's loving hockey. For hockey, she's got the rainbow tape on her stick and her helmet and stuff. So again, it's silent, not actual judgement, but the silent "Well, yes, the gay moms. Of course, their kid has rainbow tape on her stick"—I feel some of that.

And I also feel the pressure to make our rainbow community proud of us as we blast apart gender roles. There's a part of me that is really proud that our daughter isn't concerned with gender norms and that we are doing our LGBTQ community proud. But, for swimming lessons, we couldn't find her a typical girl bathing suit. So, she ended up wearing shorts and a shirt, and I'm sure there was some judgmental looks in the change room because they couldn't tell if she was a boy or a girl. Nothing was ever said to us, and I'm not sure that our daughter noticed, so I couldn't tell you if it was all in my head and I was waiting for judgement. Feeling that pressure—and it's very subtle—but it doesn't change anything we do.

So far, our daughter's extracurricular activities have been very inclusive. One of the best memories I have is when my wife coached our daughter her first year playing soccer. It was so exciting that my daughter was in soccer. My dad was my soccer coach when I was a kid, and my wife's mom was her soccer coach. It was a nice sort of generational thing. It felt like a milestone. They were both so happy in it. So I got to see my wife in her role not only as a coach but also as a mom and as an athlete. I got to see all of these identities of my wife all at once, and our daughter was so excited that her mom was there and coaching her.

We've never had any actual concerns or issues. The only tangible issue that has come up is the forms that are noninclusive, which is surprisingly sensitive for us. It's just frustrating because forms are so simple to change. And then I think they are so black and white. It's very "othering" to have to continually change and modify paperwork. Our daughter notices that, too, and it bothers her.

Once they are aware, people are often apologetic and embarrassed, which I think is interesting. My wife is more likely to let them off the hook. I'm more likely to rock the boat and not worry about offending people. I've learned from her to be kinder and gentler to people over the years. But we always bring it up. We even took on the school board for three years in a row trying to get them to change their forms to more inclusive language, and they did eventually change them. Even after-school care was using forms with noninclusive language, and they were really clear that "it wasn't their form," but they were embarrassed.

For the most part, her activities have felt safe. Hockey felt safe, surprisingly. I think maybe because it was focused on girls' hockey. So, I think there was already a different culture and the feeling around it. And even the change room was a great culture. We were told to be aware of what your kid is wearing because there is going to be a bunch of moms, dads, and grandparents. It was surprising because hockey culture is not something I associate with being super open.

At other times, as I mentioned earlier, change rooms have felt pretty uncomfortable—and, in particular, I'm thinking of when she does swim lessons at the city pool. The change room felt like an unsafe space for me as a parent of a kid who identifies herself as a cisgendered girl ... although she'll always make a qualifier "for now". Being around other parents, I did not feel comfortable because I felt the pressure of their judgment. I'm guessing it's because I did not want her to feel unsafe. I don't think she ever did. I don't know if that will change as she grows up. I don't know if it will change as her hair changes, as her style changes.

And we, as a family, teach others about our family by just showing up. So, we don't even really have to be talking to people to be educating about our alternative family. And by educating, I mean, we are not really any different in a lot of ways. So, we show up. We don't need to say anything. Just to be like, yeah, we are the same kind of family unit that everybody else is.

But there is a part of you that gets tired of educating after a while. You just kind of want to show up and do your thing and not have to comment on forms or not have to feel like you're getting stared at by other people. I think kids are more likely to stare; parents are just better at hiding it. There are times when you are just tired of having to take it on.

It would be nice if community recreation programs could access some kind of service around being aware of the language that they use. So, forms are one thing. Because then it's just simple, neutral language. But

it's hard to get people aware, to become aware of things like heteronormativity. How pervasive it is. I think it's also been hard to make them
understand how "othering" it is.

Conclusion

This three-part story illustrates that sexual stigma, heterosexism, and
sexual prejudice persist, despite a shifting cultural narrative of away
from heteronormativity (Herek et al.; Kivel and Johnson). The persistence of stigmatization and its impact are particularly noteworthy
considering this family resides in a medium-sized city that is perceived
to be vibrant and open to diverse family structures and within close
proximity to Toronto, Canada, which celebrates one of the largest
annual Pride festivals. This family also identifies as white with a
middle-class income. Within the context of the larger project, the
findings called attention to the intersectionality of diverse social
identities and the significance of race, geographical location, and
socioeconomic resources. It was clear that the relatively privileged
social identities of families and their ability to reside within socially
progressive areas may reflect an overarching positive culture while
participating in community leisure and sport experiences (see Trussell
et al., "LGBTQ Parent's Experiences").

Despite positions of social privilege, certainly, heterosexism and
stigma were reflected in the altered experiences of this lesbian-parented
family. Leanne Norman reminds us that everyday injustices and
homophobia remain pervasive. The assumption of heterosexuality and
sexual prejudice were embedded within leisure programs and facilities
through noninclusive forms and negotiating public censure when
performing gender nonconforming behaviours. As this family's story
illustrates, negotiating everyday microaggressions (Sue) of sexual stigma
and heterosexism takes an emotional toll on lesbian-parented families.

Clearly, too, the anticipation of stigmatization pervaded this family's
leisure and sport experiences through perceptions of silent judgment
and the public gaze. Within this context, the family challenges the
dominant, romantic conceptualization of the family and domesticity as
refuges from the outside world, and, in turn, it highlights the public and,
sometimes, contentious aspects of performing and constructing family.
Moreover, the inculcation of important familial values with their child

(e.g., feeling pride and not shame) compelled the lesbian parents to come out in the public sphere, despite having earlier concealed their romantic relationship to friends and family.

This story is also consistent with Shaw's ("Resistance") framework on resistance, which refers to "an act or series of actions that enhance freedom of choice and personal control" and "is closely tied to the idea of challenging hegemonic processes through the critique of dominant ideologies and of the political ideas, beliefs, and practices of the dominant hegemonic group or class" (534). Indeed, the agency of the lesbian parents to support their child's gender nonconformity within leisure and sport spaces (e.g., the change room) as well as being present within their child's leisure and sport programs (e.g., as a spectator or coach) serves to destabilize heteronormative organizational policies and programming. Moreover, despite the invisible emotional labour and challenges they experienced, their narratives illustrate the significance of advocacy to help build inclusive communities and change public policy (see the chapters by Larios and Labman in this volume).

Despite the difficulties illustrated through this three-part story, the potential for leisure to facilitate relationship building and construct a sense of family is also emphasized. Lesbian-parented families are able to construct a sense of family identity through shared experiences and memory making. Activities integrated within inclusive sport and leisure spaces (e.g., rainbow tape on a hockey stick) and LGBTQ Pride events facilitate a sense of family unity. The story also illustrates the diversity of meanings within the same family unit (e.g., the role of advocacy) and reveals the complexities and nuances between individual family members' perspectives and experiences.

Finally, municipal governments and nonprofit organizations may not overtly discriminate or display prejudice assumptions, yet a culture of heteronormativity is prevalent. Developing partnerships and collaborative relationships with local and national LGBTQ advocacy groups may help municipal governments and nonprofit leisure organizations create necessary resources and diversity sensitivity training. When discussions concerning issues related to LGBTQ families (as well as other diverse social identities) occur, a more open and inclusive dialogue may emerge, which could have a large impact on the experiences of families that access community leisure programs and services.

Endnotes

1. This work was supported by a Social Sciences and Humanities Research Council of Canada, Insight Development Grant (#430-2013-001081).

2. Throughout this chapter I intentionally use the term "lesbian-parented families" rather than "lesbian mothers" due to the social construction and fluidity of gender expression.

Works Cited

Berkowitz, Dana and Maura Ryan. "Bathrooms, Baseball, and Bra Shopping: Lesbian and Gay Parents Talk about Engendering Their Children." *Sociological Perspectives*, vol. 54, no. 3, 2011, pp. 329-50.

Butler-Kisber, Lynn. *Qualitative Inquiry: Thematic, Narrative and Arts-Informed Perspectives.* Sage, 2010.

Canadian Sport Policy 2012. *The Sport Information Resource Centre*, sirc.ca/app/uploads/files/content/docs/Document/csp2012_en.pdf. Accessed 29 July 2020.

Canadian Parks and Recreation Association/Interprovincial Sport and Recreation Council. *A Framework for Recreation in Canada 2015: Pathways to Wellbeing.* www.cpra.ca/about-the-framework. Accessed 29 July 2020.

Coakley, Jay. "The Good Father: Parental Expectations and Youth Sports." *Fathering through Sport and Leisure*, edited by Tess Kay, Routledge, 2009, pp. 40-50.

Davison, Kevin G. and Blye W. Frank. "Sexualities, Genders, and Bodies in Sport: Changing Practices of Inequity." *Sport and Gender in Canada*, 2nd ed., edited by Kevin Young and Phil White, Oxford University Press, 2007, pp. 178-93.

Fraser, Nancy. *Justice Interruptus: Critical Reflections on the "Postsocialist" Condition.* Routledge, 1997.

Fink, Janet S. "Hiding in Plain Sight: The Embedded Nature of Sexism in Sport." *Journal of Sport Management*, vol. 30, no. 1, 2016, pp. 1-7.

Frisby, Wendy, et al. "Levelling the Playing Field: Promoting the Health of Poor Women through a Community Development Approach to Recreation." *Sport and Gender,* edited by Kevin Young and Philip White, Oxford, 2007, pp. 120-36.

Harrington, Maureen. "Families, Gender, Social Class, and Leisure." *Leisure, Women, and Gender*, edited by Valerie J. Freysinger et al., Venture, 2013, pp. 325-41.

Hays, Sharon. *The Cultural Contradictions of Motherhood.* Yale University Press, 1996.

Havitz, Mark, et al. *The Diverse World of Unemployed Adults: Consequences for Leisure, Lifestyle, and Wellbeing.* Wilfrid Laurier University Press, 2004.

Hebblethwaite, Shannon. "Understanding Ambivalence in Family Leisure among Three-Generation Families: 'It's All Part of the Package.'" *Annals of Leisure Research Special Issue: Children, Families and Leisure*, vol. 18, no. 3, 2015, pp. 359-76.

Herek, Gregory, et al. "Internalized Stigma among Sexual Minority Adults: Insights from a Social Psychological Perspective." *Stigma and Health*, vol. 1(S), 2015, pp. 18-34.

Interprovincial Sport and Recreation Council. *National Recreation Statement.* Fitness Canada, 1987.

Iwasaki, Yoshi, et al. "Building on Strengths and Resilience: Leisure as a Stress Survival Strategy." *British Journal of Guidance and Counselling*, vol. 33, no. 1, 2005, pp. 81-100.

Johnson, Corey W. "Feminist Masculinities: Inquiries into Leisure, Gender, and Sexual Identity. *Leisure, Women, and Gender*, edited by Valerie J. Freysinger et al., Venture, 2013, pp. 245-57.

Kane, Emily W. "'No Way My Boys Are Going to be Like That!' Parents' Responses to Children's Gender Noncomformity." *Gender and Society*, vol. 20, no. 2, 2006, pp. 149-76.

Kivel, Beth Dana, and Corey W. Johnson. "Activist Scholarship: Fighting Homophobia and Heterosexism." *Leisure, Women, and Gender*, edited by Valerie J. Freysinger et al., Venture, 2013, pp. 439-50.

Mair, Heather, et al. "Exercising Our Leisure Imagination." *Decentring Work*, edited by Heather Mair, Susan M. Arai, and Donald G. Reid, University of Calgary Press, 2010, pp. 251-57.

Norman, Leanne. "The Concepts Underpinning Everyday Gendered Homophobia Based upon the Experiences of Lesbian Coaches." *Sport in Society*, vol. 16, no. 10, 2013, pp. 1326-45.

Nussbaum, Martha. "Women's Capabilities and Social Justice." *Journal of Human Development,* vol. 1, no. 2, 2000, pp. 219-47.

Pennington, Jarred, and Tess Knight. "Through the Lens of Hetero-Normative Assumptions: Re-thinking Attitudes towards Gay Parenting." *Culture, Health & Sexuality,* vol. 13, no. 1, 2011, pp. 59-72.

Saint Martin, Denis. "From the Welfare State to the Social Investment State: A New Paradigm for Canadian Social Policy?" *Critical Policy Studies,* edited by Michael Orsini and Miriam Smith, University of British Columbia Press, 2007, pp. 279-98.

Shaw, Susan M. "Conceptualizing Resistance: Women's Leisure as Political Practice." *Journal of Leisure Research* vol. 22, no. 2, 2001, pp. 186-201.

Shaw, Susan M. "Family Leisure and Changing Ideologies of Parenthood." *Sociology Compass,* vol. 2, no. 2, 2008, pp. 688-703.

Shaw, Susan M. "Resistance." *A Handbook of Leisure Studies,* edited by Chris Rojek, Susan Shaw, and A.J. Veal, Palgrave Macmillan, 2006, pp. 533-45.

Shaw, Susan M., and Don Dawson. "Contradictory Aspects of Family Leisure: Idealization versus Experience." *Leisure/Loisir,* vol. 28, no. 3-4, 2003-2004, pp. 179-201.

Shaw, Susan M., and Don Dawson. "Purposive Leisure: Examining Parental Discourses on Family Activities." *Leisure Sciences,* vol. 23, no. 4, 2001, pp. 217-31.

Shaw, Sally, and Wendy Frisby. "Can Gender Equity Be More Equitable? Promoting an Alternative Frame for Sport Management Research, Education, and Practice." *Journal of Sport Management,* vol. 20, 2006, pp. 483-509.

Sparkes, Andrew C., and Brett Smith. *Qualitative Research Methods in Sport, Exercise and Health. From Process to Product.* Routledge, 2014.

Sue, Derald Wing. *Microaggressions in Everyday Life.* John Wiley & Sons, 2010.

Trussell, Dawn E. "Parents' Leisure, LGB Young People and "When We Were Coming Out." *Leisure Sciences,* vol. 39, no. 1, 2017, pp. 42-58.

Trussell, Dawn E., et al. "LGBTQ Parents' Experiences of Community Youth Sport: Change Your Forms, Change Your (Hetero) Norms." *Sport Management Review,* vol. 21, no. 1, 2018, pp. 51-62.

Trussell, Dawn E., et al. "Revisiting Family Leisure Research and Critical Reflections on the Future of Family-Centred Scholarship." *Leisure Sciences*, vol. 39, no. 5, 2017, pp. 385-99.

Trussell, Dawn E., and Susan M. Shaw. "Organized Youth Sport and Parenting in Public and Private Spaces." *Leisure Sciences*, vol. 34, no. 5, 2012, pp. 377-94.

Chapter Sixteen

Storytelling Motherhood with Katniss, Hermione, Tanya, and the Warrior Cats, or Owls and Ravens Raising Wrens[1]

Gillian Calder

When you live with the reality of intergenerational trauma and your caregiving flows from that trauma, having access to stories to read aloud with a child is immeasurably important. Connections between law, love, and healing can inform a child's views on healthy ways to be part of a family, which, in turn, fosters resilience in mothers and others who care. Embedding diverse opportunities for children to learn healthy ways to be in relationships of care interweaves the welfare of their mothers with the adults, perhaps parents, they will be grow to be. Stories hold the power to disrupt the linear notion of time, to strengthen ties to a child's communities, to challenge their understanding of privilege, and to complicate what it means to thrive.[2] Curious? This is a story I imagine:

The Cover

The book's cover is a girl with braids looking in a mirror. On the table behind her are stacks of books. Her room is blue, jarringly at odds with the orange carpet that permeates the rest of the house. On a shelf beside the mirror are family photographs, but the faces are not quite clear. The title of the book is "Storytelling Motherhood with Katniss, Hermione, Tanya, and the Warrior Cats." Or it might be "Owls and Ravens Raising Wrens"—I'm still not sure.

The book has two acknowledgments: first, to my parents, who read to me when I was a child and instilled in me the great love of books that I carry to this day; second, to L.M. Montgomery, for creating my favourite book from childhood, *Anne of Green Gables*. It wasn't until I was a parent reading to my own child that I realized the influence of Anne's story on my understanding of "family." Anne was an orphan, adopted by a brother and sister,[3] with whom she created a loving family. This disruption of normativity, encountered in children's literature, is how I first came to embrace that family isn't just inherited; for many of us, family is created and negotiated.

Dust Jacket

On the inside cover, the question that this chapter asks is laid bare. What happens to law when we read aloud and, in particular, what happens to law's hold on the normative family when bedtime reading becomes the medium for transmitting stories about parenting?

Dedication

For Qannik[4] and for all our ten-year-old, story-loving selves.

Chapter One: Everyone Has a Gigi

When I was helping in the library at school, one of Qannik's friends asked me if I was Qannik's mother. "No," I said. "I'm their Gigi." "What's a Gigi?" she said. "A Gigi is someone who loves you and cares for you but may or may not be related to you," I responded. "Do you have a Gigi?" "Yes," she said, wide-eyed. "I have a Gigi."

Chapter Two: Telling a Story

The bedroom door closed, leaving her in darkness. Tanya lay back on her bed, too shocked even to cry. The look on her mother's face had said it all. How many times had she been warned, how many times had she been told about the so-called last straw? Because now, as she listened to the muffled sobbing from the room across the landing, she knew that tonight really had been the last straw for her mother (Harrison 18).

My own extraordinary experience of parenting shows how reading children's literature aloud works to construct and tell the law of parenting, creating in the process insiders and outsiders. In my early forties, I became the single parent of an eight-year-old Inuit, Inuvialuit, Gwitch'in, and Kaska Dena fireball. My commitment at the time, in a formal agreement I have with their mother, was to be their legal guardian on a year-to-year basis.[5] I stepped into Qannik's life as a caregiver in a world where others in their family could not, for reasons primarily connected to the systemic racism faced by Indigenous peoples in Canada today.[6]

Dominant colonial, legal, and ideological processes continue to support the removal of Indigenous children from their home comm-unities.[7] Marlee Kline urges us to counter these processes ("Child Welfare Law"), and my caretaking decisions have followed her urgings and have largely aimed to safeguard the ties between Qannik and their home communities (Mehmoona 1-21; Suzack). In a world where I often get constructed as Qannik's mother and where there isn't a legal category to describe our relationship with each other[8] I find myself more aware of the world that people living outside dominant expectations of parenting move through—a world infused with the ideology of motherhood (Kline, "Complicating" 306-42). As Kline writes, "A mother is expected to operate within the context of the ideologically dominant family form, one that is 'heterosexual and nuclear in form, patriarchal in content,' and based on 'assumptions of privatized female dependence and domesticity'" (310-11). Stories offered one possibility for counternarratives, deconstruction, and hope.

On the first day that Qannik and I lived together, we started the first book in the *Harry Potter* series, and before long, we entered multiple worlds inhabited by clan cats, flying girls, vampires, Inuit sea-creatures, werewolves, fairies, and time travellers—worlds of murder, mayhem, mystery, and magic.[9] Almost all this reading happened out loud, most usually at bedtime or in the morning, and always as a catalyst to conversation.

As a parent working to reimagine family and confront the systemic barriers of colonialism in an embodied way, I have joy and angst about how law is taught, constructed, contradicted, and experienced. Through books and their extraordinary characters, Qannik and I have negotiated with each other some of what is unspoken, traumatic, and unparalleled about the world we are living in together. I have also struggled when difficult issues like Tanya's abandonment[10] inevitably arose. But something extraordinary happens when you read aloud. What law is and where it lives become real, and the notion of requiring legal recognition to be a family gets displaced.

Chapter Three: Colonialism

My eighth birthday had only just passed. I did not yet understand how long a year was. It had not crossed my mind that the same ice that allowed my people to travel only in the brief weeks of summer would keep me from going home. I did not know that an unusually short summer in 1945 would hold me prisoner for a second year with the Sisters, the Fathers, and the Brothers. They were not family. They were like owls and ravens raising wrens (Jordan-Fenton et al 26).[11]

On March 18, 2013, the Family Law Act (FLA) came into effect in British Columbia. A long-overdue overhaul of provincial family law, the *Act* effected some profound shifts in law around ideas of family. Progressively, the last barrier for unmarried cohabitants to have formal equality with married cohabitants—lack of presumptive equal division of property—was eliminated (FLA Sections 81-97); parents whose child is conceived as a result of assisted reproduction are included in the regime and may be recognized in law as parents (FLA Sections 23-33); a child may have up to five parents in law given the change in definition of "intended parents" (FLA Sections 27 and 30); and the definition of best interests of the child is changed to make it clear that it is the *only* consideration in making an order or an agreement for the care of a child (FLA Section 37[1]).

Yet the new Family Law Act remains informed by colonialism. Whereas the previous law recognized a separate category for people who had legal authority through agreement to raise children, the new regime in British Columbia eliminates this distinction. When a child's parents live together and then separate, each parent is the child's guardian (FLA Section 39[1]), and only a guardian can have parental responsibilities and parenting time (FLA s 40[1]). If a guardian is temporarily unable to exercise any of the parental responsibilities that the statute identifies, the child's guardian may authorize another person to exercise some—but not all—of those provisions (FLA Section 41 and 43). In effect, a child's guardian cannot transfer by agreement sole legal guardianship to someone who is not a parent. The only way this kind of agreement can be effected is on application by a guardian to the court (FLA s 45[1]).

The purpose underlying this change is tied to the safety and the best interests of the child, which are undoubtedly important considerations.[12] But the effect of this change in the law, (Section 43(1)), is to eliminate a mother's agency, particularly an Indigenous mother's ability to make choices that she knows to be in the best interests of her child.[13] The change in the law cements permanence as necessary to parenting while setting to the side the welfare of mothers within realms of choice. In so doing, this revised section of the FLA reinforces normative ideologies of motherhood and delegitimizes caregivers who defy these norms by excluding them from the legal protections and benefits available to those that the law privileges.

The Truth and Reconciliation Commission of Canada released its final report in 2015 in a process driven by the need to take seriously the legacy and the ongoing consequences of the imposition of residential schools on Indigenous families in Canada. Stories like *Fatty Legs*, an autobiographical story of a residential school survivor told through her eight-year-old voice, are addressing this legacy and appearing on lists of school curricula throughout Canada. When you live with the reality of intergenerational trauma and your caregiving flows from that trauma, having access to stories to read aloud with a child is immeasurably important. Connections between law, love, and healing can inform a child's views on healthy ways to be part of a family, which, in turn, fosters resilience in mothers and others who care.

Chapter Four: Law and Literature

But I knew, too, where Voldemort was weak. And so I made my decision. You would be protected by an ancient magic of which he knows, which he despises, and which he has always, therefore, underestimated—to his cost. I am speaking, of course, of the fact that your mother died to save you. She gave you a lingering protection he never expected, a protection that flows in your veins to this day. I put my trust, therefore, in your mother's blood. I delivered you to her sister, her only remaining relative (Rowling Order of the Phoenix 736).[14]

In a law school setting, challenging students to think with their whole bodies, not just their brains,[15] requires moving "beyond text"[16] and engaging diverse learners to exercise their ethical imaginations.[17] It also makes visible that constructions of parenting and the law and how they inform our understandings of legitimate and illegitimate forms of motherhood are set way before students arrive at law school. My own experience of what happens at bedtime reinforced this revelation. Reading children's literature aloud, I argue, is a tale of how law, parenting, poverty, and pedagogy are all interwoven through the intimacy of the bedtime story.

At the heart of the law and literature movement is the notion that "[stories] inscribe behaviour: they lay down ways of being in us" (Manderson 90).[18] This power of stories is all the more reason to look closely at stories read to and by children as a primary means of conveying the myths and calcifying the taboos of the world we live in.[19] As Desmond Manderson has written, "children's books often hold a powerful place in our emotional memory precisely because they harbour between their covers myth in its first and purest form" (Manderson 92), which is made all the more important due to the significance of the mythic in the everyday lives of children as they work to develop their sense of the world. Law is "learned, and practiced, in specific cultural contexts, in diverse and disparate fashions, on an everyday basis" (Manderson 93). Children's literature both tells stories about law and becomes law, often by attaching value to the presence or absence of parents. These stories matter in our shared conceptualization of the law of the marginalized parent and, in particular, the way law is engaged in the question of what it means to be someone's mother.

By understanding the relationship between literature and law as a process of instillation, *Harry Potter* in its "relentless socialization" is law (Manderson 95). What do children learn about law, about parenting, and about mothering in particular from bedtime stories? How do these stories run alongside law's formal stories? Simply cast, the parents of Harry, Ron and Hermione, the three central *Harry Potter* protagonists fit the image of the ideal parents: they are all coupled, heterosexual, and not dependent upon state supports. The most prominent character in the *Harry Potter* books without an actively present or caring mother is Voldemort, arguably the most heinous character in the history of children's literature. Deeper still, the premise of the book involves the choice of what counts as family for infant Harry. Even with all the magical families at his disposal, Dumbledore reinforces biology by placing Harry with the Dursleys (his aunt, uncle, and cousin by birth) instead of in a wizarding family. Who might Harry have grown to be if offered a childhood without abuse, where he could have been raised to know the culture, practices, and traditions of where he was from? More profoundly still, being placed at a residential school, even one as magical as Hogwarts, demands interrogation.[20]

Chapter Five: Foster Parenting

Firestar padded forward and leaned close to Lionblaze. "It's time you shared your destiny with your kin. They are here now. Tell them." Lionblaze backed away. "It's none of their business!" Heart racing, he glanced from Brambleclaw to Leafpool. "And they're not my kin!" Firestar's breath touched his muzzle. "Leafpool kitted you. Squirrelflight and Brambleclaw raised you. Without them, the prophecy would never have been fulfilled (Hunter 197-98)."[21]

Law continues to privilege certain families over others in a way that continues to reflect dominant narratives, colonial ideologies of parenthood, privilege, and caregiving. In the Employment Insurance (EI) benefit regime, and particularly in the provision of maternity and parental leave benefits, we see an example of how law regulates our understanding of family.[22] Under our current EI system, foster parents[23] are not entitled to take leave from work with benefits when a child is placed with them. Like birth parents and adoptive parents, balancing the care of a foster child with paid work when the child is new to the family is incredibly challenging work. However, the provisions of the EI benefits regime are tied solely to parents who give birth or adopt.

This exclusion was challenged in a case called Canada v Hunter. The Federal Court of Appeal found that the foster parent in the case—the grandparent of the child placed with her—was intending to adopt and, thus, fit the eligibility parameters. Although on the surface the case appears to support foster parents and others who are caring for children who are not born to them, it in fact reinforces the notion that the relationship between a parent and child requires some form of legal permanency in order to be legitimate. Nowhere does it ask why the law requires this form of parent-child relationship in order to provide benefits.

The inclusion of the language of "foster parents intending to adopt" likely fits with many peoples' understanding of the significance of the parent-child bond and the need to ensure that children raised outside of their birth families are raised safely and well. But it also says that families by choice are not legitimate, at least within the purview of this legal regime. And like in the *Warrior Cats* saga, where great significance is placed on the question of who is a real parent, being relegated as an "other" can have long-lasting consequences.

Another example of law's regulation of our understanding of the family comes from the polygamy debates. In a November 2011 reference on the constitutionality of Canada's polygamy prohibition, Chief Justice Bauman found that polygamy was inherently harmful: "The prevailing view through the millennia in the West has been that exclusive and enduring monogamous marriage is the best way to ensure paternal certainty and joint parental investment in children" (para 884). The current condemnation of polygamy may be tied to many sources, including colonialism, fear of the religious other, condemnation of abuse (and particularly child abuse), and feminist concerns about consent. But privileging monogamous marriage in the way this judgment does is deeply troubling (Calder, "To the Exclusion" 228-229).

As a result, marriages that are not monogamous, or practices that recognize nonmonogamy, are othered and, in some circumstances, criminalized. The stories about who is legitimate and who is alternatively so illegitimate that we need the criminal law to regulate their behaviour are deeply embedded in legal landscapes, legal culture and legal judgment. How law can ever shift in the face of this understanding of what counts as "family" requires a rethinking of where law lives and how we learn it.

Chapter Six: Reading Aloud

What happens next is not an accident. It is too well executed to be spontaneous because it happens in complete unison. Every person in the crowd presses the three middle fingers of their left hand against their lips and extends them to me. It's our sign from District 12, the last goodbye I gave Rue in the arena (Collins 61).[24]

My argument is that formal law—statutes and judgments—and the stories told to children are equally law. Something different happens to our understanding of law when we read aloud. Reading to children shapes their understanding of parenting's status in law while allowing us, as parents, to see what they learn and what this means for legal practice and pedagogy. As Manderson writes, "The young child finds [themselves] in a medieval world. They do not read; they attend to the reading of others. They listen to sounds, and they listen over and over again." At the same time, "The text is not just aural; it is also kinetic: a phenomenon connected in the life of the child to the room in which it is read, by whom, and under what conditions (Manderson 57)."

Reading to a child, or being the recipient of that reading, gives the child an active means of being in the learning; it presents the kind of transformational experience that seems only possible through children's stories (Manderson 58). Just as Paulo Freire views the educator "as a catalyst, or animator, with the objective of facilitating an educational process in which oppressed people become creative subjects of the learning process rather than passive objects (qtd. in Blackburn 8-9)," so, too, can be the relationship between adult and child while reading together. In this way *The Hunger Games* and *Harry Potter* were essential to the way Qannik and I negotiated our early, unexpected relationship of parent and child.[25] There is something profound and life altering in the embodied practice of reading aloud—a form of engagement that can transform the way we understand law and family.

Epilogue

Qannik's newest book series is the *Maximum Ride* series, by James Patterson. It is a series of books about a rebellious group of teenaged avian-Americans, who though unrelated are linked as family. They save the world and each other. Qannik is reading this set of books voraciously and on their own.

Acknowledgments

Gillian Calder is an Associate Professor in Law at the University of Victoria's Faculty of Law. She is grateful to the three audiences where she has performed this paper—at LSA in Honolulu, Hawai'i in June 2011; at After Equality in Montreal, QC in April 2013; and at Interpellations in Canberra, Australia, in December 2013—for their feedback and engagement. The paper has been supported by the research assistance of Debra Danco, Jennifer Bednard, Kendra Marks, and Kristen Lewis. Thank you to Sharon Cowan and Rebecca Johnson whose support, friendship, and wisdom informs my own understanding of family.

Endnotes

1. This is not a conventional form of scholarship. It has been written in a form that will feel unsettling, just as some forms of other mothering are also uncomfortable. It has also been written to be read aloud, just as the stories at the heart of this chapter were too. See the introduction to this volume for further context.

2. For more on the connection between mother's welfare, colonialism, and continuity of care see Calder, "Finally I Know" 173-89.

3. The law on adoption in Prince Edward Island, the province in Canada where *Anne of Green Gables* was set, does not permit a brother and sister to adopt a child. The current law says that "an order shall not be made for the adoption of a child by more than one person, except in the case of a joint application by spouses" (Adoption Act, RSPEI 1988).

4. Qannik is an Inupiaq word for "snowflake" and is a pseudonym.

5. The concept of guardianship changed in British Columbia on March 18, 2013, with the introduction of the *Family Law Act*, RSBC, SBC 2001, c 25. Up until that time, legal guardianship of a child could rest in a nonparent being delegated all the rights, duties, and responsibilities of a parent, in the best interests of a child.

6. See the discussion of the legacy of colonialism in Canada today, *TRC Executive Summary* 183-236.

7. There are more Indigenous children in care today than were in residential schools at the height of that system See the important work of Cindy Blackstock on the ongoing practices of colonialism in child welfare in Canada today.

8. In law, parents who foster through agreement are rarely recognized as legal parents. For example, the tax definition of "dependent" is someone who is related to you by birth, marriage, or adoption. But everyday law is also enforced by having "Mother's Day" and "Father's Day" assume prominence in our society, or in the chall-

enges of helping a child fill in their school family tree project. See: (Macdonald 5-8).

9. The books that followed included: *The Hunger Games* trilogy by Suzanne Collins; *Warrior Cats* by Erin Hunter; the *Inkheart* trilogy by Cornelia Funke; *Tanglewreck* by Jeanette Winterson; the *Abarat* trilogy by Clive Barker; *Charmed Life* by Diana Wynne Jones; Forester, *The Girl Who Could Fly* by Victoria Forester; *Wintersmith* by Terry Pratchett; and so many more.

10. Like in many children's novels, there is a reason that a child is sent off to stay with relatives, or cousins, or to school where the adventure of the story happens. In *13 Treasures*, for example, Tanya's mother cannot see what is special about her and does not believe that she can see fairies, an inherited gift (Harrison). So she sends her to live with her grandmother, where her true identity is ultimately revealed.

11. Please read aloud pages 24 to 26, beginning at "My parents led me ..." and finishing with "... raising wrens."

12. Section 43 is designed to enable a parent who is temporarily unable to act as a parent to authorize another individual to exercise some, but not all, of the parental responsibilities set out by the Act. The ability to transfer guardianship can only be effected by court order. This, in principle, will keep children safe and will keep parents from transferring guardianship. However, it denies agency to the parent who cannot parent and who wishes someone to act on their behalf with the full responsibilities of parenting.

13. The particular effect of the residential school system on Indigenous women is embodied in Call to Action 41 and draws the connection between the harmful effects of the child welfare system and missing and murdered Indigenous women and girls (*TRC Executive Summary* 226-27).

14. Please read aloud the full passage at page 736 beginning with "You might ask ..." and ending with "... her only remaining relative."

15. This idea, drawn from the work of theatre activist Augusto Boal, is a mantra of my teaching. Boal writes that "Chess is a highly intellectual, cerebral game. And yet good chess players also do physical training before a match. They know that the whole body thinks—not just the brain" (Boal 49).

16. See the discussion of the significance of the art to legal education (Bańkowski et al., "Arts and the Legal Academy," "Moral Imagination")

17. The idea of developing the ethical imagination of law students as critical to legal education is drawn from the *Beyond Text* project (Bankowski et al., "Arts and the Legal Academy").

18. For key texts to the law and literature movement, see White and Amsterdam. For popular culture more broadly, see MacNeil. For a counternarrative, see Posner.

19. I am grateful to Kristen Lewis for connecting myths and normativity to shame, taboos and bodies.

20. For a peek into what being sent away to school meant for the sons of Harry Potter and Draco Malfoy, see Rowling, Thorne, and Tiffany, *Cursed Child*. This nineteen-years-later story was written as a play.

21. Please read aloud pages 200 and 201 starting at "As hurt flashed across Leafpool's gaze..." and ending with "... *I am one of the Four.*"

22. Maternity and parental leave in Canada are delivered within a legislative framework that is tied to work, which leaves many families outside of the regime and othered in the process (Calder, "A Pregnant Pause" 116-117).

23. These are, generally, people caring for children that are not their birth children or not placed with them for the purposes of adoption.

24. Please read aloud *Catching Fire*, at page 61 beginning with "The crowd has fallen silent now..." and ending with "... who defied the Capitol."

25. There is a privilege in having the time, resources, abilities, and energy to read to a child on a daily basis or to live in a community with easy access to a library. The intent of this chapter is not to marginalize those who cannot parent in this way but to raise questions about the value that can flow when one can.

Works Cited

Adoption Act, RSPEI 1988, c A-4.1, s 15.

Canada (Attorney General) v Hunter, 2013 FCA 12

Employment Insurance Act, SC 1996, c 23, ss. 22–23

Family Law Act, RSBC, SBC 2001, c 25

Amsterdam, Anthony G. and Jerome Bruner. *Minding the Law*. Harvard University Press, 2000.

Bańkowski, Zenon, and Del Mar, Maksymilian. "Introduction," *The Moral Imagination and the Legal Life: Beyond Text in Legal Education*, edited by Zenon Bańkowski and Maksymilian Del Mar, Ashgate, 2013, pp. 1–9.

Bańkowski, Zenon et al. "Introduction," *The Arts and the Legal Academy: Beyond Text in Legal Education* edited by Zenon Bańkowski, Maksymilian Del Mar, and Paul Maharg, Ashgate, 2013, Surrey, pp. 1-13.

Barker, Clive. *Abarat*. Harper Collins, 2002.

Barker, Clive. *Absolute Midnight*. Harper Collins, 2011.

Barker, Clive. *Days of Magic, Nights of War*. Harper Collins, 2004.

Blackburn, James. "Understanding Paulo Freire: Reflections on the Origins, Concepts and Possible Pitfalls of His Educational Approach" *Community Development Journal*, vol. 35, no. 3, 2000, pp. 3-15.

Boal, Augusto. *Games for Actors and Non-Actors*. Routledge, 1992.

Calder, Gillian. "Finally I Know Where I am Going to Be From: Culture, Context and Time in a Look Back at Racine v. Woods." *Justice Bertha Wilson: One Woman's Difference*, edited by Kim Brooks, University of British Columbia Press, 2009, pp. 173-89.

Calder, Gillian. "A Pregnant Pause: Federalism, Equality and the Maternity and Parental Leave Debate in Canada" *Feminist Legal Studies* vol. 14, no. 99 at 116-17.

Calder, Gillian. "To the Exclusion of All Others—Polygamy, Monogamy, and the Legal Family in Canada" in *Polygamy's Rights and Wrongs: Perspectives on Harm, Family, and Law*, edited by Gillian Calder and Lori Beaman, University of British Columbia Press, 2014, pp. 215-33.

Collins, Suzanne. *Catching Fire*. Scholastic Press, 2009.

Collins, Suzanne. *Hunger Games*, Scholastic Press, 2008.

Collins, Suzanne. *Mockingjay*, Scholastic Press, 2010.

Forester, Victoria. *The Girl Who Could Fly*. Macmillan, 2008.

Funke, Cornelia. *Inkdeath*. Scholastic Press, 2007.

Funke, Cornelia, *Inkheart*. Scholastic Press, 2003.

Funke, Cornelia. *Inkspell*. Scholastic Press, 2005.

Harrison, Michelle. *13 Treasures*. Simon and Schuster, 2009.

Hunter, Erin. *Omen of the Stars: The Last Hope*. Harper, 2012.

Jordan-Fenton, Christy, and Margaret Pokiak-Fenton. *Fatty Legs*. Annick Press, 2010.

Kline, Marlee. "Child Welfare Law, 'Best Interests of the Child' Ideology, and First Nations." *Osgoode Hall Law Journal*, vol. 30, no. 2, 1992, pp. 375-425.

Kline, Marlee. "Complicating the Ideology of Motherhood: Child Welfare Law and First Nation Women." *Queen's Law Journal*, vol. 18, no. 2, 1993, pp. 306-42.

Macdonald, Roderick. *Lessons of Everyday Law*. McGill-Queen's University Press, 2002.

MacNeil, William P. *Lex Populi: The Jurisprudence of Popular Culture*, Palo Alto, Stanford University Press, 2007.

Manderson, Desmond. "From Hunger to Love: Myths of the Source, Interpretation, and Constitution of Law in Children's Literature" *Law and Literature*, vol. 15, no. 87, 2003, pp. 87-141.

Maude Montgomery, Lucy. *Anne of Green Gables*. L.C. Page, 1908.

Posner, Richard A. *Law and Literature: A Misunderstood Relationship*. Harvard University Press, 1998.

Pratchett, Terry. *Wintersmith*. New York, Doubleday, 2006.

Rowling, J.K., Jack Thorne and John Tiffany. *Harry Potter and the Cursed Child*. Scholastic, 2016.

Rowling, J.K. *Harry Potter and the Chamber of Secrets*, Bloomsbury, 1998.

Rowling, J.K. *Harry Potter and the Deathly Hallows*, Bloomsbury, 2007.

Rowling, J.K. *Harry Potter and the Goblet of Fire*, Bloomsbury, 2000.

Rowling, J.K. *Harry Potter and the Half-Blood Prince*, Bloomsbury, 2005.

Rowling, J.K. *Harry Potter and the Order of the Phoenix*, Bloomsbury, 2003.

Rowling, J.K.. *Harry Potter and the Philosopher's Stone*, Bloomsbury, 1997.

Rowling, J.K. *Harry Potter and the Prisoner of Azkaban*, Bloomsbury, 1999.

Suzack, Cheryl. *Indigenous Women's Writing and the Cultural Study of Law*. University of Toronto Press, 2017.

Truth and Reconciliation Commission of Canada. *Final Report of the Truth and Reconciliation Commission of Canada, Volume One: Summary, Honouring the Truth, Reconciling for the Future*. Lorimer, 2015.

White, James Boyd. *The Legal Imagination*, University of Chicago Press, 1985.

Winterson, Jeanette. *Tanglewreck*. Bloomsbury, 2006.

Wynne Jones, Diana. *Charmed Life*. Macmillan, 1977.

Notes on Contributors

Heather Bergen lives and works in Tkaronto. She is currently doing her doctoral research on alternatives to the child protection system at York University. She would like to thank the young parents that participated in this research. Without their insights, humour, and generosity, none of this research would have been possible. To learn more visit *teenmomstalkback.ca*.

Stephanie Bustamante is the executive director of the Saskatchewan Youth in Care and Custody Network (SYICCN) and has a strong background in advocacy, community engagement, human rights, antipoverty work, restorative justice, the youth criminal justice custody system, and domestic violence prevention, as well as experience with several boards involving community and child welfare.

Gillian Calder is an associate professor at the University of Victoria's Faculty of Law. She holds an LL.M. from York University and teaches constitutional law, family law, and related seminars. Her research examines the ways that law shapes our understanding of the family, through performative, feminist, and critical pedagogy lenses.

Sara Cantillon is professor of economics and gender at the GCU Glasgow School of Business and Society and director of the WiSE Centre for Economic Justice. Her research areas are equality, poverty and intrahousehold distribution. She has published widely on these topics including in *Hypatia, Feminist Economics, Journal of Social Policy, Journal of Family and Economics,* and *Res Publica.*

Darlene Domshy is the research coordinator and former executive director of Saskatchewan Youth in Care and Custody Network (SYICCN). A previous background in cultural studies, combined with years as an advocate for youth voice, inclusion, and participation, have led Darlene to a strong interest in the health and wellbeing of youth with care experiences. She now explores these areas and the broader social determinants of health as a registered nurse.

Roberta Garrett is a senior lecturer in the department of arts and digital industries at the University of East London. She writes on representations of gender, class, and race in popular literature and film. She is the author of *Postmodern Chick-Flicks: the Return of the Woman's Film* (Palgrave, 2008), coeditor of *We Need to Talk about Family: Essays on Neoliberalism, the Family and Popular Culture* (Cambridge Scholars, 2016), and is finishing another monograph.

Rachel Lamdin Hunter is a registered nurse specialising in child, family, and women's health. She teaches undergraduate and postgraduate students at the Centre for Health and Social Practice at the Waikato Institute of Technology in Hamilton, New Zealand. Her PhD dissertation, titled *"She Watches over Her Household": Wellbeing of Mothers and Children in Motherled Households* was conferred at the University of Waikato in 2017. Rachel is mother to three daughters.

Martina Hutton is a senior lecturer at the University of Winchester and holds a PhD in Equality Studies. Her research focuses on poverty, deprivation and marketplace stress and exclusion examined through a psychological health, political economy and egalitarian theory lens. A qualitative PEFT researcher (Participatory, Emancipatory, Feminist, Transformative), she engages with diverse groups of people experiencing poverty/deprivation.

Nathalie Reis Itaboraí has a PhD in sociology (University of the State of Rio de Janeiro) and is an associated researcher at the Centre for the Study of Wealth and Social Stratification (CERES-IESP-UERJ). She researches about social inequalities, families, and public policies. She has published chapters in two other books of Demeter Press: *Maternal Geographies: Mothering In and Out of Place* and *Mothers in Public and Political Life*. She is also mother of three children.

Tara Kainer attended the University of Regina and Queen's University. Currently employed in the Justice, Peace & Integrity of Creation Office of the Sisters of Providence of St. Vincent de Paul, she works on projects and campaigns to eliminate poverty and increase food and income security. She is the mother of three grown children and the author of a book of poems, *When I Think on Your Lives* (Hidden Brook Press, 2011).

Shauna Labman is a lawyer and an associate professor of human rights at the University of Winnipeg, Global College. She writes and speaks extensively on refugee issues and her published work covers questions of human rights, discrimination, refugee protection, gender, resettlement, and the government-citizen dynamic in private refugee sponsorship.

Lindsay Larios is a PhD candidate in the Department of Political Science at Concordia University. She has a background in community research and a master's of social work from McGill University. Her current project as a Bombardier Doctoral Fellow focuses on the politics of pregnancy and birth, precarious migration as an issue of reproductive justice, and the radical potential of reimagining citizenship and im/migration policy through the lens of care ethics.

Karine Levasseur is an associate professor in the Department of Political Studies, University of Manitoba, and a stepmother. Her research interests include state-civil society relations, accountability, and governance. She is author of "In the Name of Charity: Institutional Support and Resistance for Redefining the Meaning of Charity in Canada," which won the J.E. Hodgetts Award for best article (in English) published in *Canadian Public Administration* in 2012.

Marie Lovrod is the program chair of Women's and Gender Studies at the University of Saskatchewan. Combining humanities and social science frameworks, she researches youth trauma and resiliency and mobilizes institutional resources to help heal the diverse lived effects of social violence. She values communities of practice that respect research, learning, and social environments as inclusive spaces.

Jenni Mays is a senior lecturer at the Queensland University of Technology. She is the lead author of *Basic Income in Australia and New Zealand: Perspectives from the Neoliberal Frontier*, with Greg Marston and John Tomlinson; and "Disability, Citizenship, and Basic Income, and Australia's Disabling Income Support System: Tracing the History of the Disability Pension from 1908 to Current." Her research interests include critical social policy and protection.

Stephanie Paterson is a professor in the Department of Political Science at Concordia University, where she specializes in feminist and critical policy studies. Her research interests include feminist governance, including state feminism and gender mainstreaming, and the politics of reproduction and motherhood.

Jacqueline Potvin holds a PhD in women's studies and feminist research from Western University, where she currently teaches in the School of Health Studies. Her research examines how sexual and reproductive health and rights are understood and addressed within global development policy and programming, and interrogates how development interventions have both contributed to and undermined reproductive justice within the Global South.

Lynsey Race holds a master's degree in gender and social justice studies and a master's of science in occupational therapy (MSc OT) from the University of Alberta, where she analyzed interviews with community support workers who were working with mothers with intellectual or developmental impairments experiencing domestic violence. She works in mental health services for incarcerated individuals as a registered occupational therapist.

Lynda Ross is a social psychologist and professor emeritus of women's and gender studies at Athabasca University. Her research and publications focus on the social construction of theory and disorder, attachment, and motherhood.

Lorna Stefanick is a professor at Athabasca University. Lorna writes on public administration and policy topics for an international audience. Her 2013 book *Controlling Knowledge* looks at state surveillance of marginalized populations. Her 2015 co-edited volume *Alberta Oil and the Decline of Democracy in Canada* (with Meenal Shrivastava) includes a co-written chapter comparing women's equality in Canada and Iran.

Dawn E. Trussell is an associate professor in the Department of Sport Management at Brock University. Her research focuses on sport and leisure culture in the lives of individuals, families, and communities. Dawn's work has a social justice orientation and seeks to address issues of power and social inclusion.

Lorna A. Turnbull is an activist mother of three and a professor in the Faculty of Law at the University of Manitoba. Her research is focused on the work of care, its importance to carers and those who depend on the care, and how legal frameworks support or fail these important relationships through the lens of Canada's constitutional guarantees and international obligations. She is the author of *Double Jeopardy: Motherwork and the Law* (2001).

Rebecca Wallace is a PhD candidate and a Joseph Armand Bombardier CGS doctoral fellow in the Department of Political Studies at Queen's University. Her primary research interests include Canadian social policy, political behaviour, and political communication.

Shauna Wilton is an associate professor of political studies at the Augustana Campus of the University of Alberta. She has a PhD from the University of Alberta. She has published articles and book chapters on immigration, national identity, gender, media, popular culture, and pedagogy. Her current research focuses on work/family balance and on popular representations of motherhood.

Deepest appreciation to
Demeter's monthly Donors

DEMETER

Daughters
Myrel Chernick
Naomi McPherson
Summer Cunningham
Rebecca Bromwich
Tatjana Takseva
Debbie Byrd
Fionna Green
Tanya Cassidy
Vicki Noble
Bridget Boland

Sisters
Kirsten Goa
Amber Kinser
Nicole Willey